The Transient and Permanent in Liberal Religion

◆

Reflections from the UUMA Convocation on Ministry

EDITED BY

Dan O'Neal
Alice Blair Wesley
and
James Ishmael Ford

Skinner House Books
Boston

Published by Skinner House Books, an imprint of the
Unitarian Universalist Association, 25 Beacon Street, Boston,
MA 02108-2800.

Printed in Canada.

ISBN 1-55896-330-8

10 9 8 7 6 5 4 3 2 1
99 98 97 96 95

Contents

A Lifetime of Learning

Doing Justice and Mercy

Developing Theology

Preface

Whatever else this collection of essays concerns—the ministry, our Unitarian Universalist movement, the present cultural and global situation—it is first and foremost about one thing: *transcendence.*

My saying this may surprise you. But as Vaclav Havel put it on a recent visit to the United States, "In today's multicultural world, the truly reliable path ... must start at the root of all cultures, and in what lies infinitely deeper in human hearts and minds than political opinion, convictions, antipathies, or sympathies. It must be rooted in self-transcendence. Transcendence as a hand reached out to those close to us, to strangers, to the human community, to all living creatures, to nature, to the Universe; transcendence as a deeply and joyously experienced need to be in harmony even with what we ourselves are not, what we do not understand, what seems distant from us in time and space, but with which we are nevertheless mysteriously linked because, together with us, all this constitutes a single world. Transcendence is the only real alternative to extinction."

In a keynote address at the 1995 UUMA Convocation for which these papers were prepared, members of the Unitarian Universalist ministry heard from the Rev. William Sloane Coffin. Coffin agrees with Havel. He declares that the chief religious question can no longer be, "What must *I* do to be saved?" It is rather, "What must we *all* do to save God's creation?"

In that sense, the challenge to Unitarian Universalists is to live up to the vision inherent in the very name we bear: a vision of human unity, universal and eternal. It is not a new vision with us. It is as ancient as the prophets and seers of many traditions. Nor is it even now exclusive to us. But according to it, whatever our differing views of spirituality, we belong to one another. Nor is it a unity that we are called upon to create. That's the good news. It's already given. We have only to recognize it and then make it more manifest in how we live our lives.

At times, reading this collection, you may feel that you have encountered a modern version of the Buddhist parable of the blind ones and the elephant. Each grasps a different part of the whole and proclaims it the essence of the whole: covenant, pluralism, partnership, and so forth. "And yet, O mortals," ends the parable, "there is the Unborn and the Uncreated." The transcendent, that is.

If there is a second theme, it is that of history. Does history warrant hope in us? Not in itself, I'm afraid. But then, perhaps history never did. The historian and social activist Howard Zinn, in *You Can't Be Neutral on a Moving Train*, published by our own Beacon Press, also echoes Havel in saying that true hope—that is, hope that is not squandered on this ideology, that leader, or even such-and-such a movement—simply cannot be foolish, because it is based on a fact: that "human history is a history not only of cruelty, but also of compassion, sacrifice, courage, kindness." This is what Havel means by "self-transcendence," when he says that the choice today is between such things and extinction.

The choice in how we see our own history, says Zinn, is similar. (And this is perhaps the problem with the tendency today for so many groups to see themselves only as victims.) "If we see only the worst, it destroys our capacity to do something. If we remember those times and places—and there are so many— where people have behaved magnificently, this gives us the energy to act, and at least the possibility of sending this spinning top of a world in a different direction. And if we do act, in however small a way, we don't have to wait for some grand utopian future. The future is an infinite succession of presents, and to live now as we think human beings should live, in defiance of all that is bad around us, is itself a marvelous victory."

Can hope itself be our path? Listen to the words of the Chinese poet Lu Xun, who teaches that hope *is* a path.

Hope can neither be affirmed nor denied. Hope is like a path in the countryside: originally there was no path—yet as people are walking all the time toward one horizon, a way appears.

So may it be. And may we have the courage to take our part, step by step.

John A. Buehrens, President
Unitarian Universalist Association
January 1995

Introduction

Dan O'Neal

All predictions are unreliable—particularly those that deal with the social and technological future. When I was a child in grammar school, some of my favorite moments were those occasional breaks in the grind of school routine when our teacher would haul out the ancient, creaking projector to show us educational movies such as Disney's "World of Tomorrow" films. Not having to do math or geography was reward enough, but the scenes depicted on the wobbly classroom screen were fascinating in themselves. We saw such marvels as cars fully automated, running on tracks, programmable for destination and speed. All you had to do after punching in your desired town and address was to sit back and enjoy; technology would do the rest.

Introduction

If my memory is correct, the future depicted in those films is now. Yet all too often these days I find myself muttering in bumper-to-bumper traffic, hands clenched around my own steering wheel. So much for predictions.

And yet, sometimes predictions are startlingly accurate. Just published in the fall of 1994 was a novel written by Jules Verne in the 1860s that depicted Paris in the 1960s. It was only recently unearthed by his grandson in an attic. The novel was never published in Verne's own day because his publisher thought it too fantastic with images of combustion engines, electric chairs in which people were executed, and underground trains. "My dear Verne," the publisher wrote in his rejection letter, "no one would believe your prophecy."

I don't think Verne was clairvoyant. I think he was an astute and perceptive observer of his times. His proficiency in making accurate predictions of the future resided not in some psychic capability, I suspect, but in a highly developed talent to peer deeply into his current situation. After all, I'm no genius in predicting that a seed will blossom into a sunflower if, after examining it at some length, I discover that it is my old snack-time treat.

It is wise to be cautious in these sooth-saying realms. Perhaps this seed is some exotic South American squash that I have never before encountered. My predictions should always be offered in a spirit of possibility rather than certainty. Perhaps the only mistake more foolish than believing in predictions is failing to make any predictions in the first place. To look sagely into the future is merely to look into the present with care and passion.

Over 150 years ago, on May 19 of 1841, Unitarian minister Theodore Parker did a little careful and passionate predicting himself. He delivered a landmark sermon titled "The Transient and Permanent in Christianity" in which he asked, and answered, a very simple but important question about the Unitarianism of his day: What was permanent and enduring about that movement as it attempted to address the needs and conditions of the age in which it lived; and what was transient, tied to passing beliefs and circumstances, and therefore not to be held onto tightly?

As we approach the end of the twentieth century, Parker's question is still a critical one to be asking. The arrival of a new millennium is an appropriate time to look at the transient and permanent in present-day Unitarian Universalism. This book is an attempt by contemporary UU observers to do just that.

All new millennia bring on a sense of impending transformation. Medieval Europe was obsessed by the expectation of Christ's imminent return around the year 1000. As the year 2000 approaches, our own premillennialists are similarly expectant. This time I believe more than just psychological factors are driving our sense of an approaching period of radical change. Many dynamics, long in developing, seem to be coming to a head in this era. The human population explosion cannot continue at its current rate forever, perhaps not very much longer. The many indications of environmental destruction—from the unprecedented rate and number of species extinction to massive pollution of the earth's air, water, and soil; to the deforestation of the globe; to global warming and the destruction of the ozone layer—portend a frighteningly unsustainable scenario.

Add to this the ever-present threat of nuclear annihilation, the accelerating pace of life with the accompanying decay of traditional cultural structures, the rapacious growth of the world economy with its seeming intent to transform the entire planet's surface into commodities, the development of global communications linking all parts of the world together for the first time in history, and the invention of ever more clever and unimaginably powerful technologies; and it is easy to see why this particular millennium has us holding our collective breaths with expectation.

Near the end of his life, the great historian Arnold Toynbee wrote about the accelerating rate of change:

> Present-day man has recently become aware that history has been accelerating—and this at an accelerating rate....The approach of the climax foreseen intuitively by the prophets is

being felt, and feared, as a coming event. Its imminence is, today, not an article of faith; it is a datum of observation and experience.[1]

Amidst all this expectation, it is wise for us as a denomination to ask Parker's question anew. It could even be that his answers might serve us well. Parker, like Emerson before him and all the other transcendentalists, was clearly a romantic. His goal was the reunion of spirit with matter, the human soul with the transcendent soul, and the intuitive dimension with the intellectual dimension.

Romanticism has ever been the minority voice in the modern Western dialogue, never going away but never holding sway either. Nevertheless, in our denomination, the Transcendentalists had an interesting effect. Both their extreme emphasis on the individual as the final authority of matters religious, as well as their uncoupling of Unitarianism from the doctrinal tenets of Christianity, were eventually adopted by the denomination. But their belief in divine immanence and their emphasis on direct intuition as the primary way of knowing were not. Our denomination has usually been on the *bevel* of progress—not directly on the cutting edge but back a little distance. We seem to follow the general flow of Western philosophical and intellectual history, but with a time lag built in, often constituting many decades. This flow since Parker's time has been more and more in the direction of a nearly total embrace of Romanticism's dominant cousin, the Enlightenment, and its stepchild, modern science.

Reason and empiricism have been adopted as the chief, or in many instances only, ways of coming to know reality—not intuition, contemplation, devotion, or a hundred other ways of arriving at knowledge. Issues of divinity have been relegated to the supposedly inferior disciplines of religion and theology. The assumptions and tenets of science have formed the ruling paradigm of Western thought and thus of our denomination.

Of course, because we are noncreedal, numerous other threads are present in our midst. Most importantly, the beliefs and values of Christianity continue to inform our thinking in a myriad of different ways. By and large, however, we fairly accurately reflect the dominant beliefs of our age. This age has embraced Enlightenment thinking.

But there is always a bit of a lag factor built in; Unitarian Universalists are seldom right *on* the cutting edge. And that cutting edge is doing some mighty interesting exploratory surgery these days, as Richard Tarnas ably describes in *The Passion of the Western Mind.*[2]

Although the scientific world view is certainly still the dominant outlook, it no longer holds unquestioned loyalty among the intelligentsia. The limitations of this way of knowing, as well as those of other mainline Western philosophical traditions, are well understood by now. Deconstructionism, which dissects and disassembles traditionally accepted knowledge by analyzing and exploding underlying prejudices and assumptions, is now the dominant voice in a variety of academic fields. A certain relativized and critical empiricism and rationalism has become commonplace. This is due not only to acknowledged epistemological limits (such as Heisenberg's Uncertainty Principle in the empirical realm and Godel's Theorem of Incompleteness in the rational) but also to the recognition of cultural, ethnic, linguistic, and gender lenses that render so-called "objective" investigation considerably less than objective.

There is also a widespread recognition that the very practical manifestations of the dominant scientific paradigm, which so dazzled us during its first few centuries of application, are showing themselves as less than positive; indeed, there is widespread fear that the long-term consequences might be catastrophic. Our very efforts to control every aspect of existence might be leading to a situation where everything is *out* of control. This pulling back from allegiance to the dominant scientific paradigm without any other paradigm ready to take its place was recognized by John Dewey at the start of the century as a historically unique situation. He observed that "despair of any integrated outlook and attitude (is) the chief intellectual characteristic of the present age."

That sounds like the bad news. But there is good news coupled with it. The situation has encouraged a widespread conversation between different viewpoints. Even as the current system shows potential for breaking down, anything seems possible.

Parker's submerged romanticism is reemerging in the latter half of this century, along with numerous and varied voices from within the Western tradition: systems thinking, the paradoxical findings of quantum science, resurgent Judaism and Christianity, mythology, paganism; underground Gnostic and mystical traditions, cultural feminism, and the emerging ecological movement. In addition, a multitude of voices from outside the Western tradition, including Eastern religions and indigenous spiritualities, are likewise finding a receptive audience.

Thus, the postmodern age that we find ourselves in has this dual dimension to it: deconstructive and dissembling as well as integrative and reconciliatory. On the one hand, there is a widespread fear of breakdown and apocalypse. As Charlene Spretnak put it, "Ours is an age of fading utopian dreams and looming dystopian nightmares."[3]

Amidst all this ferment and potentiality, Parker's question becomes all the more important. What in our own tradition is enduring enough to serve us well in this exciting and fearful time and what can be gently left behind, honored for having performed its purpose? We should also ask, What elements from *outside* our tradition can be incorporated to enable us to create healing new life?

It has been said that there are two categories of people in the world: those who divide the world into two categories and those who don't. I've got to admit being an inveterate member of the first group, for I often see the modern age as dividing into several bipolar categories. Specifically, I see two critical visions operating on the planet today. One is a vision of separateness and competition and mastery; the other is a vision of unity and interrelatedness and participation.

We can find the first vision all about us. It is the dominant outlook on the planet today. It sees a universe of separate entities interacting at a distance. It posits a strong subject-object duality. Its epistemology is typically confined to rational and empirical modes of knowing. Its method is the manipulation of the world through a detached functionality. Its principal tool is technology. And its primary manifestation on the planet today is the global economy. In fact, economic considerations have been elevated to a place of centrality in this vision. Most other human endeavors, such as art and religion, are either relegated to the sidelines or yoked to the service of the economy. It is only in this age, for example, that the accounting term "bottom line" could come to stand for that which is most important. It is only in such an environment that people could be described by the cold term *Homo economicus.*

Introduction

To those who practice the second vision, of course, this situation is completely topsy-turvy. They believe that economic considerations must always be placed within a larger framework that provides guidance and direction. This larger framework is one that speaks of an impeccable interrelatedness as the fundamental truth of the universe. Even the word interrelatedness doesn't quite capture the essence of this viewpoint. The modern day Buddhist teacher Thich Nhat Hahn has coined the term "interbeing" to more accurately portray this vision of a living universe in which every part interpenetrates every other part.

The second vision is represented by indigenous peoples: emerging Western ecologists; mystics of all religions; twentieth–century philosophers such as Whitehead, Bateson, and other systems thinkers; Eastern contemplatives such as Buddhists; reemerging pagans; cultural feminists; and prominent quantum physicists. In this vision, people are sometimes described as *Homo religiosus*, because the experience of being an essential but dependent part of a sacred whole gives them their fundamental identity and direction.

It should come as no surprise that I think the second vision is the one that must be increasingly embraced in the exciting and yet vulnerable world in which we live. This does not mean overthrowing the first vision. There is much of value in it, such as the power and clarity of rationalism and empiricism, the practicality of science and technology, the refining genius of deconstructionism. And yet this vision is clearly materially unsustainable, as any sober look at the catastrophic data coming in from all ecological fronts would indicate. And, just as fundamental, it is psychologically and spiritually unsustainable. As religious historian Robert Bellah observed, "That happiness is to be attained through limitless material acquisition is denied by every religion and philosophy known to humankind, but is preached incessantly by every American television sct."[4]

While keeping that which is sustainable in our current vision and using the purifying power of such critical new disciplines as deconstructionism to sift out the destructive elements, we need to incorporate the beneficial aspects of this second vision on the planet. Guarding against casual dabbling, we can draw on the fresh insights of cutting–edge philosophy and science, the deep knowledge of reemerging Western traditions—including Parker's romanticism—as well as the age-old wisdom of Eastern and indigenous traditions.

This is not just a nice thing to do. I am increasingly convinced that we are at another watershed moment in human history. This time it is not a dress rehearsal. The future of the current planetary biological system, which includes all human culture, is critically dependent on the direction that this generation chooses to go. More of the same will lead us down the path we are currently on, a path whose destination is becoming disturbingly clear. Many sober observers of the modern scene, including the majority of the world's Nobel Laureate scientists alive in 1992, estimate that we have only one or at most a few decades to reverse the current destructive course. After that, it will be too late.

Unitarian Universalists could play a small but important part in presenting a healing and integrative vision for the future. This will require letting go of some elements from our tradition that have served us well in the past but whose usefulness in the coming age is limited. Although I honor rationality and empiricism deeply, our overreliance on them in the past, has often meant eschewing any other ways of knowing. I see this overreliance as a transient element in our tradition. I also see our tentative posture regarding the sacred as another dimension that perhaps helped cast aside magical and arbitrary thinking in the past, but that is now a hindrance in an era when reverence and awe must be reclaimed if we are to survive.

But let me concentrate on the permanent elements of our faith, for we have much of value to draw on. Our openness to new ways of thinking, our resistance to the premature closure of truth, our insistence that words cannot fully and finally capture reality— these dimensions will serve us well in an age when established ways of thinking and being must be substantially transformed. Our past willingness to soberly confront the realities of the day and address them with bold and practical initiatives are important traits to bring with us into the next millennium. Our notion of the interdependent web, the most popularly gripping of our seven principles, leads us right into the heart of a vision that will sustain humanity and the rest of the planet for ages to come. And our tradition of spiritual practices—prayer, service, worship, ritual, meditation, devotional reading—is essential in the implementation of the second vision, for there is almost universal agreement among its adherents that this is not merely an intellectual position to espouse but an experience to live. The realization that we exist in a participatory universe is awakened by practices that reveal our true identity as partakers in a sacred immensity.

Not every contributor to this collection would agree with me. Some will vehemently disagree with any number of my contentions. But all are doing something very important: they are peering passionately into our present tradition to assess its relevance to the future. They are following the old advice given by religious educator Angus McClean:

> We are not merely the bellhops of history, passing the baggage of one generation on to another. Yet culture makes it possible for human relations to bridge the grave, for individuals who are so short of days to live with

a wisdom derived from the dawn of time. Our job, however, is not to worship history and culture like fetishes, but to feed them into our living, creative stream of personal life for spiritual and intellectual reprocessing.[5]

In the final analysis, there is no telling ahead of time whether any of our prognostications will be accurate or not. I'll tell you what. Let's have a cup of tea thirty years from now and laugh over the things I've said in this essay; no doubt some of them will show their age and their prejudices. But let us still honor the unpredictable endeavor we are about in this book: to plumb the depths of our current tradition so as to gauge its ability to take us into the era that is to come. What is permanent and enduring in our movement as it attempts to address the conditions of the age in which we live? What is transient, tied to passing beliefs and circumstances and therefore not to be held onto tightly? Let us join together in asking Parker's important question anew. Surely this is a worthwhile task, however the particulars turn out.

Our Covenant

The Covenant of Spiritual Freedom

George Kimmich Beach

———————◆———————

The twentieth century is the age of the crisis of liberal democracy. The prospect of our liberal faith is intimately bound up with that crisis. We face this one question in many guises: Is freedom the right of individuals to think and to do as they please, or is it the human capacity to respond creatively to the possibilities and limits of human existence?

The idea was planted in the eighteenth century, and flourished in the nineteenth century, that people could come together and govern themselves intelligently, virtuously, and with good will. Given liberty, they would recognize each other's "inalienable rights," exercise their individual franchise, and form majority governments. Democratic governments would respect the rights of the minority. These ideals seemed self-evident, and the human prospect seemed bright with promise. Jefferson called participation in the affairs of the common weal "the public happiness." Troubling questions of slavery and racism were bypassed by all but a few.

Today's Unitarianism and Universalism were born in this bold "Age of Enlightenment," and nursed on its cultural and political ideals. "I am always young for liberty," declared William Ellery Channing. Cradled in the early years of the American republic, we grew to vigorous young adulthood in the nineteenth century, an era of expanding confidence in the human destiny. Earlier generations spoke of faith in divine Providence; James Freeman Clarke announced Unitarian faith in "the progress of mankind, onward and upward forever."

Today, however, we are reticent about "progress" and wary of rationalistic answers to the deep, emotion-laden issues of psyche and society. For instance, when we hear Ralph Waldo Emerson's words, "He who would be a man must be an individualist," we cringe: arrogant, male individualism is the problem, not the answer. These are symptoms of how far we have traveled into liberalism's age of crisis. Our nineteenth–century forebears called theirs "the great century." Raymond Aron called the twentieth, "the century of total war"—for now whole populations take up arms against each other. W.H. Auden called our age, "the age of anxiety."

The twenty-first century will bring a new social context and, in consequence, a new meaning of "freedom": sharper awareness of the human limits and a narrowed sense of human possibilities. Does this mean an end of personal and social freedom as we know it? As an ideology of individualism, yes; as a socially embodied spiritual reality, no. Abraham Lincoln called for "a new birth of freedom" in the crisis of his age; we must call for a new covenant of freedom in the crisis of our age.

We Unitarian Universalists remain the children of the age of reason and democracy, of science-driven human progress and the discovery of human rights. We remain, also, the heirs of a noble tradition of liberal concern for civic values, social justice, and peace. This secular heritage is rooted in a theological affirmation: the dignity and sanctity of the every person as a bearer of the image of God.

A fundamental re-formation of the human spirit is emerging in our time. We must understand ourselves as engaged in that historic mission. We must believe that history is the story of freedom, agonized by the global struggle for justice. Or else our salt has lost its savor and may as well be cast out.

We too easily wrap ourselves in the cocoon of our own congregational life and forget that we are part of a world-historical movement. We dwindle into coziness and forget what brought us together in the first place: the keen sense that what we want most is to be part of something great—a historical drama in which we are actors and everything we cherish is at stake.

Birthright anti-traditionalists though we be, we are the bearers of a cherished tradition: liberalism has been the costing commitment of many before us. We believe in ourselves, but we are not sectarians who believe only in "we few." We affirm our congregations as agents of the church universal, the covenant people.

We are a covenant people, a spiritual community that is found wherever people come together in faithfulness to values that sustain and renew the common life of the public world. We must be explicit about what those values are. They are expressed in every age and tradition; the prophets of ancient Israel announced them in ringing tones: justice, faithfulness, steadfast love, mercy, truthfulness, good will, and peace.

These prophetic, covenantal values constitute us as a people. We did not choose them; by eliciting our commitment, they "choose" us. They are not optional ("preferences"), but essential to (creators of) our being. The covenant people is found everywhere around the globe and in all ages. It comes into being wherever people form communities dedicated to sustaining and renewing this vision—whenever they say, "This is the very meaning of our life together."

Transient is the reduction of "freedom" to "personal preference" and "do your own thing." Transient is the confusion of "liberal" with "lax," an ideology of freedom from shared obligations. Transient is the liberal church that is no more than a refuge from "orthodoxy," no more than a club for "our kind of people," a monoculture of the like-minded.

Permanent in liberal religion is this: devotion to spiritual freedom, the human capacity to act with creative good will in any situation, however dire. Freedom is a miracle, something inexplicable. It is demonstrated in our capacity to surpass ourselves. It is a spiritual reality that enables us to create a new thing under the sun, when we fulfill its conditions, its covenant.

What are the conditions—the requirements—of this covenant? Micah asks, "What does Yahweh require of you?" and he answers in terms of the prophetic, covenantal values: "to do justly, to love kindness, and to walk humbly with your God." Freedom is not free for the taking. We have it on exacting conditions: That we remember our finitude, our frailty, our fallibility—and therefore our interdependence. That we remember that we have personhood only in community (or we'd have died in infancy) and community only with commitment (or we won't have it for long). That we remember that liberation begins with ourselves, for it means freeing ourselves from whatever stands between us and the divine image—the creative good will—in which we are made. That we remember the principle of humility: "This I cannot do alone, nor for myself alone, but only with your help, by the grace of God."

That we live within a sacred covenant, and when we have broken it, we can renew it, in faith that this too is the promise of "the love that will not let us go."

Having made spiritual freedom central, our difficulties with "freedom"—reducing it to a manageable and appealing ideology—are almost inevitable. We are no exception to the general rule: What is celebrated as central in "every" religion is what gives it the most trouble. For instance, Jews rejoiced in being the chosen for Yahweh's covenant, and what it got them was Yahweh's denunciation, in Amos's prophetic interpretation: "You only have I known of all the families of the earth; therefore I will punish you for all your iniquities." (Amos 3:2) Our brave new covenants are forever degenerating into contracts—manageable "deals." Prophets, then, will arise, calling us to rediscover the miracle of freedom and renew the covenant of spiritual freedom.

Every religion worth its salt is founded on a miracle. This may seem disconcerting in a church that has made a specialty out of denying the existence of miracles. By reducing "miracle" to something contrary to science and reason—rather than the reality of spiritual liberation given through divine grace, clothed in ancient story—we denude the imagination. We become incomprehensible even to ourselves.

We are not free to believe whatever we want, any more than we are free to do whatever we want—unless, of course, we choose instant gratification and utter transience. We are free to believe what we must and to do what we must, in order to fulfill our human vocation, our calling to a larger humanity. The phrase, "in order that," signals an often-forgotten truth: freedom is only meaningful within a framework of purposeful action. The word "covenant" signifies a framework within which intentionality takes effect. Spiritual freedom seeks authentic self-transcendence.

Within this framework we enjoy much latitude for individual expression. Our religious communities should enjoy a diversity as various as humanity itself. But the covenantal framework itself is not optional; it is necessary, fated, and inescapable: "That's the deal," as Joy Gresham said to C.S. Lewis. We stumble over this truth again and again: Human possibilities emerge and shine most brightly in the face of limitations.

In other words, freedom emerges against a background of necessity, like a meteor in the night sky. Nicholas of Cusa spoke of "the coincidence of opposites"; freedom and necessity seem to be near opposites that nearly coincide. In time and history they are dialectically related, polarities of the kind Plato had in mind when he spoke of the one and the many, "one form pervading a scattered multitude, and many different forms contained under one higher form...." (*Sophist* 253d)

This abstract matter can be made concrete by considering the process of creating pottery on a wheel. When as a potter you form a lump of clay, you make many decisions, exercising your freedom both consciously and instinctively, to one end, a finished ceramic. The first step is highly self-conscious: "What do I want to make? Well, the possibilities are infinite—within the limits of the material, the tools, and my skill. Still, these limits are not absolute: I might venture a wholly new form, and succeed!"

The original decision in pottery making is not unlike the original decision of faith: once a direction has been set, soon it will be too late to change your mind. Choosing a bowl excludes a pitcher. Now choices are being made within an ever-narrowing range; necessity is closing in on the maker. But this is the miracle of creation: a reversal is also in progress, for the embrace of necessity gives birth to a greater freedom. With each choice, new, more refined choices arise; creative freedom is growing exponentially.

As in pottery making, so too in life: the process of making is also a process of discovering, for as the form takes shape, it begins to gain a life and an integrity of its own. As our gross, material freedom is narrowed, *mirabile dictu*, our refined, spiritual freedom grows by leaps and bounds. Suddenly we remember Nicholas of Cusa's principle: opposites coincide. The perfect end to the exercise of freedom is perfect necessity. We think: This bowl, or this life, can only be what it must be!

Do we romanticize the creative artist in us to say so? No doubt we do, but we think it anyway: Intentionality and practice conspire together to produce what is inevitable, "just so," complete and perfect. Although it never quite turns out that way—although the result is, by turns, both humbling and exalting—still, the miracle of having a hand in making a new thing has occurred. Spiritual freedom is like that: it exalts and humbles us again and again.

◆ ◆ ◆

James Luther Adams said, in *The Prophethood of All Believers,* "I call that church free which in covenant with the divine community-forming power brings the individual, even the unacceptable, into a caring, trusting fellowship that protects and nourishes integrity and spiritual freedom. Its goal is the prophethood and the priesthood of all believers—the one for the liberty of prophesying, the other for the ministry of healing."

Adams wrote these words for the 1975 sesquicentennial celebration of the American Unitarian Association, founded in 1825. They echo Channing's famous lines on the theme, "I call that mind free," from his Election Sermon of 1830, titled "Spiritual Freedom." But where Channing's heroic individualism exalted "the free mind," Adams's chastened liberalism, having imbibed the political and cultural crises of the twentieth century, exalts "the church that is free."

Between the Channing and the Adams there is both a continuity and radical break: both speak of

25

spiritual freedom, but with Adams, no longer the individual but "the dedicated community" (Paul Weiss) is the matrix, the sacred birthplace, of freedom. The dedicated community itself is the liberating reality, and our task as a liberal church is to model that for the world.

This accent also marks a renewal of theological awareness, for beyond the social vision lies a cosmic and sacred vision: "the interdependent web of existence of which we are a part." Jim Adams named it "the covenant of being." This is an unaccustomed way of thinking, for us, and it will provoke resistance. Nevertheless, this paradigm shift will transform our free faith in the new millennium, rescuing our permanency, the covenant of spiritual freedom, from our transience, the church as way-station en route to the golf course.

We covenant in spiritual freedom for a new humanity. We covenant: We freely commit ourselves to high and holy aims, aims that transcend us, aims of the Spirit. Not in freedom from obligations to others, but in freedom to enter into common endeavors for the common good. Not in freedom from the nourishing roots of our faith in ancient ages, but in freedom to give fresh interpretation to ancient symbols and stories. Not in freedom from being called to aims that surpass us, but in the freedom that springs from knowing that "we've caught a moving train" (Johnny Ray Youngblood), and, together, we're on our way.

We covenant in spiritual freedom: We find at the center of our faith an energizing mainspring, a drive for meaning and dignity implanted in every soul in every land—the wonder of being alive and awakened to life, the grace of beginning anew. Not in the self-enclosing isolation of the self, but in the quest for a more inclusive covenant. Not in narrow-mindedness or in mean-spirited debunking of things cherished by others, but in listening for the spirit of life and truth wherever it arises. Not in fearfulness that life runs out and nothing can be done, but in the courage to turn every crisis of life into an opportunity for growth and spiritual depth.

We covenant in spiritual freedom for a new humanity: We seek a better world where all peoples can flourish, sharing in the resources of planet Earth and sustaining her natural ecology, a new humanity within the covenant of being. Not closing our eyes to the awesome tasks that stand before us, but committing ourselves to labor tirelessly for the physical, moral, and spiritual well-being of all. Not despairing of the human prospect, but affirming hope, and the sacredness of the image in which we are made. Not stone-hearted when we are called to make a new beginning, nor giving up when our need is to persevere, but affirming our quest for wholeness and holiness.

Congregational Polity and the Covenant

Conrad Wright

———————————◆———————————

Although he has graciously allowed us to include it, Profes-sor Wright's paper was not written especially for this collec-tion. It does address our theme. North American Unitarian congregations grew directly from those gathered by seven-teenth-century New England Puritans. Over time, parts of the Puritans' understanding of the church proved transient. Yet the Puritans also bequeathed to us the heritage of the freely entered covenant, of abiding, continuing, and central importance.

The polity of Unitarian Universalist churches is con-gregational, rather than Presbyterian or Episcopal. To be sure, there can be considerable variation in actual practice among churches adhering to congregational polity. Unitarian Universalists like to think of themselves as more properly congregational than the Congregationalists now part of the United Church of Christ, who have accepted some elements of Presbyterian hierarchical control. On the other hand, there are many conservation churches that reject any denominational organization comparable to the UUA as much too centralized, as well as quite unscriptural. The essential principle of congregational polity, however, is found when ultimate authority rests in the local society.

Our way of practicing congregational polity goes back to the great Puritan migration to New England in the 1630s. Some of our older churches were gathered at that time and have been self-governing ever since. The Puritans set forth the principles of their polity in *A Platform of Church Discipline* (1648), commonly referred to as the "Cambridge Platform." It carefully defines both the "matter" of the visible church—that is to say, the qualifications of those who are the material of which the church is composed; and the "form" of the visible church—that is to say, what it is that transforms a collection of religiously concerned individuals into a religious community. The language of the Puritans is not ours, and some parts of their definitions have been discarded in the course of generations; but certain basic essentials are to be found there, which are as important today as they were then.

The "matter" of the visible church was defined

in the Platform as "saints by calling"—those who, there is good reason to believe, will be numbered among the righteous at the Day of Judgement. We no longer believe in the Day of Judgement, at least in that sense, nor do we accept the Calvinistic doctrine of election. But we still would agree that full church membership, involving both privileges and obligations, depends on a conscious, voluntary decision. Our children may be born with the watch and care of a religious community, and we may acknowledge that fact by a ceremony of baptism, or christening, or consecration. But it is only when they approach adulthood, and are made aware of the significance of the act, that we may decide to seek membership.

Adopting the typology made familiar by Ernst Troeltsch, we may say that congregationalism is the polity of religious groups of the "sect" type, as contrasted with the "Church" type. For Troeltsch, the "Church" is that form of religious organization that seeks to be coextensive with a whole society. A national church, like the Church of England in the early seventeenth century, would be the example most closely conforming to the ideal type. All inhabitants of the realm were presumptively part of the established church. Those who lived in a particular parish were part of that parish by birth and domicile, not by their own choice. The "sect," on the other hand, is formed by the voluntary association of like-minded believers. Thus the Puritans, who protested what they saw as corruption in the established church, sought one another out for mutual aid and comfort, and found the true church in small communities of faithful souls. The "sect" was their type of organization; congregationalism or "independence" was their polity.

For a community of the faithful to come into being, however, pinquity is not enough. "*Saints by calling*," says the Cambridge Platform, "must have a Visible-Political-Union amongst themselves, or else they are not yet a particular church." There must be some organizational basis, or "form," so that individual believers may be orderly knit together. This form is the visible covenant, or agreement, commonly called the "church covenant." From the church as a community, one is entitled to expect care and concern for one's own well-being; but one is equally obligated to express care and concern for others. So there is an element of commitment in the act of joining a church, which the covenant expresses.

The authors of the Cambridge Platform acknowledge that a covenant might be implicit, expressed by silent consent as people walk together and show concern for one another. But an explicit covenant is far better, they argued, as reminding the members of their mutual duty and stirring them up to it. When a church was gathered, therefore, the covenant would be read, and all would give their assent to it. When the church exercised discipline over its members, offenses would be understood as breaches of the covenant. If a member removed to some other community, he or she did not silently disappear, but sought dismissal and release from the obligations of the covenant.

The earliest New England covenants were simple statements of agreement to walk together. The Salem covenant of 1629 is only one sentence long: "We Covenant with the Lord and one with an other; and doe bynd ourselves in the presence of God, to walke together in all his waies, according as he is pleased to reveale himself unto us in his Blessed word of truth." The Boston covenant of 1630 is slightly longer, but expresses the same intention: "to walke in all our wayes according to the Rule of the Gospell, and in all sincere Conformity to His holy Ordinaunces, and in mutual love, and respect each to other, so neere as God shall give us grace."

These early covenants did not take the form of creedal statements, nor did they prescribe doctrinal standards for admission to church fellowship. That is not because diversity of doctrinal belief was acceptable, but because theological uniformity could be taken for granted and did not need to be spelled out. But uniformity of belief cannot be maintained indefinitely, and later on the simple covenants were rewritten to include creedal formulations. In the eighteenth century, when religious liberalism began to appear, and Arminian and antitrinitarian views found expression in some quarters, the orthodox fenced in their churches with very explicit creedal covenants.

The covenant gave form to the particular church, but the church was not the only ecclesiastical body in early New England. Until the demise of the Standing Order (Connecticut in 1818, New Hampshire in 1819, Massachusetts in 1833), it was the town, or the parish as a subdivision of a town, that was obligated to support the public worship of God. All inhabitants, not just church members, were liable to be assessed for the construction and maintenance of the meeting house and for the salary of the minister. The church—the covenanted body of those admitted to the Lord's table and were subject to church discipline—was a much smaller number than the whole body of inhabitants of town or parish.

For obvious reasons, the church members would often be more concerned to maintain standards of theological orthodoxy than the inhabitants at large. Hence the liberalism that came to be known as Unitarianism tended to develop in the large ecclesiastical community of the parish rather than in the smaller ecclesiastical community that was the church. In such cases, the church declined in importance, and the parish became the true religious community. The covenant, with its creedal coloration, tended to be associated with orthodoxy; while some liberals made it a mark of their liberalism that their religious organizations no longer used covenants.

The organizing function performed by covenants was not abolished by disuse of the term, however. Substitutes began to appear, such as "Bond of Union" or "Bond of Fellowship." One formulation adopted in a number of Unitarian churches was composed by Charles G. Ames in 1880 for the Spring Garden Church (now extinct) in Philadelphia. His original wording was: "In the freedom of the truth, and the spirit of Jesus, we unite for the worship of God and the service of Man." Such a statement is a covenant in everything but name; indeed it is closer in spirit to the primitive covenants of Salem and Boston than to the creedal covenants that had become common in more orthodox circles.

While Ames's Bond of Fellowship includes words with theological significance, it is not a creedal statement. The operative words are "unite," not "we believe." The difference is significant. A creedal covenant sets up a test by which the fitness of prospective members may be judged, and some may be denied admission. A noncreedal covenant, like Ames's Bond of Fellowship, suggests the purposes of the community of faith, but leaves it to the individual to decide whether to unite. We long ago rejected creedal tests for membership as a way to exclude any whose views may be eccentric or even heretical. We have no mechanism by which one seeking to join may be examined or tested by some ecclesiastical authority for orthodoxy of doctrine. The boundary lines of our churches are drawn by many acts of individual choice, not by official judgement.

A Bond of Union, a Bond of Fellowship, a covenant, or even a statement of purpose as a preamble to a set of bylaws, may be functionally the same thing. But there is something to be said for the word "covenant," quite apart from the fact of its long currency. It emphasizes that the church is a community of mutual obligation, which involves a sense of commitment. Even the freest of free churches needs that much discipline if it is to last long enough to accomplish anything of value in this world.

Worship and the Spiritual Life

Theodore Parker Speaks

Edited, written, and arranged by Richard M. Fewkes

———————◆———————

I must admit that I was indeed flattered to be asked to write an address for a book to be titled *The Transient and Permanent in Liberal Religion*. Your theme, is, as you know, close to the title of my now famous discourse at the ordination of Charles Shackford in South Boston, on the 19th of May, 1841. "The Transient and The Permanent in Christianity" was the first ordination sermon I ever preached and the first separate document I ever published with my own name.

It was a raw, cold day in May that day, and was perhaps a sign of how my remarks were to be received. At the time it brought me not fame, but infamy and cost me my reputation in the so-called "Christian Church." Even the Unitarian ministers, who were themselves reckoned but the tail of heresy, denounced me as "no Christian," and an "Infidel." They did what they could to effect my ruin—denied me all friendly intercourse, dropped me from committees of their liberal college, in public places refused my hand extended as before in friendly salutation; mocked at me in their solemn meetings; struck my name out of their Almanac—the only Unitarian form of excommunication. So you can understand why it gives me such great pleasure to have my thoughts and reflections welcomed and appreciated by my ministerial colleagues. It may have taken more than 150 years, but I have learned to be patient, and can now say that at long last I have been vindicated. After all, it took the Papacy more than 350 years to vindicate the views of Galileo, so who am I to complain about a mere 154 years.

Permit me, if you will, to say a few words about the context of events leading up to my ordination address of 1841. A few years before I happened to be present on the occasion of Mr. Emerson's Divinity School Address at Harvard on the 15th of July in 1838. I shall give no abstract of that sterling discourse—it being well known to all of you—except to say that to my aspiring mind it was so beautiful, so just, so true and terribly sublime in its picture of the faults of the Church in its present position. I considered it the noblest, the most inspiring strain I ever listened to. Others considered it inappropriate to the occasion, unchristian in its views, and verging on pantheism.

I did not agree with all of its sentences, but I delighted in its poetic sentiments and the declaration that the Spirit of God was more alive in our own life experience and the laws of nature than in the dead hand of tradition. To me it was a breath of fresh air in a stale and stagnant institution. If that made me a Transcendentalist then I was glad to own the name. I returned to my parish in West Roxbury with my soul deeply stirred and with the resolution fixed afresh in my mind to reflect on the state of the Church and the duties of the times.

In the controversy that followed Mr. Emerson's address, I entered into the public debate with the publication of a pamphlet, under a pseudonym, Levi Blodgett. In it I defended the Transcendentalist doctrine of the "instinctive intuition of the divine," which required neither the testimony of Scripture nor the belief in miracles for its authority. I wrote under a pseudonym because I wanted truth to speak for itself above the contention of personalities. Many suspected that I was the author, which I neither confirmed nor denied. I was a young minister serving his first parish, and few would care what Theodore Parker thought or said. My pseudonym gave me an entree into the public forum, and I was satisfied to have my views considered without the trumpet of self-approbation.

It was the furthest thing from my mind that I myself would become the center of yet another Transcendentalist controversy within the Unitarian church and ministry, even more heated than that occasioned by Mr. Emerson's Divinity School Address. Nor was it my intention to issue a Manifesto of Transcendentalist Unitarianism when I was invited to preach at the ordination of Mr. Charles Shackford. I preached the kind of sermon I had often preached to my own congregation and the views expressed were ones I had written and spoken of publicly in the recent past.

The title of my sermon was taken from an essay by the German New Testament scholar David Strauss, and I endeavored to show that the theologies and doctrines about Christ were transient and changeable from one generation to another, while his moral teachings of love to God and love to humankind were permanent and true whether he ever spoke them or not. Even if he never existed, his teachings were still true. That is the gist of what I said and even many of my more conservative Unitarian colleagues seemed courteous and well disposed to my remarks.

Indeed, the whole matter might have been forgotten, but for the response of some orthodox clergy—a Congregationalist, a Methodist, and a Baptist—who happened to be present for the occasion. They prepared a critical summary of my discourse for publication in several of their journals. Unitarianism was already considered "a halfway house to infidelity" by the orthodox and they believed that my discourse was "proof of the pudding." They had no doubt that I was an infidel and an atheist and asked whether other

Unitarian clergy considered me to be a Christian preacher. They even expressed surprise that no one had asked Mr. Shackford to disavow my opinions as a condition for continuation of the ordination service! Later they suggested that I might be considered as a candidate for public trial of blasphemy as was done to Universalist Abner Kneeland only three years before.

And how did my Unitarian brethren in the ministry respond to these outrageous charges of the orthodox? I am pained to say that they were only too willing to agree, with few if any reservations. If the objective of my orthodox critics was to turn my colleagues in the Unitarian ministry against me, to have them ostracize me and to disavow my right to preach Christian truth as I saw it from Unitarian pulpits, other than my own, well then, I am ashamed to say that, for a time, they succeeded. Even some of the Unitarian laity joined the chorus of closure. A certain Mr. Bradford declared that he would rather see every Unitarian congregation in the land dissolved and every one of our churches razed to the ground, than to permit a man with the sentiments of Theodore Parker to speak from our pulpits.

The repercussions and aftermath of that ordination sermon in 1841 were greater than I ever would have anticipated or believed possible. Before that occasion I was well liked and respected by my ministerial colleagues. Afterwards I was shunned and finally asked to resign from their distinguished Boston Association. Matters came to a head in January 1843. I had recently published an elaboration of my theological views in a book, *Discourse of Matters Pertaining to Religion.* I was invited to meet with the Association so that we might discuss my opinions.

It became apparent from the start of the meeting that they were displeased with my theological views. I was accused of being "vehemently deistical" and that the difference between us was a case of "Christianity and no Christianity." I argued that differences of theological opinion ought to exist and had always existed within the Boston Association. Moreover, I wished to know "the precise quiddity" that must be added to my view of Absolute Religion to make it "Christian." The answer given was belief in the miracles as set forth in Scripture which established the authority of Christ. The doctrinal line had been drawn.

Because I did not believe in supernatural miracles, that made me no Christian in their eyes. It was therefore suggested that in view of the lack of sympathy with the opinions of the other members it was my duty to withdraw my membership in the Boston Association. I refused to accede to their wishes, told them I had no intention of resigning, that I considered the principle of free inquiry to be at stake, that I was as personally committed to the ministry as any of them, and that unless they were disposed to prescribe a doctrinal test for membership, I would stay. I suppose this was the closest the Unitarians ever came to a heresy trial.

I confess that I was deeply hurt and moved to tears by their charges. Later I wrote in my journal: "I once thought them noble; that they would be true to an ideal principle of right. I find that no body of men was ever more completely sold to the sense of expediency." Had it all come to this because I spoke my mind in an ordination sermon in 1841?

I recall that one of the critics of my sermon said that it was not appropriate to the occasion. Not appropriate to preach the truth about the church and religion one is soon to embark upon? That was the very thing they said about Mr. Emerson's Divinity School Address. At least I was in good company. Mr. Emerson, however, had left the ministry because of certain philosophical disagreements, which he set forth admirably in his address three years before. I was determined that I would stay the course and not be forced out by those who could not bear to hear other views of Christian truth spoken from their Unitarian pulpits. Though they would refuse the courtesy of pulpit exchanges, I was intent that I would preach and lecture in the city and the glen, by the roadside and the field-side, if need be, and wherever men and women could be found. They would have my voice silenced in Boston. I would rise and go eastward and westward, northward and southward, and make the land *ring*.

The opportunity to do just that came in February of 1845 when several Unitarian laymen from Boston invited me to lecture and preach at the Melodeon Theatre. Week after week we filled the theatre. By December I was persuaded to leave my pastorate in West Roxbury and to become minister to the newly formed 28th Congregational Society in Boston. The focus of my preaching shifted from theological reform to social and political reform. I became increasingly involved in the antislavery movement and urged opposition to the Fugitive Slave Act. The audiences at the Melodeon Theatre had grown to such numbers that a move was necessitated in 1852 to the new Music Hall, whose seating capacity of 2,700 persons was soon to be taxed to the limit.

The distance between me and my more conservative ministerial colleagues was not to be bridged except for a kind of strained cordiality between us. I was referred to in some of the Unitarian publications as a "lecturer...formerly recognized as a Unitarian preacher." That I still considered myself to be a Unitarian preacher mattered not. I began to feel some sense of vindication of my views in that a growing number of young Divinity School graduates were partial to my opinions and deigned to call themselves "Parkerites." I neither sought nor needed personal approbation, but I was secretly delighted to note the growing diversity of theological views within the Unitarian church.

In the summer of 1853, in a futile attempt to stem the tide of change, the Executive Committee of the American Unitarian Association, which was headed by my conservative opponents, secured the adoption of an elaborate "declaration of opinion" that strongly resembled a creed. It declared "the Divine origin (and) authority of the religion of Jesus Christ" and that God did raise him up "to aid in our redemption from sin." It was hoped that the declaration would relieve the Unitarian body of the "excessive radicalism and irreverence of some who have stood nominally within our own circle." To whom do you suppose they might have been referring? Though individuals were at liberty to dissent from the declaration of opinion, it is clear that they wanted to make my religious and spiritual companions feel less than welcome in the Association. Well, just as they were unsuccessful in their attempts to make Theodore Parker withdraw from the Boston Association so were they unsuccessful in forcing the Parkerites from the Unitarian church.

I take no satisfaction in the fact that Parkerism or Transcendentalism eventually prevailed in the Unitarian movement. I sought no following nor followers of the person of Theodore Parker. What I wished for was free inquiry in the church and the right to pursue religious truth as one's heart and mind and conscience would lead one and the willingness of the Unitarian clergy and laity to consider new views and ideas of religion, even those considered radical and unpopular.

Theodore Parker the person is perhaps not read or quoted much by Unitarian Universalists today. That is all well and good. I am satisfied that in the course of time Theodore Parker's ideas received a fair hearing before the throne of truth and that others have taken up the quest for religious truth in directions I had not thought of nor considered. The best testimonial to my ordination sermon of 150 plus years ago is to continue the quest and to seek those permanent truths of religion that will stand the test of time.

In terms of the Unitarian Universalist Association today, I am pleased to see that your new statement of principles and purposes is inclusive and welcoming to a wide variety of religious and theological sources—Christian, theist, humanist—as well as the insights of science and the contributions of other world religions. You have put up a wide umbrella. But in your eagerness to embrace new views and new sources of spirituality do not forget your origins and roots in the religion of Jesus, else you may find yourself intentionally or unintentionally making Christian Unitarian Universalists feel unwelcome in your midst. You did not create this new and inclusive faith for the new millennium with the intention of forcing anybody out.

One of the things that utterly delights me in terms of the changes that have taken place in the liberal church of your day is the entrance of women into the ministry and into the arena of theological thought and debate. But there is still much work for you to do to right the wrongs of the centuries against the role of Woman in church and society. She was shut out of the choir, barred from the priest's house, banned from the pulpit, and told to keep silent in church. If Woman had been consulted, it seems to me theology would have been in a vastly better state in both my time and yours. I do not think that any woman would ever have preached the damnation of babies new-born—why, you could not get a woman who had intellect enough to open her mouth to preach such things anywhere. For centuries theology left us nothing feminine in the character of God. How could it be otherwise when so much of the so-called orthodox theology was the work of men who thought Woman was a "pollution," and barred her out of all the high places of the Church?

I said it to my generation and I say it again to yours that Woman has the same individual right to determine her aim in life and to follow it; has the same individual rights of body and of spirit, of mind and conscience, and heart and soul; the same physical rights, the same intellectual, moral, affectional, and religious rights that Man has. This is true of womankind as a whole, and of each special woman who can be named. In domestic affairs she is to determine her own sphere as much as Man, and say where her function is to begin, when it shall begin, with whom it shall begin; where it shall end, when it shall end, and what it shall comprise. Moreover, there is no reason why women should not vote, hold office, make and administer laws, and have the same right to freedom of industry that men have. You, at least, have made progress in these areas, but do not become complacent in your accomplishments, for there are those who would take away the rights you have won for yourselves as women and men.

To every woman let me say, Respect your nature as a human being, your nature as a woman; then respect your rights; then remember your duty to possess, to use, to develop, and to enjoy every faculty that God has given you, each in its normal way. And to men let me say, Respect—with the profoundest reverence respect—the mother that bore you, the sisters who bless you, the woman that you love, the woman that you marry. As you seek to possess your own manly rights, seek also to vindicate her rights as Woman, as your own as Man. Then may we see better things in the Church, better things in the State, in the community, in the home. Then the green shall show what buds it hid; the buds shall blossom; the flowers bear fruit; and the blessing of God be on us all.

I would say to your generation what I said to mine. The church that is to lead the new millennium will not be a church creeping on all fours; mewling and whining, its face turned down, its eyes turned back. It must be full of the adventurous spirit of the day, but keeping also the good of times past. But the church that did for the fifth century, or the fifteenth, or even the nineteenth century, will not do for the church of the new millennium. The church of the new millennium must have the smell of your own ground, and grow out of the religion of your own soul.

A church that believes only in past inspiration will appeal to old books as the standard of truth and source of light, will be antiquarian in its habits, and ward on the new age. A church that believes in inspiration now will appeal to the Holy Spirit here present and alive, try things by reason and conscience, aim to surpass the old heroes, baptize its children with a new spirit, and using the present age will lead public opinion and not follow it.

Let us have a church that dares imitate the heroism of Jesus; seek inspiration as he sought it; judge the past as he; act on the present like him; pray as he prayed; work as he wrought; live as he lived. Let our doctrines and our forms fit the soul, as the limbs fit the body, growing out of it, growing with it. Let us have a church for the whole person—truth for the mind, good works for the hands, love for the heart and for the soul—that embraces the aspiring after perfection, the unfaltering faith in God which, like lightning in the clouds, shines brightest when elsewhere it is most dark. Let our church for the new millennium fit the human soul as the heavens fit the earth.

If your ministers are filled with this new religion of the spirit, it will not let them rest. They must speak, whether people hear or whether they forbear. No fear can scare, no bribe can charm, no friends can coax them down from speaking the truth in love. The church, the state, the world oppose them, all in vain. You may have to pay a price, as did the prophets who went before you, of exclusion, rejection, misunderstanding, even martyrdom. But in the course of the centuries, truth will be vindicated, and love will embrace even those who feared its touch and transformation.

In closing I would reiterate the basic message of my sermon on "The Transient and Permanent In Christianity." The permanent truths of religion, the truths of absolute morality, of love to God and love to humankind, set loose upon the world without let or hindrance, are still true, whether spoken by Jesus of Nazareth, Theodore Parker, Levi Blodgett, or unattached to any name. They are as true today as they were yesterday and will be tomorrow. And so let us be about the practice of these truths, not because Jesus taught them two millennia ago, or Theodore Parker preached them 150 years ago, but because they are the eternal moral truths of God and of the human spirit. All of the changing and transitory theologies and christologies of the Christian church will do us no good if we do not put the enduring moral teachings of the Nazarene into practice and make them our own.

May I close with a blessing and a prayer: O thou Creating and Sustaining Power, who art our Father, yea, our Mother not the less, help us to use this world which thou hast given us, to build up the being that we are to a nobler stature of strength and beauty. And may we educate and cultivate our powers of mind, conscience, and heart till we have attained the measure and stature of a whole and perfect humanity and have passed from glory to glory. May thy truth be our thought, thy justice our will, thy loving-kindness the feeling of our heart, and thy holiness and integrity the course of our daily life. Amen.

The Passionate Enduring Center

John Alexie Crane

Individual Unitarian Universalists may describe themselves as Unitarian Universalist, Christian, Jewish, humanist, atheist, or theist. The movement as a whole, however, is not identified by any belief system. The movement is identified by persisting and powerful underlying dynamics. What is the passionate, enduring center of Unitarian Universalist faith?

Near the end of one of his essays, William James made a provocative observation. He said that deep within us is a "region of the heart in which we dwell alone with our willingness and our unwillingness, our faiths and our fears.... In these crepuscular depths of personality the sources of all our deeds and decisions take their rise. Here is our deepest organ of communication with the nature of things."[1]

Many other thinkers have pointed in this direction. Joseph Campbell used the phrase "our own most secret motivating depths."[2] The language of James and Campbell is inexact, to be sure, but they both call our attention to this significant, though elusive, level of the self. Classical scholar Gilbert Murray also referred to this area of our being when he said, "A creed or a catechism is, of course, not at all the same thing as the real religion of those who subscribe to it."[3]

Our deepest and most practical beliefs are those on which we act without question. Other terms are used in philosophy and theology to point to this part of the self, such as faith assumptions, cognitive set, world view, standpoint, prereflective knowledge, mindset, and tacit knowledge. I will use the term mindset.[4] I refer to that subliminal structure in each of us that underlies our thoughts, perceptions, feelings, and actions and is their primary source.

Our mindset—made up of a set of attitudes, assumptions, ideals, values, preferences, prejudices, beliefs—is so much who we are that we are unable to approach the world in any other way than we do. Because our mindset is who we are, we are only partially aware of it. Its contents cannot be listed exhaustively. Yet by observing the behavior of oneself and others over time, it is possible to infer many of the characteristic elements in the mindset of an individual or of a given institution or culture.

It has often been noted, as scholar Glen Fisher points out, that mindset varies from culture to culture, making cross-cultural communication difficult. Members of a subculture will give evidence of being moved by a different mindset than people in the large culture. Those who find their way to a UU church have, it seems to me, a different mindset than people in more conventional churches.

Most of the people in any culture find meaning in a religion defined largely by tradition. Both Judaism and Christianity are founded upon a body of truth revealed centuries ago. The message and practice in these groups are determined by traditions centuries old with some ongoing revision in response to contemporary knowledge.

A minority in any population does not find meaning or reward in a religion defined largely by tradition. Many have grown up within one or another of the traditional religions, but at some point found they no longer responded to the ancient message. They began to feel like outsiders among those who did find meaning and reward in the traditional church or temple. Some of these find their way to a liberal church where they are surprised to discover they feel entirely at home.

In a UU church people exceedingly diverse in their beliefs come together around a shared search for truth. They share a quest for continuous growth and renewal of their understanding of themselves and their world. A UU church is a community of seekers.

Both conventional and liberal religions are important to society, though in different ways. Joseph Campbell in *The Masks of God* pointed out that "The paramount concern of a popular religion cannot be, and never has been 'Truth' but the maintenance of a certain type of society, the inculcation in the young and refreshment in the old of an approved 'system of sentiments' upon which the local institutions and government depend."[5] The aim of popular religion is not truth but order, essential in any society.

UU religion is of another sort. We exist within an established social structure, but our principal aim is not order; it is truth. Ours is an extremely valuable cultural construction: an institutionalized form of philosophical religion.

Each of our congregations is a community of people who provide stimulation, support, and love for each other as, together, they seek ever growing understanding of their existence. The gathering itself of a UU community to share in this quest is its primary sacrament.

UU religious communities have some traditions, of course, but they are not constituted by their traditions. UU religion is defined by a tacit commitment to truth progressively realized in the present life of each person. This has implications for worship.

In the Christian tradition, worship has been defined as "the exhibition to God by some act of the mind or body or both, of the honor and reverence due to him by reason of his supreme dominion."[6] Worship understood in this way has generated majestic art, architecture, and music. The God referred to is the God of Our Fathers, seen for centuries as the Emperor of the Universe. Alfred North Whitehead made a striking observation. "When the Western world accepted Christianity," he observed, "Caesar conquered." The tradition committed the idolatry of "fashioning God in the image of the Egyptian, Persian, and Roman imperial rulers.... The church gave unto God the attributes which belonged exclusively to Caesar."[7] This deity, well suited to the maintenance of social order, was also well suited to serve as an object of worship as worship is traditionally defined.

Philosophical religion found its way to other, less conventional conceptions of God. These have generated in UU religion a tacit definition of worship as an art form. It aims at the creation of meaning, verbal and nonverbal, and at the creation of understanding and insight bearing on the conduct of life.

Worship is an art form whose substance is meaning. Meaning is experienced in the symbolic, linguistic, and institutional forms through which we find direction for our existence, thoughts, feelings, judgments, and actions. Epiphany figures large in UU worship services. An epiphany is "a sudden, intuitive perception or insight into the reality or essential meaning" of some aspect of existence.[8] In worship, epiphany is an intense experience of expanded understanding in the individual. The epiphany may be so sweeping, so deep that it may carry insight out beyond the reach of language. The person may be able only partially to express the insight in words.

A wonderfully rich sense of community is generated in many of our congregations. You feel it at District meetings. At the annual General Assembly. At retreats. At summer conferences. On Sunday mornings in our societies all over the continent.

Which is odd: We are extreme individualists. Yet a sense of community among us is rich and deep. Why should this be when we are so strongly committed to individual freedom of belief?

It is because the sense of community springs, not from a body of shared beliefs, but from the underlying mindset we hold in common. It springs from the tacitly held set of values, conceptions, assumptions, ideas, ideals, and goals we carry within us, which generates resonances in us when we come together. We are a community of seekers, committed to the search for truth. We are joined at the level of our existential roots, at the deep level of the mindset.

Our religious beliefs are diverse. They are transient. Permanent is the dynamic, creative mindset we share. It is a mindset that has repeatedly thrust us into a heretical role. It is a factor in new insight, in unconventional thinking, a source of cultural evolution.

All mindsets will continue to be shrouded in

mystery. It is possible, however, to infer elements of a people's mindset by closely observing over time the behavior that flows from it.

A survey of Unitarian Universalists was developed by the National Opinion Research Center in the mid-1960s. The data are reported and analyzed in a book by Robert B. Tapp, published in 1973.[9] When asked what rewards they most looked for in their worship services, 97 percent of Unitarian Universalists, given a multiple choice, opted for intellectual stimulation. Our religion does not offer ultimate answers. This indicates that in the mindset of Unitarian Universalists is a willingness to tolerate ambiguity. "Beware ultimate answers" is a tacit UU maxim.

Distrust of final answers also suggests that Unitarian Universalists take for granted that their religion is not in the mind alone, but in their whole being. The nineteenth- and twentieth-century phrase "salvation by character" bespoke this assumption.

A conviction in the mindset of a community of seekers is that human beings shape their lives by their actions, choices, and decisions—within limits imposed by natural order. Neither God nor Satan determine our fate; nor do we look for the intervention of a divine savior. A faith assumption is part of the UU mindset, faith in human power and potential. Unitarians and Universalists are inclined to celebrate humanity, what it is and what it may become.

Another element in the UU mindset is a com-

mitment to self-government, as opposed to governance by others. Autonomy is a major goal for Unitarian Universalists. Unitarian Universalists want to
govern themselves rather than be passive before their
social conditioning.

A study of UU values was carried out in 1975 by
Robert L'H Miller.[10] Miller noticed that a sociologist,
Milton Rokeach, had made a comparative study of the
values of Catholics, Protestants, Jews, and the unchurched. Miller took the same survey instrument,
administered it to Unitarian Universalists, then compared the results with Rokeach's findings. The outcome was interesting. For example, Miller learned that
though Unitarian Universalists are widely diverse in
their stated beliefs, they share a remarkably homogeneous set of values in a distinct and unique configuration.[11]

Even more strikingly, he found that rich Catholics and rich Protestants held a different set of values
than poor members of their churches held; new members held different values than long-term members.
But neither wealth nor any other variables affected
the typical UU value configuration. Poor Unitarian
Universalists had the same values as rich ones. New
Unitarian Universalists had the same values as members of long standing.[12] Miller said at the end of his
study, "The data supports the conclusion that being a
Unitarian Universalist is characterized by holding a
constellation of values which differentiates such per-

sons from other kinds of religious communities and, at the same time, develops an internal sense of community and a homogeneous community.

"The UU set of values is marked by the uniquely high ranking of a constellation of terminal values: self-respect, wisdom, inner harmony, mature love, a world of beauty, and an exciting life."[13]

In Rokeach's design were two sets of values of eighteen each. He designated the second set as Instrumental Values. Unitarian Universalists here chose values "largely focused on competence, [and] also ranked uniquely high: loving, independent, intellectual, imaginative, and logical. This distinctive quality of being religious in the Unitarian Universalist paradigm reflects a religion of personal realization, individual self-fulfillment, and self-actualization."

Miller ended his article by pointing out that,

The value survey data gives added detail to observations articulated in 1967 in the report of a denominational Committee on Goals (headed by Robert B. Tapp).

For us...the search for meaning in our personal and social lives, the experience of handling our joys and tragedies, the search for profound and satisfying human relationships, the pondering of our place in the total scheme of things, the awareness of the separation between our potential and our actions—our aspirations and our achievements—all of these we believe to be truly religious. Together they suggest to us a common commitment to the expansion of the quality of life. This roots our theology, our thinking about religion, both in life and in humanity's self-transcendence.[14]

"A common commitment to the expansion of the quality of life" and to "humanity's self-transcendence" are two other features in the UU mindset.

The UU mindset endures in our movement. It draws us together in community. It plays a significant part in shaping our thoughts, feelings, actions, and reactions. It is our passionate enduring center. And we are its servants, not its master.

The Lotus in the West

James Ishmael Ford

———————◆———————

Buddhism truly has come west. In addition to the various Asian Buddhist enclaves long established in the West, increasing numbers of North Americans of European and African descent are now finding Buddhism relevant in their lives. Starting from a few eccentrics in the nineteenth century, today a noticeable minority of Westerners have converted to Buddhism.

Also, many Westerners have discovered an ongoing interest in Buddhism without leaving their original faiths. While remaining Christians or Jews, these contemporary pilgrims have embraced Buddhist practice and perspectives as integral to their spiritual lives. And, most relevant for us, this interest in cross-religious disciplines has included a number of Unitarian Universalists.

Western religious liberals have been fascinated with Buddhism from as early as 1844, when Elizabeth Palmer Peabody's anonymous rendition of a chapter from the *Saddharmapundarika-sutra* was published in the transcendentalist journal, the *Dial.* This chapter, "The Preaching of Buddha," became the first Buddhist text available in the English language. This seminal event was for years credited incorrectly to Henry David Thoreau,[1] which may account partly for the mystique Buddhism has held for Unitarian Universalists since that time.

Over the years many Unitarian Universalists have found themselves drawn to Buddhism, studying its sacred writings, practicing its spiritual disciplines, and even taking the Precepts—formally becoming Buddhists. These days there is even a Unitarian Universalist Buddhist Fellowship. Only time will tell whether this is merely a fad or a harbinger of something profound happening within our movement.

It is important to consider some of those aspects of Buddhism that Unitarian Universalists have found so compelling, particularly as we reflect on the shape of our liberal faith at the beginning of a new century.

There are, of course, as many different schools of Buddhist thought as there are Christian. The range of belief among Buddhists is as wide as that between Roman Catholics and Mormons and Quakers, if not wider. Still, some basic concepts seem to be shared by virtually all Buddhists.

Buddhism is based in the teachings of a historic person, Gautama Siddhartha, who became the Buddha. There is some dispute over the actual dates, but he lived in northern India roughly between the sixth and fifth centuries before the birth of Christ. The stories say he was born into wealth and nobility. In his search for wisdom Siddhartha rejected his privileged condition to became a mendicant practicing severe privations.

After a number of years, unable to find peace or wisdom through either extreme of self-indulgence or self-privation, he took up a middle way between these extremes, grounded in a practice of silence and simple presence. The stories differ in detail, but after great effort on this middle way, Siddhartha came to some profound experience of insight. From that moment he was known as the Buddha, the "awakened one."

The Buddha's teachings are summarized as the Four Noble Truths.[2] The First Noble Truth is expressed in the Sanskrit word *duhkha*, usually translated as suffering. This is accurate, but in itself not complete. *Duhkha* means suffering, pain, unsatisfactoriness, angst, anguish. It speaks to a fundamental characteristic of our human condition. In the First Noble Truth, the Buddha proclaimed this *duhkha*, this suffering, is a foundational existential truth that cannot be escaped or ignored.

This unblinking "real world" approach may be the first element of Buddhist teachings that genuinely draws Unitarian Universalists. As with Buddhists, Unitarian Universalists try hard to live in the real world, however unpleasant it may be. This insight into ubiquitous human suffering, a common existential anxiety, has resonated as a simple and observable truth for many religious liberals.

The Second Noble Truth explains the Buddha's understanding of the cause of *duhkha* in *tanha. Tanha* means literally "thirst." It points to a particular aspect of our human condition, what may be called a "clinging consciousness."

The Buddha asserted that the human self is without ultimate substance. As with all other things, the human self is the product of numerous factors coming together, none of which are themselves permanent. He taught that our sense of permanence, and our belief that other people and things are permanent, rises naturally, but is illusory. It is this false sense of permanence for self or universe that is the clinging consciousness.

The Buddha did not mean the universe is illusion or *maya,* as the Hindus claimed. He unequivocally asserted that we live real, concrete, tangible lives in a real, concrete, and tangible universe. But, and this is the critical point: we live conditioned existences.

Our lives are relative, rising and passing in time within a play of cause and effect. The core of the teaching of *tanha* is that our perceived self has no ultimate substance. And our suffering in the sense of *duhkha* comes from clinging to what is passing as if it were permanent.

The Third Noble Truth is the "good news" of Buddhism. The Buddha asserted that in the direct empirical realization of the insubstantiality of the ego and all things, the suffering of *duhkha* can dissolve. This is not a snuffing out of our humanity, as some have suggested to be the teaching of Buddhism. Rather, the Buddha showed that when we truly see into our insubstantiality, we find not a cold withdrawal, but rather a way of freedom and of genuine value.

Another way of seeing the insubstantiality, and yet incomparable value, of things is in the reality of our complete interdependence. Within Buddhism this mutually dependent universe is sometimes called the Jeweled Net of Indra.

Some observers have noticed a parallel between the Jeweled Net and the "Seventh Principle" of Unitarian Universalism, the call for us to acknowledge and respect the interdependent web of all existence of which we are a part."[3]

Onc can find within Buddhism a deep metaphysic applicable to the already compelling image of the interdependent web. This alone is potentially of immense value for us as contemporary Western religious liberals, and I will return to it later.

The Fourth Noble Truth is about the vehicle to the realization of *duhkha*, its cause, and its cessation. It is encapsulated as the Eight-Fold Noble Path, consisting of right view, right thought, right speech, right action, right livelihood, right effort, right mindfulness, and right meditation. The Eight-Fold Path is frequently divided into the three interdependent aspects of enlightenment: morality, meditation, and wisdom.[4]

Many Unitarian Universalists, as well as other non-Buddhists, have experienced a sense of recognition in these Four Noble Truths. For forty years, the Buddha wandered throughout Northern India and taught his middle way. As he was dying the Buddha warned us not to put anyone else's head above our own, not even his. The Buddha reminded his followers that everyone has full worth in the universe. Each of us is called to see for ourselves and then to act in a sacred manner. Many Unitarian Universalists have found these ideas compelling.

Since Elizabeth Palmer Peabody's introduction of an authentic Buddhist text to our transcendentalist ancestors, Buddhism has become an increasingly influential force among Unitarians and now Unitarian Universalists. The next significant step in our liberal romance with Buddhism came about as humanism became a force within Western liberal religion.

For many humanists Buddhism appeared to be an intriguingly ancient faith not directly concerned with questions of God or gods. Buddhism was a faith not even focused on those grand cosmological speculations that so many theorists of comparative religion have posited as fundamental to any "authentic religion." Certainly Buddhism's very existence challenged the conventions of early comparative religion and gave much comfort to many religious liberals and radicals.

There is even more of value for Western humanists in an examination of Buddhism than a shared nontheistic stance. Both approaches to the great religious questions of life and death share a profound belief in the value of our human condition. And many humanists have found the Buddhist analysis of consciousness intriguing, one that speaks of the possibility of joy and peace within our human condition just as it is.

A number of humanists have taken up Buddhist practices, particularly Zen meditation. It is also worth noting that many Buddhists have been marked by the social activism they have seen in Western humanism. A multifaceted dialogue is taking place as Buddhism comes West. As time passes, I expect this particular dialogue between Western humanists and Buddhists to give the world much of value.

Of course, this ongoing interest in Buddhism among Unitarian Universalists has not been exclusive to humanists. Many liberal Christians are also interested in the details of Buddhist insight. Catholics have tended to dominate this interreligious dialogue, but many Protestants are also engaged.

For Protestant Christians this interest probably dates largely from the "death of God" era of the 1960s. At that time many people were seeking a "religionless"

Christianity, or at least a Christianity that did not demand intellectual assent to the existence of what many found to be some problematic divinity.

For those who thought about it, a "Christian atheism" and a "Christian-Buddhism" seemed to have much in common. Buddhism seemed to be a far older example of a religion that shared a common focus with contemporary spiritual concerns.[5]

In the UUA Commission on Appraisal survey, *The Quality of Religious Life in Unitarian Universalist Congregations*, three percent of Unitarian Universalist respondents professed Buddhism as their primary theological perspective. While in itself this is a significant number, on the basis of conversations with Unitarian Universalists across the continent, I suspect the real figure is in fact much higher. If we simply consider Buddhism as *a* major rather than *the* major strand in one's theological thinking, then I believe we have a very significant force shaping Western liberal religious thought as we embark on the third millennium.

Indeed, I feel there are two astonishingly important movements today challenging and possibly reshaping Western religious thought in general, and our Unitarian Universalist way in particular. One is feminism.[6] The other is Buddhism.

What is perhaps most interesting in the dialogue between Buddhists and Unitarian Universalists is that although many Unitarian Universalists are in fact becoming Buddhists, Western Buddhists are also becoming Unitarian Universalists.

It is important to consider what it is that attracts Western Buddhists to Unitarian Universalism. As I suggested earlier, this is very much multifaceted, an open dialogue. Michael Port Sensei, a Zen teacher who is also an active member of the First Universalist Church in Minneapolis, Minnesota, wrote a telling essay for the Spring, 1994, *UU Sangha*, the newsletter of the Unitarian Universalist Buddhist Fellowship. In this essay Port records a conversation between several UU Buddhists.

In that conversation he notes a number of reasons why Western Buddhists might want to become Unitarian Universalists. Significantly, the first reason cited in his essay is children. He notes "Many Buddhist centers do not have religious education programs—lack of resources, lack of priority, lack of parents in the leadership."[7]

In this he implies more than a sense of compatibility between our Unitarian Universalist religious education curricula and Buddhist principles. Port Sensei seems to suggest those traditional aspects of our UU religious education programming—acceptance of self-worth, and the encouraging of a free and critical search for truth—are exactly the same for Western Buddhists and Unitarian Universalists.

Western Buddhists decide to join UU congregations for a number of important reasons. Opportunities for social engagement are found in UU societies that are generally not available within Buddhist practice centers. Somewhat related, Buddhists can see how Unitarian Universalists have begun to integrate feminist perspectives that have also challenged contemporary Western Buddhist thinking. Each of these are incredibly rich elements in the dialogue.

Both Western Buddhists and Unitarian Universalists deeply feel the centrality of ecological concern. In general, both are attracted to issues of "economic justice." And also, although both movements are essentially white and middle class, each shares a deep concern with issues of racial justice. However tentatively, both attempt to engage the questions. All these things tend to pull Western Buddhists toward Unitarian Universalism.

I consider this highly significant: In his essay Michael Port suggests that many Western Buddhists seem to consider joining Unitarian Universalist churches as a way to reconnect with cultural religious roots. I find in myself an atheist who dreams of Moses and Miriam, of Jesus and Mary,[8] and so I see this possibility of an adult reconnection with the faith of my childhood through Unitarian Universalism very interesting and personally, deeply true.

Any way of spiritual synthesis is rife with danger. The possibility of a shallow eclecticism is always present. The temptation to take a little of this and a little of that, and to not allow genuine challenge, is always possible. But, there is something in the Buddhist analysis that can genuinely speak to our contemporary Unitarian Universalism, which I believe makes it worth chancing the dangers.

There is also something that goes even beyond a keen analysis of the nature of the world and our human condition and fifteen hundred years of exploring the image of the interdependent web that Buddhism brings to Unitarian Universalism. This is something I find to be a particularly precious gift, and something I believe we Unitarian Universalists desperately need. The one thing I find most compelling in this apparent rooting of Buddhism within Unitarian Universalism is the gift of a rationally based spiritual practice.

To think about religion is one thing, to experience the sacred with our blood and bones is another. I believe the practices of Buddhism, particularly the practices of presence associated most clearly with the Zen and *Vipassana* schools, are gateways to direct personal knowing of that sacred interdependent web that haunts so many of us.

We are finding Buddhist and Buddhist-inspired meditation practice groups growing in Unitarian Universalist societies around the country. At this point Zen has been the most common practice for the majority of Unitarian Universalist Buddhists. This fact is reflected in the existence, at this writing, of Zen meditation groups at possibly a dozen UU churches. But this may well just be the beginning of Unitarian

Universalist Buddhist practice. For instance, lay-led *Vipassana*[9] practice groups may well prove to be the next major Buddhist wave to attract significant numbers of Unitarian Universalists. Already there are several *Vipassana* groups at UU societies in different parts of the country.

The Vietnamese teacher Thich Nhat Hanh combines Zen and *Vipassana* techniques and, with his highly developed sense of social engagement, has particularly inspired many Unitarian Universalists. Also, although probably destined to remain a smaller part of the whole, there is interest in the various *Vajrayana* practices of Tibetan Buddhism.[10]

Once a great Buddhist teacher declared that enlightenment and meditation practice are the same thing. What seems to be happening for a number of us is a marriage between our Western style religious rationalism and the equally rational but more holistic spiritual practices of Buddhism.

I suggest that looking at the interdependent web through a general Buddhist understanding of mutuality—grounded in the personal insights that may be gained through disciplined spiritual practice—may well be a way for us to reclaim much of our Western religious heritage in new and profitable ways. Many of us who have rejected Jewish and Christian revelation but still feel the fundamental truths of that ancient call for justice, equity, and love may find in this UU Buddhist perspective something of immense value.

One Buddhist insight of the sacred nature of the whole, on this interdependent universe, has been called cosmotheism.[11] I suspect here we have one possible basis for understanding a naturalistic theism that is rather more subtle and possibly more sustaining than the pantheism to which it seems many Unitarian Universalists currently adhere.[12]

Indeed, in such examinations we may well find ourselves engaged in a process of synthesis, a process carrying us toward an authentic permanent in liberal religion—a permanent we can barely conceive at this time.[13] Of course, how all this may actually shape our Unitarian Universalist communities in the next few decades is very much an open question. To make any prediction is almost to guarantee one will look foolish in a few short years. Still, it seems to me that as we quest after the worth of our liberal religion, it is possible that those among us who embrace silent meditation and other practices and insights of Buddhism may well help us all sort out what is genuinely transient and what is truly permanent in liberal religion.

Four Spiritualities

Peter T. Richardson

———————————◆———————————

Unitarian Universalists have spent two centuries form-
ing a new and distinctive religion for the planet. We
can see our history from the Enlightenment to the
present as the spinning of the cocoon of a new world
faith. This faith has been gestating slowly in a small
but vibrant minority. In the turmoil of emergence a
synergy of five powerful offerings has been forged:

- affirming individual religious freedom;
- affirming independence of communal life
  in congregations;
- affirming an active tolerance in a pluralistic context;
- affirming global citizenship, which considers all branches of human religious tra-

dition to be our own inheritance; and
- affirming an open and creative attitude in the practice of worship.

For most of our history we have functioned in a Christian context as a liberal heresy. From the time of Joseph Priestley, however, there has been a lively interest in alternative contexts having their origins in the Middle East, India, and the Far East, as well as within nature–centered traditions.

In this century intellectual interest has transformed into participation and incorporation. The cocoon shows those first signs of breaking open in our current excitement with growth and demographics. I hope we will be ready for the acceleration that might follow: To do this, we must have our spiritual house in order.

To this end I propose four spiritualities for the embodiment of our vision, which if developed in parallel will give vastly more people the opportunity to travel with us than would otherwise be the case. I believe the world critically needs our religious perspective, but the forms we currently have for expressing this faith are too specialized and have too limited an appeal. We must move intentionally to develop these four distinctly different ways of being religious if our congregations are to minister broadly and effectively in the new millennium.

The Four Spiritualities are the Path of Unity, the

Path of Devotion, the Path of Works, and the Path of Harmony. Each has its own characteristics for mind, heart, and hand. All are equally important as alternative journeys, and exist in creative tension with each other.

The four paths are derived from observation of the various spiritualities to be found throughout the world, but particularly what may be seen in the traditional Hindu yogas. These parallel ways of spiritual practice are in turn compared with the insights of psychologist Carl Jung, and those inspired by him.

I have formulated each of these spiritualities in concert with the typology of the Myers Briggs Type Indicator, a Jungian system of personality assessment. As I present them, the Four Spiritualities are coordinated with what are called the cognitive functions in Jungian typology: the perceptive functions, Sensing and Intuition; together with the judging functions, Thinking and Feeling.[1]

It is not necessary to have any prior knowledge of Jungian theories of psychological types to see the possible importance of these Four Ways for us as Unitarian Universalists. However, interested readers may wish to refer to the excellent article by Rolph Gerhardt, "Unitarian Universalists and Other Personality Types" for an introduction to the Myers Briggs Type Indicator and its possible significance for Unitarian Universalists.[2]

The Four Spiritualities

The Path of Unity represents the NT or Intuitive/ Thinking perspective within the Meyers Briggs types. This is our Unitarian Universalist mainstream, populated with a cloud of witnesses: Joseph Priestley, Hosea Ballou, Margaret Fuller, Theodore Parker, Mary Livermore, Abner Kneeland, John Dietrich, and many other prominent figures in our past and present. For me, the quintessential Path of Unity approach, both theologically and mystically inspiring, can be seen in the life of R. Buckminster Fuller.

According to the Myers Briggs analysis, twelve percent of humanity falls within this category. For this population there is a profound quest for understanding the great principles of nature and human nature, for systematic and global thought, the mystic quest for clarity in spiritual practice, for competency in professional life and a systems approach to organization.

In his autobiography, Theodore Parker spoke of "remedial Justice" as above "palliative Charity" for he had hold of a large, embracing vision.[3] His epistemology was equally grand:

> To me, Human Life in all its forms, individual and aggregate, is a perpetual wonder: the Flora of the earth and sea is full of beauty and of mystery which Science seeks to understand; the Fauna of the land and ocean is not

less wonderful; the World which holds them both, and the great Universe that folds it in on every side, are still more wonderful, complex and attractive, to the contemplating mind.[4]

In Hinduism this spirituality is known as *Jnana* Yoga, the Way of Knowledge. The Buddha himself was on an NT path and in the Far East are the Bodhisattva of Boundless Conduct and the Zen tradition. In the West we can look to Origen, Aquinas, Erasmus, Russell, Thomas Merton, or (in its introverted forms) the "wintry spirituality" spoken of by Martin Marty.[5] On the neopagan compass, it is the earthen inspiration of the north.

The Path of Devotion represents the SF or Sensing/Feeling perspective within the Myers Briggs typology. It is the polar opposite of NT spirituality and is the least common of these spirituality types among Unitarian Universalists.

Followers of this path focus on the here and now rather than possibilities for the future, in acts of tangible piety and personal service rather than global visions of good. The real, the practical, "acting locally," present matters of the heart, move them religiously.

In a Sensing/Feeling spirituality God is near, in the embrace of care, in the tears of ecstatic joy, in traditional communal values, in the smell of incense and the sound of bells, in the arrangements of flowers and newly polished candlesticks, in patient care at the bedside of the sick, in sustained acts of kindness and consideration.

Our most prominent SF personalities may include Thomas Potter, the charismatic Caleb Rich, Eleanor Forbes, Quillen Shinn, and Sarah Flower Adams, author of "Nearer My God to Thee." In the story of Mary and Martha, both are followers of the Path of Devotion. The epitome of this path may be found in the hymn, "Dear Mother-Father of Us All":

> forgive our foolish ways.
> Re clothe us in our rightful mind,
> in purer lives thy service find,
> in deeper reverence, praise.[6]

Hindus find the Path of Devotion through the myriad forms of *Bhakti* Yoga. In Buddhism we find the Bodhisattva of Pure Conduct and the practice in countless home shrines honoring Kwan Yin, goddess of mercy and compassion. Mo Tzu, in early China, worships a Heaven of universal love. Mohammed lived profoundly in this Sensing/Feeling spirituality as expressed in *Surah* I:

> Praise be to Allah...
> the All-merciful, the All-compassionate...
> You alone we worship,
> and to You alone we turn for help.[7]

In Catholic Christianity powerful examples of the Path of Devotion can be found in the shrines and stories of St. Francis of Assisi and in the healing center at Lourdes. Studies of the Myers Briggs indicators suggest approximately thirty-eight percent of humanity center their spirituality in this. On the neopagan compass, this is the way of the summery south.

The Path of Works is the Sensing/Thinking pair within Myers Briggs typologies. ST spirituality has given us such leadership as Ezra Stiles Gannett, Thomas Whittemore, Julia Ward Howe, Henry Whitney Bellows, Richard Eddy, Edward Everett Hale, Clinton Lee Scott, and Dana McLean Greeley. For this path, action, production, one's work is one's identity. Work is the center and location of the spiritual journey.

God, or the purpose, destiny, and structure of society and nature, rules and leads us "Forward through the Ages." Commitment to the right way; loyalty to the institutions for implementation of that way; order, fairness, and rationality in human relationships; responsibility for the traditions of ethics and law; steady action to maintain the world order from the simplest routines to the most complex administrations of our lives; these all motivate the religious journey of the ST pilgrim.

Here duty becomes a sacred ritual, stewardship of the world's material and human resources a divinely sanctioned honor. Brother Lawrence, a Carmelite monk, carried on a dialogue with God through the daily work of his kitchen, in what he called "The Practice of the Presence of God." Or, we may find this same insight in the words of Epictetus: "What would you wish to be doing when you are found by death? I for my part would wish to be found doing something that [is] beneficent, suitable to the general interest. If death surprises me when I am busy and these things, it is good enough for me if I can stretch out my hands and say: the means which I have received for helping the world I have not neglected; I have not dishonored the world with my acts. That I have been given life, I am thankful."[8]

This spirituality can be tinged with a sense of the tragic, particularly appropriate inasmuch as on the neopagan compass it is the direction of the setting sun, the west, the season of autumn. There is a sense that fealty to the right often goes unrewarded along with a powerful inner sense of justification. There was great pathos when Moses stood on Mt. Nebo and looked westward toward a promised land he would never see. But what he stood for endured!

Unitarian Julia Ward Howe penned one of the most triumphant expressions of this Sensing/Thinking spirituality in her "Battle Hymn of the Republic." George Washington and Mahatma Gandhi walked this ST path. Myers Briggs studies suggest another thirty-eight percent of humanity are inclined to this spiritual way.

In Hinduism the Path of Works is known as Karma

Yoga. Picture Arjuna, the archer and hero of the *Bhagavad Gita*, guardian of righteous order, about to do battle. In Buddhism this is the path of the Bodhisattva of Steadfast Conduct. In Chinese religion this is the way of Confucius, Mencius, and Hsun Tzu. The ancient Chinese *Book of Odes* mainstreams ST spirituality. It seems the Path of Works has been in decline among Unitarian Universalists for more than a century.

The Path of Harmony is Intuition/Feeling in the Myers Briggs typology. NF is the polar opposite of the Path of Works. This way is well represented among us with such luminaries as Judith Sargent Murray, William Ellery Channing, Ralph Waldo Emerson, Lydia Maria Childe, Clara Barton, Clarence Skinner, Sophia Fahs, and Jesus himself.[9]

For those who walk the Path of Harmony, life is an experiment in spiritual discovery and growth; we exist that the possibilities of our human nature may move toward fulfillment for all. Here, the ideal is to hold the opportunities open for all life to become what it is and can be. In the words of Emerson: "Our life is an apprenticeship to the truth that around every circle another can be drawn, that there is no end in nature, but every end is a beginning; that there is always another dawn risen on mid-noon, and under every deep a lower deep opens."[10]

Here, a strong mystic component is lifting the earthly into mystery, the practical into the poetic. The

NF mystic quest is matched with a deep idealism as portrayed in the terse humanism of the *Tao Te Ching:*

> Surrender yourself humbly;
> then you can be trusted to care for all things.
> Love the world as your own self....
>
> Good weapons are instruments of fear;
> all creatures hate them.
> Therefore followers of Tao never use them.[11]

In Hinduism those on the Path of Harmony practice Raja Yoga, or the way of actualization. Rabindranath Tagore in his life of poetry and Sri Aurobindo in his development of integral yoga are examples of NF spirituality. In China we find the Bodhisattva of Eminent Conduct and the Taoist tradition of Lao Tzu and Chuang Tzu. On the neopagan compass, we find the dawning sun in the east and the season of springtime hope. Myers Briggs studies suggest this is the spiritual path for twelve percent of humanity.

I warn the reader of these too-brief summaries that each path is deep and universal. Any religion aspiring to wide appeal must include all four. Most religious violence through the ages has been caused by a lack of appreciation by those in any one path of others who journey in one of the three alternative paths.

Sorely lacking has been a substantial imperative

for active tolerance such as is found in the *Bhagavad-Gita*. I hope we will develop this spiritual tolerance in a form palatable for the twenty-first century in our own Unitarian Universalism. Clearly seeing the differences and complementarities in these four ways may be that form.

Each of the Four Spiritualities is needed as a stimulation for the others. Each has a polar opposite that exerts centrifugal and centripetal force on the other. I have observed those on the Path of Unity, for example, drawn to hours of Buddhist chanting or to the repetitive Anglican or Catholic rituals, as examples of practices in the Path of Devotion.

Those on the Path of Harmony may be drawn to the structured spirituality of the Path of Works, or to their sometimes tragic sense of steadfastness. Those on the Path of Works may find the hopeful, idealistic, and even Gnostic longing for harmony by those on the Path of Harmony to be an attractive balancing for their own spiritual seriousness.

Mencius, in the mainstream of the Confucian tradition of Works, reached across to stress the quest for harmony in life and the right of revolution, which usually would be found in the idealism of the path of Harmony.[12] Channing, a paragon of the Path of Harmony, was revered by his Path of Works parishioners.[13] Always, one's own spiritual home base, the journey that moves you, is complemented by influences that can deepen and broaden that path.

You doubtless have seen the reticence with which we ministers and our people share the "good news" of Unitarian Universalism with our neighbors or even those who have already visited our congregations. "Let people decide for themselves. Don't be pushy with them." We seem to be saying don't invite them to participate, give, or even speak, when we declare "We do not proselytize."

We frequently feel the truth of our religion, the openness of process, is invitation enough. These perspectives represent our dominant spiritualities, in the Path of Unity and the Path of Harmony. We, by and large, seem to specialize in introverted forms of these two paths, which, if the Myers Briggs studies are correct, appeal to approximately four to seven percent of the general population. In our bold and extroverted moments we may add another twenty percent who can hear us.

Along with a sprinkling of others to manage our Property and Finances and to chair our Flower and Caring committees, we could continue indefinitely a noble and stimulating ministry of visioning and exploring in microcosm what the world around us so desperately needs to make manifest in the lives of its millions. I hope for more. With intentional sponsorship of all Four Spiritualities, through the accompanying pain and dislocation, we may yet grow into our destiny to serve a world that awaits us.

Saved By a Song

Carl Scovel

This sermon was preached at the author's home church, King's Chapel, two weeks after delivering the Berry Street Lecture.

One evening a year ago last May our phone rang. It was Rudi Nemser, minister to our church in Cherry Hill, New Jersey. "Good evening, Carl," he said, "I'm calling to ask if you'd like to give the Berry Street Lecture next year in Fort Worth. That's in Texas."

The Berry Street Lecture! Once a year a UU minister addresses colleagues at the UUMA annual meeting, following a tradition begun in 1820 when William Ellery Channing spoke to the Boston Unitarian clergy gathered at the Federal Street Church. The door of the parish house opened onto Berry Street, hence the name.

Now at last I could deliver my credo, my *summa*, my *apologia pro sua*. Now I could tell my colleagues what it was all about. Without even thinking about the air fares from Boston to Fort Worth, I said, "I'll do it!"

Rudi said, "It's all honor, you know."

"Honor's enough," I answered. "I'll do it."

And so it was that evening that I took out a new manila file folder, wrote Berry Street Lecture in large black letters on the tab and began the thirteen-month preparation of my *magnum opus.*

My manner of preparation was primitive. I had no topic, no title, and lots of time. Whenever I had an idea on any subject that might be remotely useful, I wrote it down on a napkin, file card, envelope, shopping bag or, once, the back of my hand, and on returning home transferred it to the Berry Street file folder.

When the folder got too fat, I sat down, pulled out the scraps of paper, chucked some, saved others, wrote salient thoughts on a large sheet of paper, and stuffed it all back into the folder. But what would be my theme? What would be my focus? Around what central thought would I organize my forty-five to fifty minutes worth of words? People would expect me to talk about spirituality. That's pretty vague. What is spirituality? Does anyone know? Is it more than a guess or a fad? Should I even mention the word? I didn't know.

Collectively, Unitarian Universalists have a great openness and also a great resistance to matters religious. How could I, a Christian, say so and analyze this contradiction without seeming to attack people for not being Christian? How could I get people to talk about their resistance? I didn't know.

I knew I had to say something about what is at the heart of my own faith, at the heart of Universalism, and at the heart of Christianity itself: the love of God. But how could I name this truth without sounding trite? How could I re-articulate God's love in convincing words? I didn't know.

How could I speak to my colleagues so that for a moment we could forget that we are ministers and realize that our personal quest and our personal faith is a source of strength? More than that, how could I help them to see how important it is that our religious community, our own church, and our own tradition often determine what we do or do not believe. You simply cannot believe certain things in certain communities. Several times I wanted to call Rudi and say, "I'm sorry. I just can't do it." Each time I remembered that Rudi had already announced my acceptance to all my colleagues.

In late May at the Weston School of Theology Commencement, I heard Brian Dailey, Vice Rector, say, "We are called to witness to the good intent at the heart of reality, to know it, and to name it." Moved by his words I scratched them down on the program and decided to use them as my thesis. What an irony, that a Jesuit should proclaim the Universalist gospel!

Two weeks before I was due to give the lecture, I made one final pass through the folder, cobbled together an outline and chose a title, "Beyond Spirituality." I sent a three–page letter to my two respondents who were hoping, of course, for the full text. Then my wife, Faith, and I packed our bags and went off to a high school reunion at the Adams Mark Hotel in Indianapolis where for three days we ate, chatted, and slept without a thought of the impending oration. We arrived in Fort Worth on Monday night and found a Days Inn near the convention hotel. After supper with friends we returned to our room, and I began my two-and-a-half days' preparation for the lecture.

First, I tried a laptop computer with WordPerfect, but I found its software fast and tricky; I fished my thick, bright red fountain pen from the briefcase and worked by hand. It felt right. Then I sorted through the folders. By Tuesday night I had an outline. On Wednesday after coffee and a bagel I was back in my room and wrote all day, stopping only to scratch my head, stare at the corners, check the World Cup series on television, and occasionally walk around the block. By Wednesday night I had written all but the last section. I photocopied what I'd produced and left copies for my two respondents at their hotel.

On Thursday Faith, but not I, went to hear the morning speaker, a brilliant UUC minister, Tex

Samples. He told stories and told his listeners how to tell stories.

I stayed in my room and wrote the last section, photocopied it, and delivered copies to my two respondents. I reviewed and revised the manuscript one last time, jogged, showered, shaved, dressed, and was at the hotel by 3:45 P.M.

Rudi Nemser was waiting at the podium. He adjusted my tie, stuffed my bright red fountain pen in a pocket where it couldn't be seen, shook his head and at 4 P.M. called the assembly to order. Perhaps four hundred clergy, spouses, and church school directors were there and a few lay delegates as well.

After a prayer and introduction by my good friend Libby Smith, I stood up and for the next forty-five minutes read my text with rarely a departure from it. I cite the two paragraphs which felt most "right":

> The Great Surmise says simply this: At the heart of all creation lies a good intent, a purposeful goodness, from which we come, by which we live our fullest, and to which we shall at last return. This is the supreme mystery of our lives. This goodness is ultimate—not fate, not freedom, not mystery, energy, order, nor finitude, but this good intent in creation is our source, our center, and our destiny. . . . Our work on earth is to explore, enjoy, and

share this goodness. "Too much of a good thing," said Mae West, "is wonderful." Sound doctrine.

I followed this with a brief history of Universalism and then I continued:

But what changed my life and moved me to speak today and brought me down from my private Olympus was my own discovery (or the divine disclosure) that I, who trusted least, could trust this love; that I, who believed so little, could believe this love; that I who wished above all to be self-sufficient, could receive this love, and sometimes even live a small piece of it. . . . I discovered with the psalmist that we can know the goodness of the Lord in the land of the living.

There was more, but I need not relate it now. I ended with a prayer that Thomas Merton read at a conference of Hindu, Buddhist, and Christian contemplatives in 1967.

As I was giving the lecture and afterwards, I felt a sense of incompleteness about it. I'd worked as hard as I could on it. I knew that. But something was missing, and I didn't know what. I was disappointed but did not berate myself.

When I was finished, I introduced my two respondents. The first was Suzanne Spencer, a Boston lawyer for several years, and then an intern at King's Chapel while she was a student at Harvard Divinity School. She served churches in Los Angeles and Vancouver before taking a pulpit in Studio City, California. She gave a quiet, reasoned disquisition, gently questioning some of my assumptions, but appreciative and sympathetic.

The second respondent, Deane Starr, a friend of more than thirty years, agnostic and iconoclast, spoke. I can only paraphrase what he said. It went something like this: "Carl says that he sees goodness at the heart of the universe. I don't see that at all. I look into the universe and all I see is conflict, conflict and indifference, a sublime indifference, to our human species, or any other species for that matter."

Deane went on with the grand eloquence of a Robert Ingersoll and other great naysayers. Then he described going to Portland, Oregon, for his son's funeral and after the service going on an evening cruise. Deane said, "I didn't find peace in a church or in prayer. I looked into the sunset, and I found peace there." Then Deane took a tack that I did not expect. He said, "I am now going to lead you in singing a hymn. It's a hymn I learned as a child in the Nazarene church. You don't have the words in front of you, but I'll bet you know it." And then Deane in his lovely resonant baritone began to sing:

I come to the garden alone
While the dew is still on the roses;
And the voice I hear falling on my ear
The Son of God discloses.
CHORUS
And he walks with me and he talks with me,
And he tells me I am his own;
And the joy we share as we tarry there,
None other has ever known.

I was wondering to myself, "What is Deane doing? Why is he singing this hymn?" Deane pitched right into the second verse, which no one knew so he sang it alone, until we joined him in the chorus. Deane was right. Almost everybody knew it. Well, it was quite a sight and quite a sound to see and hear four hundred Unitarian Universalist ministers and spouses singing an old chestnut like "In the Garden"! And this isn't the end of the story.

About a week later I was sitting in my office when Deane called me on the phone and told me he was retiring that very day, and that his previous week's speech had been his last chance to address his sister and brother ministers. So he had been pleased that I had asked him to respond. Then Deane told me this. (Again I paraphrase.)

"I noticed that many people were crying when we sang that hymn, which surprised me. After it was all over, someone came up to me and said, 'Did you hear Tex Samples speak this morning?' I said, 'No, I was writing down my remarks for this afternoon.' He said, 'You mean, no one told you what he said about that hymn?' I said, 'No, I told you, I was working.' So this person told me what Tex Samples had said." [Remember, please, that Tex had been the morning speaker on the same day that Deane and I spoke in the late afternoon.]

"Tex had said, 'I used to really hate fundamentalists and I used to hate that hymn, 'In the Garden.' It seemed so sentimental, so self-indulgent, so sticky, such bad music, you know. And once I was speaking to a fundamentalist group, and I sang that hymn in a high forced falsetto. I really stuck it to them.

"After my talk, when people came up to speak to me, I noticed one woman was waiting some distance from the others. Only after everyone else had left did she come up. She said, 'You know that hymn you sang?' I said, 'Yes.'

"She said, 'I want to tell you something about that hymn. From the time I was about ten years old until I was about fourteen, my father raped me almost every day of my life. After he was finished I'd put my clothes on, and I'd go out into the backyard, and I'd walk slowly about the yard, and I'd sing that hymn. It was the only thing that kept me sane, the only thing that kept me from killing myself. Because when I sang that hymn, I knew I was somebody. I hope you'll remember that the next time you sing it.' "

That's the story Tex Samples had told the UU clergy on Thursday morning. Deane, who had not heard the story, chose that hymn to sing on Thursday afternoon. And that's what Deane had called to tell me after we got back to Boston.

After Deane hung up, I realized why I had felt the lecture was incomplete. It *was* incomplete. The lecture alone could not make the point. It took that song to complete it. And that gave me a new angle on Unitarian Universalism. It's a community where Christians give the lectures and humanists lead the hymns.

It seemed as though God had used all of us, me, Sue, Deane, Libby, Rudi, Tex Samples, 400 UU clergy, and a woman whom none of us will ever know, to point to the goodness at the heart of life and to remind us that nothing in heaven or earth—not death, not life, not powers, not principalities, not even a drunken father who raped his daughter—can separate us from the love of God, the good intent at the heart of reality, which is in Jesus Christ our Lord, and which fills all creation too.

In a changing world, that good intent is permanent, changeless, lovely, sure.

Thanks be to God.

Our Children Ask for Bread

Arvid Straube

———————◆———————

At the Central Midwest District Meeting, on November 11, 1978, Irving Murray delivered an address about the future of our movement, still relevant for us today. He took as his text Matthew 7:9, "Who among you, if your children ask for bread, would give them a stone?" We have been, in a manner of speaking, said Murray, feeding our own and our children's spiritual hungers with a dry, hard, and indigestible faith, the spiritual equivalent of a stone. Scorn is a spiritual stone; too often we seem to approach life and faith with a distancing, condescending scorn. We "tolerant" Unitarian Universalists too often spend far more energy deriding our neighbor's faith than we do articulating a sustaining faith.

The spiritual bread we need, Murray suggests, is

in satisfying answers to the questions of meaning. How do I face death? What is the meaning of tragedy? What are my obligations? What are the ways of love? What can I know? What ought I to do? What may I hope? Answers to these questions engage the heart and the will as much as the head. They are shaped in community more than in isolation. A diet of light music and lecture/discussions is meagre fare. We long for answers we can live by.

In the American Revolution, the transcendentalist renaissance, and the civil rights movement, Unitarians and Universalists were leaders. In the development of new religious and social ideas, Unitarians and Universalists led. But names of famous Unitarian Universalists on those T-shirts are names of long ago. The question is: Will Unitarian Universalism influence the world in face of the frightening religious revival now going on all over the world? In the midst of religious ferment of a scope seldom seen in history? It seems to me our movement is at a critical point. We are deciding now whether we will be a historic anomaly, a tiny cell of cranky intellectuals, or an important voice in shaping the next millennium. We are deciding right now whether the Unitarian Universalist religion in the new millennium will be vital or trivial.

I see in our institutional behavior of today the seeds of both kinds of faith. We could continue as a small group of upper-middle-class, white intellectuals who constantly talk about openness and inclusiveness but only have time for and interest in people quite a lot like ourselves. People of all skin colors would be welcome, as long as they share our accents and lifestyles.

We would proclaim our multisyllabic, left-brained, abstract gospel to the well-fed, politically correct, many–degreed individualists who would smugly listen to sermons most of the population couldn't understand. Prayer would continue to be suspect. The irrational truths of dreams, ritual, imagination, and emotion would be suspect. We would live in fine homes while our meeting rooms were shabby and cluttered. We would furnish our businesses and offices with state-of-the-art equipment while our churches make do with cast-offs. We would continue to pledge to the church, on average, less than we spend on one weekend away. We would be quick to condemn our neighbors' irrational beliefs and practices in scornful and merciless terms while we fall prey to trends and fads that are incomprehensible to most of the population. We would be quick as ever with solutions for the problems of the poor and the oppressed, who, of course, do not live near us, work with us, or go to school with our children.

As we became ever more isolated, we would feel ever more hurt that the world, not recognizing our superior wisdom and greater intelligence or our churches, persists in its intolerant, reactionary, and unenlightened ways. Most of the world, of course, will never hear of us. If it did and understood us, it would despise us as earnestly as we patronize and look down upon it. I see the seeds of this future in much of our present institutional behavior.

I also see the seeds of a much brighter future in some emphases of our movement. These are fragile and controversial, but they are signs of growing institutional and spiritual health.

Our churches and fellowships will be exciting places where all ages and classes of people will embark on the adventure of spiritual exploration. Our congregations will be as individual as fingerprints. Yes, there will be upper middle-class suburban congregations in the woods, made up primarily of academics. And there will also be inner city congregations of people of all races and classes called to ministry in our inner cities. There will be mostly black congregations or Hispanic or Asian congregations as well as mostly white congregations. Gospel hymns will be favored in one and Earth rituals in another. Rather than scorning the faiths of neighbors, we will be deeply involved with the more tolerant and compassionate among them. Our theological differences will not matter much, because we have come to know and respect each other from shared experiences of feeding the hungry and housing the homeless together.

The communities wherein our congregations are located will know us well. They will have no doubt about who we are and what are our values because our works will be apparent to all.

In our buildings will be a huge variety of activities and classes: meditation, prayer, journal writing, and support groups of all kinds. Study groups on the Bible and on a wide variety of religious topics as well as church-sponsored social action and service projects in such areas of community need as child or adult day care, after-school programs for children at risk, and learning centers for the elderly. Worship services will vary widely, but will be uniformly joyful and celebratory, yet dignified. The entire person will be addressed: mind, body, heart, and will. The importance of relationships and community to healthy spiritual life will always be lifted up. Programs will be there to help people strengthen relationships: parenting classes, courses on sustaining friendships, spiritual growth groups, and enrichment opportunities for people in committed relationships.

And we will not ever forget our children. We will have for them not only Sunday school but programs throughout the week and over the summer that UU parents may raise whole, healthy, tolerant children in community.

In the past, as all thoughtful mainline religious thinkers acknowledge, we have contributed much to religious thought in the United States. We need now to acknowledge that other religious groups may teach us. We need to talk with them, respectfully and as equals. Churches and synagogues, working together, can do much to work toward health, wholeness, and healing of our society. The only way to overcome the forces of reaction now raging among some religious people is for those of us who stand for the liberating, healing power of religion to work together. We cannot stay aloof from the struggle. Nor can we fruitfully engage it by ourselves. We need not approve of every article of our neighbors' faiths. We do need to feed the hungry and work for justice together that our combined voices be heard, voices insisting and demonstrating that the authentic religious impulse drives forward love, justice, and compassion, not reactionary hatred.

To be heard in the religious culture in which we live, we must be able to use the language of our culture. The religious language of our culture is Jewish and Christian. The Bible is too great and powerful a resource to be left to the religious right. We believe in salvation, healing, and wholeness. Atonement is simply at-one-ment; we're for it. No matter what language we speak at home in our house of worship, we have important words to say to the culture at large. We must say them in the language that is most readily understood; the need for hearing our message is urgent.

We must, to be vital in the twenty-first century, feed the spiritual hunger of our people with the bread of life, the wine of the spirit, and the fruits of the imagination. We must speak this message not to the few much like ourselves, but to the whole world.

A Lifetime of Learning

Faith and Formation:
Leadership for the Next Century

Spencer Lavan

———————◆———————

James Luther Adams, scholar and teacher, died on July 26, 1994, the same day this essay was completed. Adams, who taught "the prophethood of all believers" so effectively, was my teacher. He was a major stimulus in my own decision to take up an academic ministry.

As a student at Harvard Divinity School from 1959 until 1962, I studied with him, benefiting from the stimulating Tuesday evenings with Jim and Margaret Adams at their home. Working with Jim Adams taught me and many others about the Radical Reformation, about the radical movements and sects of religious people who refused to accept sterile traditions and whose adherents were prepared to lay down their lives to challenge the political and religious order of their European context. Jim Adams began his teaching career at Meadville. His concern for vital, living, ethical religion still undergirds our curriculum.

Four major themes engage us at Meadville/ Lombard Theological School as we work to prepare women and men for the Unitarian Universalist ministry in the twenty-first century. The challenges we try to be mindful of for our ministry in future decades, are many. These four, however, are central for us in our work in many varied ways.

We believe ministry in the next century must (1) be prepared to serve congregations and communities that are multicultural, multiracial, and diverse in perspective and be prepared to address the complex issues of urban survival; (2) go beyond the narrowly parochial to understand, appreciate, and deal constructively with the issues of interfaith relations, taking other religious faiths seriously and interpreting their messages for UU congregational worship and adult education; (3) take intelligent and far-ranging life-span religious education as the heart of ministerial leadership of congregations, in a ministry using the tools of education to resolve issues within congregational life as well as to teach religious ideas and faith perspectives; and, (4) place the ethical and religious issues and values of environmental survival at the core of ministry and therefore be literate in fields bearing on these concerns: science, medicine, and sustainable economies.

How many words will we write and speak about the challenges that face us in the twenty-first century? I bring a perspective emerging from the continuing tension within theological education for our Unitarian Universalist ministry. This tension comes from competing needs, on the one hand for academic preparation necessary to a learned ministry and, on the other hand, for praxis, learning from action and reflection, which plays so large a role in *formation* for ministry.

Some colleagues question whether theological education can be truly transformative, especially for students making midlife career changes, whose vision and personalities have already been strongly shaped. Yet, the mother of one of our recent graduates humorously wrote that we have been a "finishing school" for her daughter. She went on to explain more seriously that her daughter has, by her theological school experience been "formed" for ministry because that experience has addressed issues of personal and professional development in a way earlier undergraduate and graduate education in the sciences never shaped her as a person. This case does not stand alone. I think of another mid-forties recent graduate who has been completely transformed and reshaped for ministry by theological education, especially by that education in the community and in the internship congregation.

Many writing on the challenges of ministry in the twenty-first century will continue to focus on the pastoral, priestly, and prophetic functions of our ministry. There is value in this focus. In these functions ministers address the great passages, personal crises, and issues of social justice that members of our congregations and society face perpetually.

It is my view that although these are critical dimensions of ministry that must not be omitted from theological education, emphasis on the four themes I cited earlier provides a focus on the crucial matters that our women and men will address, act upon, and live with in their ministries. These themes—multicultural and diversity issues, intercultural and interreligious connections, life-span religious education, and broad environmental concerns—can be and are adjusted and shaped to meet the needs of particular students, and also serve as the basis of continuing education for practicing parish ministers, ministers of religious education, and community ministers.

Multiculturalism and the Church

If our movement is to survive and be in touch with those persons in the United States and Canada who are prepared to receive and understand our liberal religious message, then a major focus of our work must be to attract persons of color and a greater variety of ethnic backgrounds into our ministry and congregations.

The role of theological education in this work is not only to recruit and educate persons of color for our ministry, but also to provide education for all students on racism, on the means of building effective multicultural religious communities, and on critical social justice issues as those play out in the varied urban and suburban settings of North America. Our Dean of Students is an African American UU minister. Four of our students are African American. We also have students from India and the Philippines. In our school future religious leaders make intercultural connections for our movement. Ours is the opportunity to take our all too often self-absorbed religious movement in difficult and challenging new directions.

International Connection and Dialogue

Meadville/Lombard and its presidents have had a long history of connection through the International Association of Religious Freedom (IARF) with religious liberals from India, Japan, Hungary, and elsewhere. We have served as an educational institution for students from many countries beyond the borders of North America. The school has honored leaders of other religious organizations in other countries, most recently Dr. Arpad Szabo, Rector of the Protestant Theological Institute of Cluj, Romania, and Nichiko Niwano, President of Rissho Kosei Kai of Japan.

Because of a tradition of international involvement, our students preparing for the ministry gain some knowledge and understanding of the history and practice that has long taken and does now take Unitarian Universalists well beyond both parochial missionary outreach and abstract study of world religions. All courses in UU history discuss Eastern European and English roots of North American Unitarian Universalism. Courses such as Literature for Liberal Religion include study of Brahmo Samaj literature and the *Lotus Sutra* as core texts beyond Channing, Parker, and Margaret Fuller for Unitarian Universalism. Several students have taken courses in Lakota-Christian dialogue sponsored by the Catholic Theological Union, offered in part on the Lakota reservation in South Dakota.

We participated as an institution in the 1993 Council for a Parliament of the World's Religions. We are part of Chicago-based Christian-Muslim dialogue activities. We will sponsor an intensive course in January, 1995: "Interfaith Dialogue and the Liberal Church." With all this we testify to our concern that connectedness and interfaith dialogue will be a central concern for our movement in the next century.

Religious Education and Team Ministries

Religious Education, long the poor stepchild of our ministry and often directed only to children, must now have a central place in our work with adults and children. Religious education is far more than classroom teaching of subject matter. It is also far more than an opportunity for a polemical presentation of one theological or social point of view. Religious education must be for all members of congregations. It takes place at board meetings, in meetings of the worship committee, on retreats, in adult classes, and when children are present with adults in Sunday services.

Nearly thirty years ago Crane and St. Lawrence Theological Schools, where there was an emphasis on religious education, closed. Now, at last, with gifts from the Shelter Rock congregation, Community Church of New York, the Fahs family, and the St. Lawrence Foundation, Meadville has established the Angus MacLean Chair in Religious Education, created the Sophia Lyon Fahs Center for Religious Education Study, and brought to the school from the UUA the Independent Study Program for the Ministry of Religious Education. The Independent Study Program is now accredited. Persons may earn an M.A. or an M.Div. with modified residency requirements and be prepared holistically to serve our congregations as team ministers. The intensive courses we offer in January and July as well as others which have been and will be offered on the campuses of non-UU theological schools open new possibilities for all UU ministers to review past learning and to evaluate critically its usefulness for their present ministries.

Global Issues

Our tradition of a learned and literate ministry has always assumed the minister's need for our preaching and teaching to be informed about world and national issues. Increasingly, we need to read or watch well-written and well-documented presentations for analysis exceeding the five-minute newscast with its fire and brimstone approach to coverage of events. Ministers in the next century must interpret world events and know enough to bring in guests and panelists to speak to our congregations in language that educates religiously, demonstrates an understanding of interfaith dialogue, and speaks to multicultural and diverse perspectives.

On our faculty, we have in Ron Engel a social ethicist internationally known in the field of environmental ethics and religious faith. We focus on this theme in relation to issues of population control, agricultural development, sustainable economy, and perspectives of liberation theologies. Those entering ministry in the twenty-first century will need to be literate in science and issues of greening. They will also have to be ready to address and respond to issues of medical ethics that their congregations face, both theoretically and practically, to offer honest, moral leadership. We shall have to learn to play a major part in addressing these issues publicly if our ministries in congregations are to be effective.

In the past half century James Luther Adams was our most able theoretician, theologian, and ethicist. He laid the groundwork. In the next century our religious leadership, compassionate and caring, will require all the knowledge and skills I have addressed here so briefly. I call upon all my colleagues to join the conversation in critical reflection on the ways we may learn them and live them amply.

Our Unitarian Universalist Curriculum

Colleen M. McDonald

Since the beginning of time, we humans have tried to demystify our existence. Some among us have feared the unknown and imagined the Source of Life and Death as capricious, even malevolent. Some have vilified human nature, foretold eternal misery for at least a portion of humanity, and lived with a sense of powerlessness in the face of a Greater Power.

In contrast my spiritual ancestors envisioned a moral and compassionate Creator, Source of the gifts of human freedom and possibility. Instead of focusing on human failings and failures, they proclaimed our potential for goodness and greatness. Rather than dividing the human community into the worthy and the unworthy, they affirmed all humanity as brothers and sisters. They said, in effect, "Let us devote our lives in witness to the Love by which we are all conceived and eternally embraced. Let us live together, respecting the dignity and equality with which that Love endows us. As we address problems here on earth, let us be guided and inspired by our vision of the better world that awaits us upon death."

Hope for the future, faith in humanity, and commitment to a better world for us all: these attitudes constitute the passionate center of Unitarian Universalism and the foundation and aim of Unitarian Universalist religious education. They are perspectives on life that are continuously challenged by the failures, disappointments, and catastrophes that—with our successes, rewards, and triumphs—are part of life. Dishonesty, betrayal, malice; war, pollution, crime: Each person must wrestle with unhealthy and destructive tendencies that are part of human nature. Each generation must face crises that threaten the nation or planet.

The survival and vitality of our liberal religion demands that we continue to ask and to answer these questions: How can we continue to believe in and give witness to a theology of hope? How can we proclaim the power of love and affirm human potential in a world of ever-present hatred and violence? How can we sustain our faith in humanity when people act in ways damaging to themselves, to others, and to our planet?"

Unitarian Universalist religious education in all

its forms (including classes, worship, and social action, in age-specific and mixed-age groups) must teach the following.

We need to teach our story as a people of faith, hope, and commitment—our communal history, the history of our movement: What was the context from which Universalism, Unitarianism, and Unitarian Universalism developed? How and why has our religion attracted converts and champions? In a world of alternative or competing theologies and religions, how is it distinct or unique? From what vantage points could it be considered superior? What has motivated people willing to die for it? What has been said against us by critics inside and outside our movement? What are our weaknesses and limitations? What has influenced us to change? How have we changed over time? What are our boundaries? How did our own congregation begin? What is its history? What impact has our religion had on the larger world and our particular community? What have we as a people of faith, hope, and commitment accomplished? Where have we failed by our own standards?

The point of these complex questions is neither simple nor definitive answers. They are meant to shape a Unitarian Universalist identity, a complex identity grounded in our passionate center.

The shaping of UU identity occurs within the context of our characteristic assumptions. Each of us must decide whether the passionate center of Unitarian Universalism is truly compatible with our own heartbeat. In any thoroughgoing attempt to define and distinguish Unitarian Universalism, we will deal with a variety of other faith traditions, each with its own strengths. Our educational process may direct a person to religion to which s/he is better suited, and we accept that possible outcome.

Unitarian Universalism is by no means perfect. Our hope for what it can achieve in the world must be tempered with humility.

Pain can ensue from trusting in human nature and from striving after lofty goals. Still, because our history reminds us that privileges we now take for granted—for example, freedom of worship and women's right to vote—were once deemed an absurd idea or impossible dream, we have reason to maintain our hopeful vision.

We need to teach the stories of particular and exemplary representatives of our faith. The stories need to mirror the diversity of people who have found a home in Unitarian Universalism and include both "heroines and heroes" of long ago and "ordinary" persons of our own time. We need to illustrate and spotlight the manifold ways our religion can reveal itself in our lives, from our child-raising approach, our choice of vocations and avocations, and the causes we champion as major players and supporters. The portraits we paint need to be "real," avoiding the suggestion that our role models are superhuman. We must acknowledge that people with the same foibles and flaws as the rest of us have done great good, and so can we.

These are the questions we need to ask of these persons' lives: How did their hope for the future and faith in humanity (and appropriation of our faith tradition) influence their lives? How did they direct their commitment to a better world? What were their causes or goals? What were their successes? What enabled them to succeed? What were their sources of inspiration and support? What role did other Unitarian Universalists play in their lives? How did they cope with discouragement? How did they sustain faith in themselves and their causes? What were their weaknesses? How did they come to terms with failings and failures? What can we learn from their experiences?

Our story as a people gives us a broad picture of Unitarian Universalism. Stories of our people offer a snapshot of Unitarian Universalists. Our stories don't tell us so much as they ask us, How do these tales of UU experience speak to me, to my experience, to my life? How am I to shape my religion? How does it shape me?

We need to teach ourselves to take evil, people's inhumanity, seriously. We need to stare it in the face until we can integrate it into our personal theologies. We Unitarian Universalists all too easily avoid this issue. Sidestepping the question of evil, we run the risk of espousing a "fair weather" religion of little or no worth in crisis and catastrophe. What happens when the "inherent worth and dignity of every person" goes unrealized or awry? What about Adolph Eichmann? Charles Manson? Saddam Hussein? What common factors make us human? What separates "us" from "them"? How do "they" fit into the world of "justice, equity, and compassion for all," which we say we affirm and promote?

We need to teach ourselves to use the arts as vehicles for self-expression and re-creation/transformation. We need invitations to produce and respond to symbols, to tap our intuition, to know ourselves as creative beings capable of healing and changing our world through our creativity. We need opportunities to get in touch with and express our feelings of pain, despair, longing, and exaltation. Through worship, our sacred spaces, and especially religious education, we need a range of media and modes through which we may give form to our greater vision—music and dance as performers and participants, drama, poetry, the graphic arts, crafts, and sculpture. We need the means of documenting our dreams, our achievements, our passions—all that we hope will survive us when we die. We need vehicles to enable a sense of solidarity with the larger community, which includes persons from the past, the present, and the future with whom we are joined in the glorious struggle.

We need to teach ourselves to recognize and oppose threats to human empowerment: racism, sexism, heterosexism, classism, ageism, ableism. In our homes and congregations we need to provide our children an anti-bias education that discourages bigotry and promotes acknowledgment and appreciation of human differences, recognition of unfair behavior, empathy with the oppressed, and instruction in effective action to bring about justice. We adults need to be involved in ongoing re-education; we have a model in The Welcoming Congregation. Re-education equips us to assess what we "know " about people who are "different," to see our own prejudices, biases, and discriminatory action, and to appreciate how related "isms" ultimately hurt everyone. We can also learn to take appropriate action to effect desired changes within ourselves and society.

We need to teach the skills of conflict resolution. For a world in which peace and justice prevail, we must know how to use strategies that help people approach our differences and solve our problems without violence or power plays. We need to learn the methods of "win-win" solutions, the strategies of negotiators who empower and exercise power with, rather than power over, others. We can learn to identify sources of interpersonal tension and conflict and learn to let our values and priorities guide us in determining which issues to "push." And we can become clear about those situations in which negotiation and a willingness to compromise are not appropriate.

Even as we seek to live in harmony with those who may hold beliefs or values different from ours, or with those who engage in behaviors uncharacteristic for us, we need to exercise our right and responsibility to think critically. Although it is important to appreciate others' perspectives and to respect their right to disagree with us, appreciation of and respect for differences does not lessen our obligation for moral and critical judgment.

We need to teach an ethic of social action that reminds us of what we can and cannot do in addressing issues that can seem overwhelming:

> We cannot fix complex problems simply.
> We cannot fix enormous problems quickly.
> And we cannot avoid action because it is too hard.
> We can break problems down.
> We can develop multiple, specific strategies.
> We can take a long view, setting both short-term and long-term goals.

Sustaining faith in humanity, hope for the future, and a better world for us all, this is our Unitarian Universalist curriculum. This is our agenda now and into the twenty-first century.

Rethinking Children's Religious Education

Elizabeth Parish

———————————◆———————————

"I don't think that Unitarian Universalism is right for many children. It is a religion for adults. Children seem to need something definite to hold on to and later they can reject it as they get older if they want to. If I had it to do again, I'd teach them differently."

This statement came from a woman I know who regretfully resigned her membership in a Unitarian Universalist congregation and joined a mainstream Protestant congregation, both to further her own religious growth and to provide for the religious education of her children.

Supporting her statement is the fact that only about ten to fifteen percent of our membership grew up as Unitarian Universalists. Why are we unable to retain most children who grow up in our church schools once they reach adulthood? If we want to continue to grow into the twenty-first century, if we want to have a positive impact on our society, we must address this question. (I realize some would argue that many adults do consider themselves Unitarian Universalists but just do not attend our churches. If this *is* true, it is not a particularly positive situation itself.)

I propose two primary reasons to account for the fact that we don't retain many of our children as adult members: (1) we do not offer children something definite to believe; and (2) we typically segregate children from the central act of the congregation—namely, Sunday morning worship.

Many of the new members of Unitarian Universalist congregations are parents whose children have started to ask religious questions that the parents do not know how to answer. Thus, they seek a church home that will provide religious education for their children—preferably one that relies less on dogma than the denomination in which they themselves were raised. Satisfying their own spiritual yearnings is an important bonus, but not their primary reason for coming.

Often these new Unitarian Universalist parents want their children to learn the rudiments of the Bible and other world religions, but they do not want them to be told exactly what to believe. To fulfill this goal, our religious education programs are usually designed to teach children the basics of other religions, to teach them to ask questions, and to let them make up their own minds.

This approach does not work. Although it arises from excellent intentions, its overall effect is detrimental both to children and to the future of Unitarian Universalism.

Such an approach often leaves children confused. One parent told me that after going through Unitarian Universalist religious education, her son thought that he was supposed to choose whether to be a Hindu, a Jew, or a member of some other world religion. He didn't even realize that Unitarian Universalism was one of the options, because he had no sense of what it was. Recently, we have become aware of this danger and are attempting to more actively provide children with a positive statement of our identity.

This change I feel is extremely important because children just do not have the same abilities as adults to question religious beliefs, to deal with abstract concepts, and to make discerning judgments between various claims. Yet this is exactly what we expect them to do in most of our educational programs. As the woman quoted above said, Unitarian Universalism is a religion for adults.

We also make the mistake of assuming our children have prior knowledge of religious stories and beliefs. Most of them do not, just like an increasing number of adults. Children are confused enough in our society. In an often chaotic and uncertain world, they need more structure, not less. We may be offering them knowledge, but we are not offering them faith or belief. Knowledge may inform their minds, but it does not strengthen their hearts. A faith grounded in certain core beliefs does. We are our children's role models. They *want* to know what we believe. We owe it to them to provide some definite answers.

This is hard when we ourselves do not know what we believe. Approaching religious education with the attitude that we will just let children make up their own minds communicates the message that we adults are uncomfortable, ambivalent, or uncertain about religion in general.

As a denomination composed primarily of come-outers, many of us have rejected another religion. Too often we communicate this sense to our children. In so doing, we are placing them directly into an adolescent-like stage of rejecting and questioning, without letting them go through the prior stage of learning and believing. Maya Angelou says, "There is nothing quite so tragic as a young cynic, because it means the person has gone from knowing nothing to believing nothing."[1]

We Unitarian Universalist adults who grew up in another religion and became disillusioned need to avoid passing on this disillusionment to our children.

If we have not healed from our own wounds, it is difficult to be positive about religion. Some argue that this is good. There is a common assumption among us that to be a Unitarian Universalist doesn't require openness to diverse forms of religious belief and practice as much as it requires a repudiation of religious practice in general. Such an approach is based on a negative stance; our children have a right to start afresh.

Our ambivalence about religion is not the only reason our children eventually leave our congregations; we also make the mistake of excluding them from the adult worship service. Having the church school meet at the same time as the adult worship service is a relatively new practice. Perhaps we should reevaluate this practice. Why can't the children go to the adult service? We think we exclude them with their best interests in mind, assuming that they will find worship boring. But this practice communicates our own ambivalence about religion. Worship is an activity, it tells them, about which we have misgivings.

A recent Doonesbury strip illustrates this point well. The Doonesburys are telling their son Alex that they have decided to start attending church as a family. An exchange follows in which Mike Doonesbury acknowledges that as a child he found church boring, but "you have to come by that feeling honestly. You have to put in the pew time, like Mom and I did." Alex pauses and then asks, "What if I like it?" His parents respond with, "Like it? What do you mean? We'll cross that bridge when we get there, honey." Why should children value and commit to an activity that their parents regard suspiciously?

Another effect of excluding children from worship is to weaken their commitment to Unitarian Universalism as they reach adulthood. If they have relatively little experience with attending Unitarian Universalist worship, the transition to becoming an adult UU will be difficult.

At our district's Summer Institute several years ago, I was talking to a number of young people in their late teens who wondered out loud how to make such a transition. They expressed a desire to broaden their participation beyond attendance at youth meetings, but they felt uncomfortable in the adult service and in other areas of church life.

Perhaps such a transition would be difficult under the best of circumstances; many denominations experience a decline in the participation of teens and young adults. Yet the transition to adult involvement is made even more difficult by unfamiliarity.

A third effect of excluding children from adult worship is to rob them of something necessary for the health of their own hearts and minds and souls. We all need worship. We all need a break from the constant stimulation and entertainment that our society throws at us. Worship, as Earl Holt says, "is the opposite of entertainment, time which others fill for us, a diversion. It is a time not of recreation but for re-creation. It is an hour for seeking perspective on all the other hours of our lives. At its best it invites us to empty ourselves that we may be filled."[2]

We have become accustomed to constant stimulation and continual entertainment. Worship lacks overt stimulation. We need this lack of stimulation in order to be re-created, in order to discover in the midst of stillness the wisdom and strength that dwells within and around us. Children need this, too. When this need is fulfilled, we are actually more easily entertained and stimulated by the subtle beauty that surrounds us in the everyday world.

Worship offers its own kind of stimulation anyway, one especially suited to children. It is called ritual. But because our roots are in the low-church Protestant tradition, our worship is sermon-centered and contains little ritual. Moreover, ritual actually has negative connotations for many of us; it is viewed as empty, meaningless, and even frightening.

What is ritual? It is a "pattern of behavior that is either loosely or quite explicitly repeated on similar occasions."[3] Common rituals in a worship service include a consistent order of service every week; certain words that are spoken or familiar hymns that are sung in every service; and repeated activities such as lighting the chalice or ringing a bell to start the service.

I believe that one of the purposes of worship for

children is to introduce them to ritual elements. Ironically, worship and ritual seem to be natural activities for children. Children *like* "smells and bells," liturgy, ritual, music, and other aesthetic elements. They like it because it fulfills certain essential needs. At their best, the rituals that children learn give them a sense of belonging and a sense of being rooted in the sacred.

I grew up in a Methodist church. Although my family was by no means devout, I became familiar with both Sunday school and adult worship. Now, I certainly do remember sitting through boring sermons, just as I remember that one morning when I thought the minister's prayer was going to go on forever. Methodists, after all, are low-church Protestants, too. There aren't many smells and bells.

But I also remember the music. Methodists know how to sing hymns with great gusto; good, rousing singing was par for the course. The memory of this singing as well as a love of certain hymns stays with me to this day.

I also remember other rituals such as the Lord's Prayer and the Doxology. These elements remain meaningful even though I left Methodism because they reconnect me to that past, which for me was positive.

Along with creating a sense of belonging and of being rooted in the sacred, ritual also makes order out of chaos and gives form to what is formless. In *To*

Dance With God, Gertrud Mueller Nelson relates a story of some small children standing on the beach facing the incoming waves. They could not handle the immensity of the ocean, so they dug a hole into which the waves washed; they created a smaller ocean. Nelson writes,

> What is too vast and shapeless, we deal with in smaller, manageable pieces. We do this for practicality but we also do this for high purpose: to relate safely to the mysterious, to communicate with the transcendent....We cannot head straight into the awe of the Almighty. Like the child before the ocean, we turn our backs on what is too much and slowly create the form that will contain something of the uncontainable.[4]

That form is ritual and worship. They help us relate to the transcendent, the powerful, the mysterious. Children are aware of these forces, perhaps more so than adults. They feel this power, they experience it. And children will create ritual to help themselves deal with the experience.

Bedtime rituals are a good example (though they can become so elaborate as to be obsessive). Just think of what children are facing when they go to bed: sleep, darkness, and the night. All carry great power. All are mysterious. With their sense of sight diminished or eliminated, children's sense of imagination takes over. In the darkness, the whole world becomes different. In sleep, death seems to occur. Strange dreams appear in the night that cannot be controlled. This is power, this is mystery.

Ritual is a way of imposing a structure on this mystery, of making it manageable, of helping us feel more in control. This is why children may need bedtime rituals, including bedtime prayer. Prayer helps them gain strength, comfort, and hope in the face of the power and mystery of the dark and sleep. Prayer at anytime helps them express gratitude and love, which are great strengths with which to face the mystery of the transcendent.

So why do children need ritual in church? Because religion is also about power and mystery and the transcendent. It is about the eternal, about that which is greater than we are. Children need a way to relate to this awe-inspiring mystery, a way to create form out of the immense and uncontainable. So do we adults.

It is my hope, as we move into the twenty-first century, as we face a society increasingly characterized by chaos and confusion, that we provide our children with two important offerings. The first is to include them in the central ritual of our congregations, worship, as well as other meaningful rituals. The second is to provide them with positive attitudes toward religion and positive statements of faith that contain beliefs they can hold on to. Our children need to be taught and shown that hope is real and that there is a source of sustaining life and goodness that is greater than we are but that is available to us and that our actions can and should reflect.

The words used to describe this Source are secondary. Of primary importance is the proclamation and education of the reality of this Source. We cannot allow our own negative experiences with various images of the divine to poison our children's religious beliefs.

Children need worship and faith in order to value and thus nurture their basic religious yearnings. It is critical for them to have the means to express the most basic religious impulses of gratitude, trust, praise, and love.

We adults, I believe, share these exact same needs. Perhaps, then, we and our children can enter into a reciprocal relationship. May we let them inspire us with their wonder, with their awe, with their gratitude, and with their love. May we cultivate these deeply human and deeply spiritual impulses in them, and also let them cultivate the same impulses in us. This is the sacred task before us.

Doing Justice and Mercy

Racial and Economic Justice:
Hand in Hand En *La Lucha*

Sandra Decker

As a member of the UUA's Black Concerns Working Group, I have done antiracism workshops around the country for our UU churches. Everywhere I have found a similar unawareness that we are all implicated in the racial and economic injustice around us. Mercy and Justice: How ought we relate as a people and as congregations to the larger society?

At the 1994 General Assembly in Ft. Worth, a white UU woman told me that she had traveled around the world, and that we were really lucky in this country to have the kind of democracy we do. I asked her if she had been to any of the workshops sponsored by Unitarian Universalists for a Just Economic Community (UUJEC) or The Black Concerns Working Groups

(BCWG). She had not. She was interested in UUA governance and music. I asked if she thought many people of color would agree with her statement. She believed they would, should they travel around the world as she had.

Robert Reich, in his book *The Works of Nations*, says we are rapidly becoming a country where 20 percent of the people will be "symbolic analysts," well educated and able to think independently.[1] They will live in housing complexes surrounded by high fences, completely separate from the rest of the people. They will travel from their locked garage at home to the locked garage at work and never confront the other 80 percent of their neighbors. The other 80 percent will be struggling to live on minimum wage, if they have jobs at all. Most Unitarian Universalists fall into the category of "symbolic analysts." Have we separated ourselves so utterly that we are completely out of touch with the reality of the rest of the world?

At our antiracism workshops I always hear predictable statements at the beginning of each session from white Unitarian Universalists. "Blacks only like gospel music." "Blacks will only go to Christian churches." "We're an upper middle income church so...." "We're a highly educated church so...." "There aren't any people of color who live around our church." "I only like Eurocentric music." "Blacks are just as racist as anyone else."

Most people who complete the eight-hour workshop go through a transformation. They come to understand how we grow up with blind assumptions that must be unlearned and that we have to change ourselves before we can truly have an impact on anything else or even envision a different way of being in the world. We use a form of praxis in these workshops that the liberation theologians use in their base communities in South America. Praxis is theory plus action. Shared reflection informs how we are today and helps us to act differently tomorrow. We learn to be, as Ghandi said, "the change you want to see."

The new group, Unitarian Universalists for a Just Economic Community (UUJEC), is working in similar ways in our Association to help Unitarian Universalists understand economic injustice and how we as individuals must change in order to affect the larger society.

The first time I drove through east Oakland, I was in shock. I drove by block after block. I saw the doorways filled with our African American brothers and sisters, blank and hopeless looks on their faces. I had seen this scene on TV. Seeing it in person gave me a whole new perspective on racial and economic injustice. I know the Rev. Jim Smith from the Allen Temple Baptist church in east Oakland, a church with 4,000 members doing a tremendous amount of outreach. Jim says he spends most of his time just trying to convince people they do have something to bring to the table, that they have value as human beings.

How different from the work we do in our UU churches.

Cornell West says in *Race Matters*,

> We must delve into the depths where neither liberals nor conservatives dare to tread, namely, into the murky waters of despair and dread that now flood the streets of black America. To talk about the depressing statistics of unemployment, infant mortality...and violent crime is one thing. But to face up to the monumental eclipse of hope, the unprecedented collapse of meaning, the incredible disregard to human life and property in much of black America is something else.
>
> To struggle to barely survive while others live in million dollar homes; to never have the medical care you need for your sick and dying child when you know it is available; to know hunger and very poor quality of food day in and day out while others eat at posh restaurants...crushes the will to live...virtually drives people crazy...fills people with anger and hatred and leads to nihilism...the lived experience of coping with a life of horrifying meaninglessness, hopelessness, and (most important) lovelessness. [2]

West believes the nihilism of the black community is linked to the structures of corporate institutions that affect us all and that they are inflicted by white supremacist beliefs permeating US society and culture. Just being a witness to this creates a state of nihilism for everyone. The Buddhists say you can never have enough of what you don't need. How much do we need? What are we willing to give up?

What can we do? I believe it is most important for Unitarian Universalists to be confronted with reality. We shouldn't hold our antiracism training in upper middle–class, white neighborhoods. Let us get out of the convention center at General Assembly and really *be in* the city we are visiting. Do we have to stay at only the "best" hotels? We need to know our own communities. We can support restaurants and businesses owned by people of color. If white, we can move out of our all–white neighborhood or make sure that absolutely anyone can move in. We can monitor real estate companies and banks. Our children will grow up with the expectation that they should live as they see us living. Exactly how much do we deserve?

We can also raise our own awareness. Our churches can become base communities. We can learn about solidarity with the poor and "be the change we want to see." I recommend a book by UU minister Fredric John Muir: *A Reason For Hope, Liberation Theology Confronts a Liberal Faith.*[3] In the back of the book is a curriculum to teach liberation theology in our churches. Muir points out that "the process of developing a contextualized liberation theology cannot stop there. In order for liberation theology to retain its dialectical character, awareness must give impetus to action."[4]

Bev Harrison, feminist liberation theologian, has pointed out that evil is to be found in the gap between what we say and what we do. Sally McFague, another feminist theologian, defines sin as "living the lie."

The Hispanic women of the United States (*mujeristas*) say that God is *en la lucha*, in the struggle. If we live the heritage of our religion, we live out an imperative. We are called to be in the struggle, too. We are admonished as Unitarian Universalists to go forth and sin no more, to stop living the lie and to be the change we want to see.

En La Lucha!

Can a Prophet Chair the Board?

Richard S. Gilbert

———————◆———————

"(People) are most conservative after dinner."
Ralph Waldo Emerson (Unitarian)

"A stuffed prophet sees no visions."
Clarence R. Skinner (Universalist)

A priest friend in the Catholic Worker movement once asked me: "How can a predominantly upper middle class religion escape its self-interest and be an advocate for the underclass?" The question was baldly put; I was without adequate answer then, and the question still challenges me. It should challenge all of us. Can a religious movement consisting largely of people who have "succeeded" in the American economic system be expected to give radical critique of that system, much less provide impetus for its radical reform? Can a people be "terribly at ease in Zion"?[1]

Figuratively speaking, Unitarian Universalists occupy many of the board rooms of the nation; they are often very close to the seats of power. It is not inconceivable that this power might be used as leverage for a radical critique of the existing configurations of power and a vehicle for its radical transformation. Although it is not inconceivable, it is perhaps not likely. But until the Unitarian Universalist movement resolves the contradiction of being terribly at ease in an unjust Zion, it will lack an effective praxis for social reform.

I believe the issue of economic justice is the Achilles heel in the Unitarian Universalist pantheon of social values. Despite the inexorably growing gap between rich and poor,[2] with its attendant social problems, the liberal religious voice is strangely silent. Why?

Unitarian Universalists are often in the forefront of issues that do not affect us directly—wars in which relatively few of our college educated sons and daughters fight; the civil rights movement, which by and large did not pose a threat to our security; the ecological movement, which seems safely distant from our primarily suburban homes. Our pioneering efforts in combating homophobia constitute a notable exception.

We have been trapped in what Walter Rauschenbusch called "culture Protestantism," in which the church "has simply yielded to the law of social gravitation"[3] and sunk to a cultural lowest common denominator. We are a classic case of the economic understanding of denomination so clearly articulated by H. Richard Niebuhr: "The domination of class and self-preservative church ethics over the ethics of the gospel must be held responsible for much of the moral ineffectiveness of Christianity in the West."[4]

We are an upper middle-class movement. A 1993 demographic study of Unitarian Universalists indicates ninety-five percent had attended college, eighty-three percent graduated, and sixty-five percent had some postgraduate education (including all of our clergy), all up from a similar survey in 1987. Respondents reported a median household income of $50,000, up from $42,000 in 1987, and approximately $20,000 above the national median.[5] If we were to look for a religious group that had most benefitted from the status quo, it would appear to be the Unitarian Universalists. Saul Alinsky pointed out, "Once you're on top you want to stay there. You learn to eat in very good restaurants, to fly first class. The next thing you know these things are essential to you. You're imprisoned by them."[6]

The denomination as a whole has not had any significant program to deal with the question of economic justice. "Ad hocracy" through General Assembly resolutions on poverty and related issues is the main response. The late Paul Carnes likened our resolutions to the petitionary prayers of the Methodists. There have been few attempts to enable a middle class movement to question the justice of its own prosperity or the potential use of it on behalf of greater justice.

The impact of class on religion is evident in Unitarian Universalist history. Unitarian Universalism has been a conspicuous part of the American establishment. This was true of Unitarianism from the beginning, although it was not until early in the twentieth century that Universalism, with its earlier appeal to lower middle-class people, became sociologically almost indistinguishable from Unitarianism. Our history has been the struggle of a prophetic minority against the benefits of the very class to which it belongs.[7]

A single historical illustration epitomizes the tension. William Peck, secretary of the radical Unitarian Fellowship for Social Justice in the early twentieth century, gave a somewhat biased, but illuminating, account of an American Unitarian Association meeting dealing with social responsibility. "Rev. Samuel M. Crothers, D.D. of Cambridge, gave the principal address on What Is the Social Problem? (We are still wondering).... This meeting was a mild and uneventful exhibition of skillful skating on thin ice without fracturing the ice. Evidently the public anticipated it; for whereas our two previous rallies have been before crowded houses, this was typically Unitarian. Bonnets galore and seats to spare."[8]

The issue has hardly been resolved. In his 1962 study of the Unitarian Universalist movement, Harold Taylor was prompted to write: "The danger here lies in the possibility that the liberal church may become the church of the suburban educated liberal."[9] Angus MacLean wrote in 1965: "More and more of our ministers express the fear that suburban classism and privilege outdo the faith when and where the chips are down."[10]

I can illustrate the aversion of the movement to a sharp critique of the contradictions between a prophetic church and a prosperous people. As chair of the Unitarian Universalist Task Force on Economic Justice from 1979 to 1982, I was summoned before the Board of Trustees and interrogated about the purpose of our group, a rather unusual practice. We had just released a study draft calling for a radical redistribution of income among the American people and in the world. It was clear that a number of denominational financial leaders were concerned about what effect our work would have on denominational giving. It was a tense meeting, and I feared for our future. As a result of that pressure, lack of resources, and a feeling the topic was simply too vast for our capacity, we settled for a brief theological-ethical statement on economic justice and a study guide instead of a prophetic statement for the denomination. Clearly we were walking where angels fear to tread.

Can a Prophet Chair the Board?

It would seem the prophetic edge of this movement has been dulled, that "success" has lured a comfortable people into a culture religion, that a prophet cannot chair the board. The tension between our proclamation of economic justice and our own economic security is painful, but it must be addressed.

For some, economic justice is an oxymoron—inherently self-contradictory. However, from the perspective of religion, it is clearly not! Rather, economic justice is an imperative of religious people in virtually every tradition and time.

We are a nation of "dinners without appetites at one end of the table and appetites without dinners at the other end" in the words of nineteenth–century Unitarian Senator Charles Sumner.[11] Data from the Census Bureau in the fall of 1994 flesh out these images. Nearly one in six Americans, 15.1 percent, 39.3 million, live below the poverty line, an increase of one million from 1992, the highest level since 1960. Between 1989 and 1993, the typical US household lost $2,344 in annual income—a decline of 7 percent. In 1993, median family income declined by 3.5 percent, to $30,126. The income of the middle fifth of the population has stagnated. At the same time there are a record number of billionaires, 83. The 400 richest Americans are worth $349 billion.[12] Millions of Americans are saved from falling further only because of record-breaking numbers of two-earner households and record numbers of people moonlighting.[13] Over

15 percent of all heads of households living in poverty worked year-round and full time, and 40.3 percent worked for some period of time.[14]

Although Americans are working harder and have the world's highest productivity rate, we still have less leisure than other developed nations.[15] The average American is working harder for less. Furthermore, "fear of falling"[16] abounds. We are going "up the down escalator."

Meanwhile, as the poor get poorer (the bottom fifth earn 3.9 percent of total income, having lost 5 percent between 1970 and 1990); the middle-class is squeezed (60 percent lost ground), the rich are getting richer (the wealthiest fifth receive nearly half of the total income, up from 43.5 percent in 1970, while the richest 1 percent gained 87 percent). The top 1 percent of the population (2.5 million people) have almost as much income as the bottom 40 percent (100 million).[17] We are witnessing a "waltz of the wealthy," a meaner, harsher nation, the "new American apartheid."

Our unequal distribution of income—wealth inequality is far greater—is represented by the "fairness ratio," the proportion of the income of the richest fifth in the country to the poorest fifth. Our ratio is twelve to one, compared to nine to one in France, five to one in the Netherlands, and four to one in Japan and Finland.[18] This avalanche of figures can be likened to a pyramid made out of a child's blocks, with each layer representing $1,000 of income. Although the peak would be higher than the Eiffel Tower, almost all Americans would be within a yard of the ground.[19]

What is worse, we seem to be taking it for granted, as if it were in the nature of things. There is little public outcry. We experience what Hannah Arendt called the "banality of evil," an apathetic acceptance of obvious injustice as the norm.

Religion must challenge economics on the nature of freedom, equity, community, and the meaning of life. We have learned in the last decade that mink coats do not trickle down—nor do Trump Towers. That is like assuming that if the horses are fed, the sparrows will eventually benefit.

Fundamental moral issues are involved. In a competitive society, what do we do with the losers? Are capitalism and altruism compatible? Self-interest, once considered a moral defect, has been transformed into a moral virtue. I submit that the current configuration of the American economy is unjust.

Unjust on what basis? One of our tasks as religious people is to raise questions of justice. And one of the most fundamental questions is "How much do we deserve?"[20] Are the rich rich because they deserve it, and the poor poor for the same reason? Is this inequity wrong? I submit four propositions to argue that increasing disparities of income and wealth are inherently unjust.

Proposition One: the greater the disparity in income, the less the freedom in society. The market economy is built on the assumption that each person can cast his/her economic ballots in the marketplace, thus undergirding human freedom.

To the question "How many libertarians does it take to screw in a light bulb?" the answer is "None. Market forces take care of it." No so. When income disparity is so great, a kind of market imperialism develops. Those with the most "votes" always outbid others. Political democracy is based on the "one person, one vote," principle, but market democracy is based on the "one dollar, one vote" principle. Power grows out of the end of a dollar bill. I submit there is greater freedom with ten people each having $10 than one person with $100 to spend. The Golden Rule in our nation is that "those who have the gold, make the rules." More equitable distribution of resources will broaden the base of our democracy.

Proposition Two: the greater the disparity in income, the less the fairness in society. To what extent have the rich and poor "deserved" their lot in life? Research demonstrates the income level of one's family is decisive for one's lot in life. Given two groups, one relatively poor, one relatively well off, with exactly the same educational level, poor children with IQs over 120 would earn just about as much as the rich ones with IQs below 80. Earnings consistently relate to the economic status of one's family.[21]

I suggest the argument that unequal incomes are necessary for economic incentives is greatly exaggerated. Through changing tax laws, tax loopholes, tax expenditures for the affluent, there is plenty of incentive at the top. However, as income rises, marginal utility (the extra utility added by its last unity) decreases. Each extra dollar provides a bit less incentive. The motivation to move from $100,000 to $110,000 in income is far less than to move from $10,000 to $20,000. The same potential $10,000 increase would produce very different incentives.

On the other hand, people with lower incomes are disproportionately taxed, thus dampening incentives. In reality we "soak the poor" with regressive sales and property and payroll taxes.[22] In addition, taking a minimum wage job may well bring lower income than does public assistance and make one ineligible for government medical coverage to boot. We need a more progressive tax system with greater incentives at the bottom.

Proposition Three: the greater the disparity of income, the less community there will be. American society is marked by excessive individualism. John Maynard Keynes defined capitalism as "the extraordinary belief that the nastiest of (people) for the nastiest of motives will somehow work for the benefit of all."[23]

We are in a new class war, each person fighting for a piece of the economic pie. We have become increasingly fragmented. Social Darwinism, "the survival of the fittest," has replaced our Constitution's preamble, mandating us to "promote the general welfare." It is as if we were saying, "Your end of the lifeboat is sinking."

Economist Lester Thurow once asked a Harvard alumni group from whom would they take income if given the task of raising investment in plant and equipment from 10 percent to 15 percent of gross national product. "One hand was quickly raised and the suggestion was made to eliminate welfare payments. Not surprisingly, the person was suggesting that someone else's income be lowered, but I pointed out that welfare constitutes only 1.2 percent of GNP. Where were they going to get the remaining funds—3.8 percent? Whose income were they willing to cut after they had eliminated government programs for the poor? Not a hand went up."[24]

We are "drunk on the rhetoric of individualism." We cannot survive "half suburb, half slum." As Francis Bacon said, "Money is like manure, of very little use unless it be spread around."

Proposition Four: the greater the disparity of income, the greater the potential for erosion of moral sensitivity and religious meaning. Affluence tends to corrupt, and absolute affluence corrupts absolutely, to paraphrase Lord Acton.

There is a cartoon showing three fish swimming, one behind the other. First is a small fish saying "There is no justice." Immediately behind, ready to swallow it, is a larger fish saying, "There is some justice in the world." Finally, there is a large fish about to swallow both, saying "The world is just."

"Lee Iaccoca, asked how he felt about making $20.6 million in a single year, said, 'That's the American way. If the little kids don't aspire to make money like I did, what the hell good is this country?'"[25] Religion suggests there are other criteria.

What should we do in the face of this injustice? Within the context of a market economy, we need, among other things, a much more progressive income tax system based on equal sacrifice and ability to pay. A maximum wage income tax pegged at a set ratio to the minimum wage—say ten to one—would fund a negative income tax with a guaranteed income floor and real incentives to work.[26] Unitarian jurist Oliver Wendell Holmes said, "Taxes are the price we pay for civilization." Americans are the most under-taxed people in the developed world, and it shows in our growing gap between rich and poor.[27]

In the end we must face up to "the predicament of the prosperous." We need an ethic of "class betrayal." Such betrayal requires us to be advocates, not for the prosperous, for we can advocate for ourselves and do. It will require "a theology of relinquishment."[28] That relinquishment is decidedly not mere charity or philanthropy, but a radical reform of a system in which "entitlements" gravitate not to the poor, but to the middle class.

Only twenty-five percent of entitlement spending is means tested; the rest goes to the middle class in the form of tax expenditures for business, housing mortgage interest deductions, social security benefits, and other items documented by former Commerce Secretary Pete Peterson, a self-described "fat-cat Republican."[29]

I am under no illusion this challenge to our economic complacency will be happily received by Unitarian Universalists. To have one's own prosperity called into question is distinctly unpleasant. Nevertheless, religious leaders in every age and tradition have been urged, in the words of Catholic Worker founder Dorothy Day, "to comfort the afflicted and to afflict the comfortable." One minister at midlife wrote, "Wherever the Apostle Paul went, there was a riot. Wherever I go, they serve tea." We are too often so caught up in this system from which we benefit to criticize it objectively, much less prophetically. That must change.

In the words of Walt Kelly: "There is no need to sally forth, for it remains true that those things which make us human are, curiously enough, always close at hand. Resolve then, that on this very ground, with small flags waving and tinny blasts on tiny trumpets, we shall meet the enemy, and not only may he be ours, he may be us."[30]

The New Three R's

William Jones

———————◆———————

Every project can be reduced to a specific mission or purpose, and this, in turn, dictates a specific approach or method to tackling the project. This principle also informs our topic.

The implicit motivation for the essays in this collection—"to identify the enduring center of our UU faith, and in light of the changing times to assess what we need to hold on to, reformulate, or abandon"— is an "early alert" to an acute menace to the survival and well being of our society and also our faith community. These essays are a delicate exercise in virus identification and vaccine production where we seek to identify the specific virus that threatens us and produce, in response, an effective vaccine that protects us from the effects of the threatening invader. In sum, we are engaged in social diagnosis and social therapy where the *permanent* that we isolate is advanced as a cure, as our magic bullet.

At first glance this assignment appears to be a historical and theological scavenger hunt that directs our attention to the past, scouring the nooks and crannies of our faith to separate the wheat (the permanent) from the chaff (the transient). However, the controlling phrase, *in the light of changing times,* dictates a quite different focus and accent. It rivets our attention on our present life situation and grants it coequal authority, value, and significance. In this context, the faith absolute (the permanent) that we select is based on its socio-therapeutic utility for the geopolitical megatrends and causalities that dominate today's world. Given this understanding, I will describe my diagnosis of this social reality and demonstrate its superior merit for producing a preventive/corrective therapy.

I want first to advance some general principles to guide our analysis that I have found useful in assessing the relative merit of rival norms or functional absolutes, that is, our *permanent*. Here, I will identify oppression as the geopolitical megatrend that is generating new types of conflict that call for more effective methods of conflict reduction. Accordingly, any permanent that we select from the UU core must certify its competence in conflict resolution.

The permanent in Unitarian Universalism that I

advance as the preferred therapy returns to the birth of our movement and its *raison d'etre* as a protest against oppression—a protest based on a doctrine of pluralism and its affirmation of individuals and groups as coequal centers of freedom, authority, and power. However, when our birth norm of pluralism is used to assess our faith community today, I find a radical abandonment of this permanent (pluralism) in favor of its opposite, the transient (assimilation). My thesis is this: In the postmodern world of oppression and expanding conflict, the preeminent permanent that we must endorse and incarnate is the pluralism that marked our birth.

The New Three R's

For more than two decades now, I have argued that oppression is our fundamental geopolitical megatrend, that group conflict would increase, expand, and explode, that *counter*-violence would be the growing response from the oppressed to the violence inherent in society's systemic oppression—in sum that oppression and the conflict it generates are the preeminent economic, social, and political issue that we and our children will have to cope with.

A simple exercise should persuade anyone who doubts that oppression stands at the top of the Hit Parade of human affairs. Select any major newspaper, *The New York Times, Wall Street Journal,* etc., at random.

Do a content analysis of the headlines to determine which human activity is referred to most often. Then turn to the International Summary section and repeat the content analysis. Invariably, your analysis will identify some expression of oppression.

To further verify this analysis, simply draw up a list of the ten geopolitical hot spots where there is the greatest tension or hostility between groups. Start locally, regionally, nationally, internationally, or "galactically"; it does not matter. What you will find is the following. A large subpopulation in the society has relabeled itself as oppressed and defined itself as discriminated against. It is protesting that oppression and adopting an "any means necessary" morality.

What is being described in all of this is the three new R's—not reading, 'riting, and 'rithmetic but resurrection, resistance, and revolution/rebellion. The three R's are the fever, the future warning alarm, signaling the recognition that economic, social, and political (esp) oppression has been sighted and is being attacked. The new three R's point to the resurrection of a new consciousness in the oppressed as co-equal that radicalizes them to resist (protest) and apply the "first shall be last and the last shall be first" principle of social change to the hierarchical inequalities of our "trickle down" society.

Other prophet-predictors have given us early alert warnings about the new three R's. At the beginning of this century, W. B. Du Bois identified "the color line" as the preeminent geopolitical and national issue of the twentieth century. Understand, as most do not, that he was actually identifying esp oppression— conflict between the haves and the have-nots—as the inescapable geopolitical problem for this century. He was wrong only in his failure to include the twenty-first.

Frederick Douglass also warned us, the author of *Jane Eyre* before him, and the Founding Mothers and Fathers of America too, that "Where justice is denied, where poverty is enforced, where ignorance prevails, and where any one class is made to feel that society is an organized conspiracy to oppress...and degrade [it], *neither persons nor property will ever be safe....*"

There is a intriguing review of *Jane Eyre* that identifies the historical root of this protest. "Altogether *The Autobiography of Jane Eyre,*" the reviewer tells us, "is preeminently an anti-Christian proposition. There is throughout it a murmuring against the comforts of the rich and against the privations of the poor, which as far as each individual is concerned, is a murmuring against God's appointment."[1]

The conflict associated with the new three R's expresses the same paradigm shift and new consciousness: a rejection of a belief and value system that made the position of the oppressed at the bottom of the social ladder not only moral and right but inevitable. The "murmurers" in *Jane Eyre* are today's oppressed, underclass, the wretched of the earth. They have undergone a radical shift in how they regard themselves. Casting off the world view of the oppressor that legitimated their inequalities as moral and always best for the "murmurers" welfare, they now see themselves as coequal and no longer honor the "superiority" of those above them in the social hierarchy. Make no mistake: All of this is being fueled by a moral and religious legitimation that adopts the "any means necessary" philosophy that society's power elite hypocritically reserves for itself (e.g., the just war theory), while counseling those at the bottom to turn the other cheek.

Note the impact of the resurrected consciousness for increasing the scope and level of societal conflict. Once I define my situation as oppression, I automatically divide reality into two antagonistic spheres: oppressor and oppressed. My self-awareness *as oppressed* confirms the presence of a significant other in my life environment who opposes my survival and well-being. If I reject the view that god and nature's god, the natural and the supernatural, are the cause of my "appointment" at the bottom of the social ladder, and if I refuse to blame the victim, myself, I will hold some other human culpable—who is now identified as my enemy. In all of this, the potential for conflict should be obvious.

Conflict Reduction Models

Various conflict reduction models have evolved to address this accelerating group conflict and disharmony that are seemingly immune to our traditional and time-tested defenses. I want to identify three. Model one manages conflict primarily between individuals and very small unorganized groups, for example, John hits Jim, Mary strikes Jill. The conflict here is random and sporadic. A spate of corrective and preventive techniques are in place for these circumstances, particularly in the public school system. but none successfully addresses the conflict associated with the three R's.

A second model, *Getting to Yes,* is already familiar to us.[2] Its design handles conflict involving larger organized groups, for example, labor-management units, and basically coequal in power. The anticipated conflict is reduced through in-place rules that both parties accept as supportive of their self-interest needs. If conflict does arise, a compromise model is applied, both sides give up something.

These two models, however, cannot effectively cope with the peculiar circumstances of the new three R's; a different model must be constructed to accommodate the fact that here we have considerably larger populations, indeed subpopulations, in a society. More important than the numbers factor is the fundamental inequality of the parties that must be accommodated. One group has an overwhelming surplus of power that provides monopolistic access to the society's life-sustaining and life-enhancing resources, the most of what the society defines as the best and least of the worst. The power deficit of the other group, as one would suspect, establishes a least-of-the-best and most-of-the-worst status.

Another factor that is absent in model two generates an additional layer of conflict. Here, the in-place rules/laws that are the foundation for an operational consensus in model two are themselves in dispute; the two parties disagree about the impact of observing the rules for their respective self-interest needs. One group sees the rules as helpful; the other pictures them as harmful. This impasse necessitates the creation of a new code or constitution. All of this ultimately requires the creation of a new set of rules, a new constitution, and so forth, with all of the attendant conflict that is familiar to us through daily observation of geopolitical hot spots.

But the major flaw of *Getting to Yes* is apparent when one considers the consequence of applying a compromise model to a situation of pervasive economic, social, and political inequalities. A seesaw image will illustrate that if both ends of the seesaw give up equally, the configuration of inequalities remains intact, thus replicating the conditions that spawned the original conflict. In sum, conflict reduction in the context of the new three R's requires a policy, a theology of relinquishment that obliges the party with the surplus of power and privilege to reduce the gap by reducing its surplus of power and privilege. It is this model that our research seeks to develop.

Pathways to the Permanent

The merit of the *permanent(s)* in Unitarian Universalism to address this problem is unsettled. We have received testimony from reliable witnesses that portray Unitarian Universalism as both saint and sinner, as deadly virus and vaccine, in sum, as cause and cure. It is this fundamental issue that we continue to "cuss and discuss" in projects like this one.

It is easy to show that we operate on a binary logic in the social arena. No matter who we are, where we are, or what we do, we have two and only two choices. We will choose either to continue and preserve the present situation, or we will choose to change it. Choosing to "do nothing" is obviously a choice to continue and preserve. Thus, within a concrete situation of oppression, there are two and only two broad classes of theologies: guardian theologies that preserve and continue the oppression and goading theologies that undermine the oppression. Each *permanent* that is advanced will belong to one and only one of these classes, and its location in one of these classes is a critical factor in determining its status as permanent or transient.

The binary logic means that no human action or product is neutral; each will tilt toward change or preservation. This is another way of speaking of "praxis verification." "The verification principle of every theological statement is the praxis that it enables for the future. Theological statements contain as much truth as they deliver practically in transforming reality."[3]

Permanent and transient are labels. Consider the label on a can. The label is not an intrinsic feature of the content of the can. Rather, it is something that we paste onto the can. The label is detachable and replaceable. It is also particular in the sense that it expresses a single angle of perception that reflects our idiosyncratic world picture, our subjective view of what things are, rather than a feature of the object itself. The same tenet can always "wear" a different dress or label that represents a different or opposed belief and value perspective.

The function of the label—and every word is a label—is to control and direct our response. In fact, the inner logic of labeling is to predetermine our response by making us think that the label is an accurate descriptor of the object to which it is attached. Our labels are indicators of our binary logic tilt.

The DDT (Diagnosis Dictates Therapy) principle uncovers our binary logic tilt through the application of this dictum: Successful social therapy requires accurate and adequate labeling/diagnosis of the situation, in particular its controlling causes and trends.

As an illustration: I have a headache, so I go to a doctor for treatment who diagnoses why I have a pain. The diagnosis, whatever it is, identifies a particular cause for my headache, and the therapy, in turn, is linked to that causality. If, for instance, the diagnosis/causality is constipation, you can predict the likely therapy: Ex-lax, more bulk, water, or exercise. Suppose, however, a second medical opinion indicates a brain tumor. Same therapy? No. This diagnosis prescribes a radically different therapy because it isolates a different cause.

The therapy-diagnosis principle obliges us to incorporate the concept of "false causality" in our analysis and assessment of issues. To illustrate: a suburbanite on Long Island dug a huge hole 90 x 90 x 90 feet in her/his backyard. An alarmed neighbor asked why the gigantic crater had been dug and received this answer: "To keep the elephants away." The neighbor, now even more disturbed, retorted: "There aren't any elephants within 10,000 miles of this neck of the woods." The hole-digging suburbanite came back with: "See how effective it is."

Several implications follow from this understanding for our assignment. Any corrective (permanent) that you may propose for a problem—be it a particular theological tenet, spiritual discipline, policy, program, or curriculum—will be grounded on your particular diagnosis of the situation and its implicit causality. In this sense, every policy recommendation is

171

an implicit demonstration and endorsement of the accuracy and adequacy of the diagnosis/causality to which it is a response. Accordingly, the merit or demerit of any therapy, policy, or permanent that is presented to us should be judged on the validity of its causal analysis, its successful avoidance of a false causality.

Another story illustrates a final distinction between espoused theory and theory in use: A Roman Catholic priest was conducting a catechism class on heaven that involved a series of five questions. Question one: "How many of you believe in heaven?" All raised their hands. Question two: "How many of you believe that heaven is a good place." All raised their hands. Question three: "How many of you believe that heaven is the best place?" Again, all raised their hands. Question four: "How many of you want to go to heaven?" All raised their hands again, but this time, most raised both hands. His final question: "How many of you are willing to die tomorrow and go to heaven?" Not a single hand was raised. What was their theory-in-use and what was their espoused theory? If their answer to the first four questions represented their theory-in-use, their answer to the fifth question should have been either: "Yes" or "No, I don't want to wait until tomorrow, I want to die right now." The answer given was their espoused theory, the answer we give to legitimate what we want others to think are our operational faith commitments and practices. The answer not given, their theory-in-use, is what is entailed if actual practice dovetails with announced beliefs. This distinction effectively uncovers our inconsistencies and hypocrisy. It determines whether the permanent we advance represents what we preach or what we practice.

Pluralism as the Permanent

An application of the foregoing guides yielded the doctrine of pluralism as my priority permanent for this essay. To get a fix on the argument requires an analysis of three concepts: assimilation, integration, and pluralism, each of which is a different response to difference.

Assimilation sets up *one* thing to function as absolute, as the ultimate ideal. This becomes the standard by which all things are measured and to which they are expected to conform. Assimilation then uses this one thing to measure other things. Deviations from this ideal are viewed as deficits, abnormalities, deprivations, and evil. The end result of assimilation is the establishment of a two-category system, hierarchically arranged into alleged superior and inferior groups.

The inner logic of assimilation is to get rid of the different; and it does this in a precise and predictable way—through cloning, cleansing, or confinement. The different is required to give up its difference(s) and become a clone of the assimilationist norm. A second method is cleansing or the eradication of the different through genocidal and holocaust operations. Holocausts historically are the outgrowth of assimilationist policies. Confinement of the different into a ghetto or establishing apartheid structures make up the third response to the different.

Integration is both similar and different. First the difference. Whereas assimilation establishes the norm of inequality, integration begins with the affirmation of coequality, designating things as coequal in terms of significance importance and value. To incarnate the integrationist ideal demands that all of the coequal items be present, as coequals. Given this norm of co-equality, eradicating differences through cloning, especially if it is involuntary, or extermination are excluded.

The integrationist norm also seeks to eradicate difference, but through a different method. Integration accomplishes this through blending. Example: Process a tomato, carrot, and celery in a blender. The result, as every cook knows, is an "integrated" mixture in which the original colors and textures have been eradicated.

A third model, pluralism, monopolizes the birth of Unitarian Universalism. Pluralism, like integration, affirms the coequality of the "different." But unlike integration and assimilation, it eschews both definitive blending and cloning. Rather, "the different" are retained as different, and this difference is regarded as valuable and indispensable for the new world order or however the ideal situation is defined. All of this leads to its motto: coexistence in coequality or coequality in coexistence.

Consider which of these three models the United States applied to religion and what that recommends for solving intergroup conflict. The outcome of assimilation in religion would be a single religion. Clearly the United States said no to that. An integrationist approach would also yield a single model that is a hybrid, for example, of Christian and Jew. This too was rejected. What America enshrined is a pluralist blueprint where different religions are addressed as coequal, where the Catholic is not required to become Protestant, or the Jew, Christian.

The American experience and its choice of pluralism in religion demonstrates that intra- and intergroup conflict are reduced and minimized where there is a tilt away from the assimilationist norm, and conflict is maximized where it is not. This is also the lesson we learn from a larger geopolitical and historical review of group conflict, a lesson that you can teach yourself through an exercise in which you control the variables and evidence. Draw up a list of (a) the most dehumanizing case studies of oppression in human history and (b) the most intractable geopolitical hot spots on the globe, especially where ethnic conflict is present. In every instance, the tilt will be toward the assimilationist model and away from the pluralist norm.

This leads me to conclude that only integration and pluralism are viable options to handle the spiraling group conflict that the future will inevitably manifest. And integration's ideal—blending items of coequal value not merely in *creed*, but in *deed*—cannot occur until pluralism is established. Integration involves the blending of coequal units, which means that you cannot move directly from assimilation to integration. Before the blending can occur, the items to be integrated must first be established as separate and coequal. In sum, integration comes after, not before.

If this philosophy of pluralism can inform our quest for the permanent, and if Unitarian Universalism can continue to incarnate this spirit, then the new world order can come, where the lion and the lamb will lie down together and happily the lamb will get up again.

Liberating Religious Individualism

Fredric John Muir

No doubt, an age will come in which ours shall be reckoned a period of darkness when we groped for the wall but stumbled and fell, because we trusted a transient notion, not an eternal truth; an age when temples were full of idols, set up by human folly.

Theodore Parker[1]

Reaching an Impasse

The scene is as recurrent and predictable as a New England town meeting. At this congregational meeting as at most others, the arguments reflect an ardent, uncompromising belief in individualism. The topic under debate was banning smoking in the church building.

The first several people to speak suggested that the reality was smoking is bad—for the smoker as well as those in the area. It simply did not make sense to smoke. Another person rose to say that whether it was good or bad, smokers had the responsibility to go along with the group, whatever the vote might be. She seemed to have been assuming a ban.

Finally, some of those opposed to the ban spoke, interestingly none of them smokers. "I want to defend the right of those who do smoke, to smoke," one of them said. "Since when have we been in the business of telling people what they can and cannot do?" There was some applause and then another supporter of smoker's rights spoke: "We've always protected the rights of the person here, and I don't want to start taking away those rights now. I don't like smoking either, but if allowing it is what will keep us free, then I want the ban voted down." The debate continued for another fifteen minutes and then the vote came: fifty-five for, and two against.

This congregational meeting highlights three forms of individualism. The first, Robert Bellah calls "biblical."[2] This biblical individualism recognizes the needs of the individual, but also that there are times when every person has a religious (biblical) obligation to go along with the group.

In a culture where we believe in the dignity and sacredness of the individual, biblical individualism attempts to appeal to a broader religious context. In this case "it's bad to smoke" connotes a sense of immorality. To be a good person, a religious person, would be to conform and to refrain from smoking.

The second form is described as "civic" individualism and is characterized by a straightforward call to do what is best for the group without direct appeal to the divine. Here the argument shifts from theology and morality to civic responsibility. Civic individualism emphasizes the needs of the group, and places the individual good within the context of a common good. This is essentially the utilitarian ideal that has shaped much modern ethical thought.

The third form of individualism found in that congregational meeting is "modern individualism." It holds that the individual must always take precedence over the group. Although it did not win in that meeting, this is the form of individualism that has taken over our contemporary American culture. Bellah explains: "There are both ideological and sociological reasons for the growing strength of modern individualism at the expense of the civic and biblical traditions. Modern individualism has pursued individual rights and individual autonomy in ever new realms."[3]

Even though it seems obvious, profound conflicts exist among these forms of individualism. Bellah believes the differences have generally been ignored in our times because at their core all three philosophies "stress the dignity and autonomy of the individual."[4] As biblical and civic forms of individualism have acquiesced to the tenants of modern individualism, major problems have emerged:

"The question is whether an individualism in which the self has become the main form of reality can really be sustained. What is at issue is not simply whether self-contained individuals might withdraw from the public sphere to pursue purely private ends, but whether such individuals are capable of sustaining either public *or* private life."[5]

Bellah is not suggesting here that we return to the civic and biblical traditions of individualism. He sees they also are inadequate. Each embody forms of discrimination that are not tolerable in contemporary society—sexism, racism, and a loss of individual dignity are ever present as the demands of the group become greater and stronger. The result?

We face a profound impasse. Modern individualism seems to be producing a way of life that is neither individually nor socially viable, yet a return to traditional forms would be to return to intolerable discrimination and oppression. The question, then, is whether the older civic and biblical traditions have the capacity to reformulate themselves while simultaneously remaining faithful to their own deepest insights.[6]

Paul King supports Bellah's conclusion: "some of our deepest problems both as individuals and as a society are closely linked to our individualism."[7] But King asserts that Bellah's analysis is limited.[8] It is not enough to expect an emerging new individualism or a heroism, somehow rising out of the old order. Although the strengths of civic and biblical individualism are appealing, they simply carry too many social liabilities to work.

King proposes a "heroism" that recognizes the value of individualism, yet has its roots in a social basis. He describes an individualism that can grow out of addressing the "tri-lemma" facing the modern middle class.

This "tri-lemma" is seen as coming out of an economy that has left the middle class increasingly on a par with the working class and just as vulnerable to poverty as those at the bottom of the economy. On the one hand the middle class is nearly powerless, while on the other it is tacitly expected to participate in the oppression of workers, the unemployed, and the poor. "Finally," King writes, "...our structural powerlessness as employees and our individualism create a sense of isolation and meaninglessness, of being unable to change either our vulnerability to or our cooperation in that oppression."[9]

This "tri-lemma" is ingrained in the country's identity and is revealed in our consumerism, nationalism, and religion. We need to address these ways we have come to see ourselves in order to find our identity. Of the first, King asserts: "It was Marx who suggested that 'you are what you do.' We seem to have changed that into 'you are what you consume.'"[10]

The second is nationalism. It is common to American religion, and even Unitarian Universalists, to frequently view religion as interdependent with the American experiment and experience. And third, religion, whether fundamentalism, orthodoxy, or liberalism, has given us an identity in which "the problems and their resolutions are couched in individualistic terms."[11]

The oppressive nature of the "tri-lemma" will increase and debilitate the middle class further as long as the middle class continues to be defined by consumerism, nationalism, and religion. The three forms of individualism critiqued by Bellah, and the three sources of identity put forward by King, are all oppressive and isolating. There is nothing about them that promotes liberation, community-building, empowerment, and interdependency.

The town meeting and the congregational meeting are examples of the pseudo-power King found in middle class communities. After the smoking debate and the congregational meeting, a member expressed his enthusiasm for what he heard: "Wasn't it great? We have such a variety of people here, such interesting ideas." His remarks add to a commonly expressed belief found in Unitarian Universalist congregations: they have become sanctuaries for religious eclecticism.

This perspective is summarized by the many who

repeat: "You can believe anything and be a Unitarian!" (We are the Church of the Ten Suggestions). This notion is correct in at least one sense: We embrace all three forms of individualism as suggested by Bellah. Both Bellah and King conclude that for American society, this embrace has created an impasse.

It has also created an impasse for Unitarian Universalism. In accepting several forms of individualism, even all of them, as our identity, Unitarian Universalists have avoided making a critical decision, a decision that will have a profound impact on the future. We now stand at a time when we must make a decision for continuing oppression or for liberation. But how will we decide?

Ideology and Myth

"The inherent worth and dignity of every person"[12] is sacrosanct in Unitarian Universalism. To suggest that the needs of the group are just as valid as those of the individual, let alone possibly more valid, is to prompt an inevitable look of disapproval, if not outright hostility. In some circles it can result in accusations of socialism. Where Bellah and others have explained the rise of individualism in American culture, Berger and Luckman provide a framework for understanding how individualism has reached such a near ontological and religious status.[13]

I contend that, though integral to the faith of

Unitarian Universalism, individualism is neither inherent nor ontological to our religious or national life. Individualism has achieved this near-sacred status, not because of a God-given character, but as a result of the importance people are willing to give it.

It is important to keep in mind that the objectivity of the institutional world, however massive it may appear to the individual, is a humanly produced, constructed objectivity. The process by which the externalized products of human activity attain the character of objectivity is objectivation.[14]

Understanding how the objectivation process works is not to suggest that individualism carries less value. It does show, however, that its value is sacred because a person has chosen to make it sacred. King says that objectivation is never value-free. The construction of our social reality, that is, the meaning we give to things, is always biased. Such is the nature of ideology: "ideology refers to the evaluative use of ideas in defense of a particular position, representing only the interests of one contending group against another. It does not disclose historically valid knowledge, but conceals the fact that human beings have constructed reality."[15]

We all have an ideology. There is nothing wrong with this; it is the reality of everyday life. But we do need to be aware that we process information from the perspective of our ideologies, and therefore need be aware of what they are.

Individualism is an ideology embraced by Unitarian Universalists (and, indeed, by American culture) for good reasons. Individualism has achieved its near–sacred status because it supports, encourages, and gives meaning to a particular way of life and system of faith. We simply need to remember we have decided to make it so.

As Unitarian Universalists and others have their faith in individualism, some faith traditions place their emphasis elsewhere through the same process of objectivation. For example, Richard Shaull explains that "God exists in us as we develop the right concepts."[16] He suggests that through the process of objectivation, as certain ideas are developed and then projected outward, God is created.

The important thing to remember is there is no such thing as objective reality.[17] Individualism may appear as objective reality because it is such an integral part of the Unitarian Universalist faith system. The appearance of ontological worth creates a tautology that can only preserve the status quo.

We also find ideology embodied in the form of story. When this happens we have mythology. "Myths are central in human life," writes Alice Blair Wesley. She elaborates: "All people and cultures without exception hold myths to be true. Any who believe that others—less sophisticated—may naively hold myths to be true while they themselves do not, are themselves naive."[18]

Sam Keen expands on this: "myth refers to inter-locking stories, rituals, rites, customs and beliefs that give a pivotal sense of meaning and direction to a person, a family, a community, or a culture."[19]

As myth, the objectivation of reality that has become ideology can be retold, rehearsed, and re-presented almost endlessly. As myth, it can easily be passed on from generation to generation, giving it historical validity that in turn enhances its ontological-like character. As ideology supports and nurtures the status quo, so too does mythology.

"A myth involves the conscious celebration of certain values," writes Keen, "...always personified in a pantheon of heroes.... But it also includes an unconscious, habitual way of seeing things, an invisible stew of unquestioned assumptions. A living myth, like an iceberg, is only ten percent visible: ninety percent lies beneath the surface of consciousness of those who live by it."[20]

Mythology is powerful, but it is not permanent. Individualism as an ideology for Unitarian Universalism is integral to the faith message and tradition, but it is not absolute or permanent. It exists because we have placed it there, and we continue to tell the myths that bolster, perpetuate, and give meaning to UU individualism.

This is Pluralism?

At the same time that Unitarian Universalists tell the myths of individualism, we also talk about pluralism, another integral element of our faith. Pluralism is an ideal that Americans affirm, and it is a principle that Unitarian Universalists agree is not only commendable but desirable.

In our Principles and Purposes: "We affirm and promote the inherent worth and dignity of every person...acceptance of one another...respect for the interdependent web of all existence of which we are a part."[21]

Pluralism refers to having differences that are tolerated without loss of individual or group character. Pluralism means that every person has a right to participate on every level of societal life regardless of who they are and what they think. Pluralism in religion means a diversity of people and thought all under the same name.

Pluralism is not the antithesis of individualism. Rather, pluralism supports individualism. The pluralism and diversity that are proclaimed as integral to the Unitarian Universalist faith are based on respect for the inherent worth and dignity of every person. But, we need to ask, what standard is being used to determine these? Indeed, what is the context of this understanding?

The United States now has a diversity of cultures

unparalleled in its past. This diversity has been the result of rising immigration from Latin America and Asia, in addition to Eastern Europe and the Middle East. The result? "Some Americans who were born in the United States are saying they can not identify with its prevailing culture."[22]

While diversity gains momentum on all levels, responses in local communities aren't good. Racism, sexism, and homophobia are at dramatically high levels; the rich and poor grow further apart; there seems to be a strengthening of individual self-protection and isolation.

As diversity races ahead, what about pluralism? What about respect and welcoming of individual differences? As a nation and as a religious movement, there appears the possibility that we will find ourselves on the wrong side of history because we are not prepared for the changes taking place. Unitarian Universalist church historian Conrad Wright says about the need to respond:

> Liberal religion articulated a value system that derived its strength from the social arrangements made possible by the discovery of the exploitable resources of the New World. But those resources were not limitless. The infinity of the private individual was plausible enough on the shores of Walden Pond, when there was no one closer than Concord Vil-

lage a mile away; it is hollow rhetoric on the streets of Calcutta or in the barrios of Caracas. The progress of humankind onward and upward forever may have seemed an axiom grounded in history to James Freeman Clarke; it seems something less than that to the residents of Middletown, Pennsylvania. The principle of religious toleration was easy for Jefferson, who could not see that it did any injury for his neighbor to say there are twenty gods or no god; but the principles of toleration takes on a sharper edge when the decisive differences are not in the realm of speculative theology, but on the question of apartheid and what it is that others should be forced, despite their opinions, to do about it.[23]

Moving Toward Liberation

I believe that liberation theology gives Unitarian Universalists one way to move toward a real pluralism, a living myth. Liberation theology opens a way for the needs of the group while allowing for an individualism that combines the best of the civic and biblical traditions, and even keeps in balance the demands of our modern individualism.

I explore the reasons for a liberation theology elsewhere.[24] Here it is important to understand from what we are being liberated. Why liberation? We need liberation because we are increasingly empty.

Charles Bayer refers to a "spiritual ennui"[25] that he believes has become commonplace in American culture. With the routine of daily work and personal calendars reflecting every waking moment planned, Americans settle into bed at night feeling exhausted and empty. Bayer suggests, "Perhaps to a greater degree than any mass culture in history, affluent US middle-class folk have more spare time and more money to use, as they please, but little they can do, no place they can go and nothing they can buy seems to fill the gray void."[26]

It is no wonder that our churches have members who claim their lives are empty, meaningless—they feel a dark hole that can't be lighted or filled. They turn to the church looking for fulfillment. They want to be given the meaning of life just as one might go to the supermarket to be handed packaged meat.

Not finding their needs met by an inner strength, some turn to alternatives, work, relationships, alcohol, drugs—these are just the most common choices. These all help to make up the codependencies that have taken over many lives. Some churches support the work of self-help programs: Here are opportunities for a handful who have the courage to face their reality. They gather with other codependents to share their experiences. Together, they nurture one another on the road back to recovery.

Another issue interrelated with this spiritual ennui is a life without risk or adventure. Not that one must sign up for adventures in Outward Bound or run a marathon, but just to be moved by life, to be passionate about living and compassionate for those with whom we live, could do much. Life is often structured in a way that won't allow for the adventurous, the impromptu, or the unthought-of. After the death of a parishioner, David Rankin was moved to write: "A religion that promises a life without tension, a life without conflict, life without suffering—is a religion of passivity, a religion of mediocrity, a religion of insignificance. Besides, everything worth doing in the world is a desperate gamble, a game of chance, where nothing is certain."[27]

Spiritual ennui in the form of boredom, codependency, and a lack of adventure dominate the lives of middle class church members. Liberation from these dehumanizing forces would free people to place their energies outside of themselves. But in order to make this final step, a step away from the isolation that comes from modern individualism, there has to be a recognition that this individualism is destructive.

This is not to say that individualism is per se bad. What I believe is really desired is pluralism. Pluralism embraces the inherent worth and dignity of every person—pluralism celebrates individualism. But Unitarian Universalism is not pluralistic.

We are anything but pluralistic: the membership

of Unitarian Universalism is dramatically homogeneous. For the most part we are highly educated, middle class, and white. Our churches are not the environments we say we wish for. Our churches are not at all what we like to think they are.

Confronting the discrepancy of myth and ideology with reality and our ideals might be sobering, even frightening. And moving beyond homogeneity cannot be easy. But if we do, we can liberate ourselves into a genuine pluralism; we may well achieve lives of value and meaning.

Moving beyond homogeneity will not be easy, but it will liberate us to a pluralism that can evoke a new myth. Perhaps the creation of a new story is the risk and adventure we need. King suggests "Theology is most vital and creative when a community begins to recognize that its conception of the world and the actual conditions of historical existence are at odds."[28]

If we will take notice, this is exactly what is happening to us. The Unitarian Universalist myth of individualism is antiquated and running out of steam— it is a transient belief at a time when a permanent belief, a guiding myth, is needed. A transient belief in an isolating and oppressive individualism is not facing the world situation as it is today. Even worse, it is supporting lifestyles that are destructive.

As life around us moves forward at breakneck speed, as personal lives are slipping away, can Unitarian Universalists respond? Wright concludes:

So the fate of religious liberalism rests with us. We may cling to the old paradigm, proclaim individual freedom of belief as an absolute value.... Then we may dwindle in numbers and influence until we end up a museum piece, like the Shakers, the Schwenkfelders, and the Swedenborgians. But on the other hand, we may learn how to relate to new social forces, to master a new revival as a segment of the Church Universal, but we may even contribute something to the humanizing of what threatens to be a far less comfortable world than the one you and I have known.[29]

The time is now at hand when we need to study and critique what Unitarian Universalism stands for. We need to explore the changes and patterns that keep pace with and around us; to dream, articulate, plan, and implement the future course. Our call should be nothing less than the call sounded by Theodore Parker: "Let then the Transient pass, fleet as it will, and may God send us some new manifestation of the Christian faith, that shall stir men's hearts as they were never stirred; some new Word, which shall teach us what we are, and renew us all in the image of God; some better life, that shall fulfill the Hebrew prophecy, and pour out the spirit of God on you men and maidens, and old men and children...."[30]

The Church Green:
Ecology and the Future

Robert Murphy

———————————◆———————————

Does liberal religion have a future? If we answer in
the affirmative, can we begin to imagine the outlines
of liberal religion in the next century? What will the
Unitarian Universalist movement look like in the decade of the 2090s?

In 1992 Richard Ostling responded to some similar questions in an unusual piece.[1] Ostling is *Time*
magazine's associate editor for religion. His assignment was to predict religion's future for a special report on life in the decades ahead. To anticipate religion in the year 2001 seems challenge enough.
Ostling, however, pushed ahead four generations to
the year 2092. He came back to *Time* with an intriguing mixed bag of observations and speculations.

At the center of Ostling's picture of the future, religion seems to be holding some familiar ground. In his year 2092, Christianity is still the world's largest faith. Roman Catholicism is still Christianity's larger component. In many respects little has changed over the years. Radicals and reformers have come and gone, but after each pull to the left, Roman Catholicism has moved back to the right. Women have risen to new positions of authority but are still barred from the priesthood. In 2092 the Vatican is still speaking against divorce, against most forms of birth control, and against homosexual relations. In practice, though, most parish priests look the other way. Roman Catholicism is a survivor. For centuries it has demonstrated its ability to roll with the jabs and knocks of history.

In his year 2092 there is still a Protestant mainstream. Protestant intellectuals, however, have had a difficult time in a postliterate era. Since the Reformation, the Protestant cause has found much of its support in communities valuing rationality and reading. On the new information superhighway—well, few people have the ability to read anything that surpasses *Time* magazine in length and complexity.

Among people who consider themselves "spiritual," the emphasis in Ostling's future world has shifted from theology to ritual and celebration, with theology continuing as a fine art for the cognoscenti. Many mainstream Protestant groups prominent in the 1990s seem rather small by the end of his next century, though there has been growth in the Pentecostal churches. Still, many of the cooler, more literary Protestant movements hold significant influence in his year 2092, because as Ostling says, many of their members remain book readers "and are thus inevitably leaders of the economic ruling class on all continents."

Ostling approaches the future cautiously. In his year 2092 humanity is still waiting for the Age of Aquarius, and humans still stand on the calm side of the Apocalypse. Persons who have bet on Eden and those who anticipated the Day of Doom may both be disappointed. And yet, in Ostling's future world there are surprises. The strange cults and colorful sects that often grabbed attention in our own time have, in Ostling's new age, nearly vanished. Most have collapsed, but others have evolved into comfortable obscurity. Among the missing, apparently, are the sweet imperialists who once dreamed of drawing all nations into the same prayer tent. The religious future, if I read the signs correctly, is conservative yet also pluralistic, inhabited by some communities and individuals who lie to find their own way.

Buddhism and Hinduism, which Ostling says were "once considered near-cults in the United States," have become sizable and respectable in the America of 2092. Ostling says nothing more on this topic. So we don't know whether he thinks the Americanization of the Eastern religions is to be attributed to immigration or to conversions among the old American population. Likely, a combination of both developments will be responsible. This raises a curious point for Unitarian Universalists. Since the days of the transcendentalists, many of our churches have brought the currents of Eastern and Western religious thought together. Today, we eagerly chat about our need for diversity and multiculturalism, but we seem to have turned away from involvement with Asian-American communities at the very moment when these communities are expanding and shaping new identities. How long has it been since Asian-American concerns received recognition in General Assembly workshops or in the pages of the *World*? The historians of 2092 may ponder our negligence.

Looking ahead to the year 2092, today's Unitarian Universalist may be interested in something else in Ostling's picture. A century from now, an amorphous effort Ostling calls "the World Soul Movement" has developed from the assorted neo-pagan and New Age groups which, he says, "were the rage early in the twenty-first century." Spiritual feminists and environmentalists together have moved portions of organized religion beyond familiar harbors and into new waters. The new movement, Ostling suggests, combines a generous measure of self-care with ecological celebration. Aristotle and pastoral bliss, science and easygoing religion, have again been embraced. Cowled figures from the past may be coming back into view and, not far behind, a homespun Benjamin Franklin may be amusing Marie Antoinette by showing her the latest in high-priced garden gear.

Alas, at this point the picture from the future snaps and pops and goes fuzzy. Where and how did the World Soul Movement develop? Did choirs sing hymns from *Singing the Living Tradition* while the congregations assembled? Were the covenants and confessions familiar to Unitarian Universalist ears? Ostling fails to provide details, so the story of its growth is left to the reader's imagination. Maybe our church historians in 2092 will give a prominent place to the World Soul Movement in their works. Maybe not. Some of today's Unitarian Universalists may long for the day when our movement glides easily into something like the World Soul Movement. Others may approach the church green with a healthy measure of skepticism.

As a Unitarian Universalist who has spent more than twenty years in environmental work, including some years when I tried to define terms like "earth-centered spirituality," perhaps I should be delighted by the greening of the Unitarian Universalist movement. Perhaps the World Soul Movement will yet prove to be my cup of herbal tea. Still, for now, count me among the wary. Before I plunge deeper into Deep Ecology and its offshoots, I want to know where this path leads. Other Unitarian Universalists have stood at this kind of crossroads. What kinds of questions did they ask? What points did they consider? What were the rough spots they anticipated?

The late James Luther Adams, I suspect, is the kind of guide who will be much needed by Unitarian Universalists now venturing into the theological woods to find a "green spirituality." Adams was familiar with most of the high hopes and great expectations that have swept through our liberal congregations during the twentieth century. He watched Unitarian Universalists follow cutting-edge causes from the days of Sacco and Vanzetti to the era of Earth First! shenanigans. He also saw Unitarian Universalists move from the mind–cure methods of the 1920s to the days of New Age mud baths and primal screams. James Luther Adams knew many of the twists and turns in our movement's history. His was a profound understanding of the transient and the permanent in liberal religion.

Three points in particular James Luther Adams might want to bequeath to environmentalists within the Unitarian Universalist movement. Adams would undoubtedly press for a respect for history and for an awareness of what he called "dimension." He would caution us about the kind of liberalism "that has sometimes retreated into a superficial and provincial backwash of 'progress' ideology, sometimes into a mere privatization of religion, and sometimes into an up-to-date provincial zeal for the spirit of the times."[2] "This kind of liberalism," Adams would remind us, "is impotent to deal intellectually and responsibly with the ultimate issues of life."

At a time when some Unitarian Universalists seem eager to find the end of history or to move outside of history or away from history, Adams would challenge our "historical illiteracy and debilitating rootlessness." "Nothing significant in human history is achieved except through longstanding continuities," he wrote. "No philosophy of life, no religion, can remain viable unless it possesses a sense of depth, a sense of breadth, a sense of length (or continuity) in history."

As Unitarian Universalist congregations and affiliate groups move into Earth Day events and environmental roundtables, there is something very special behind us. We are not just another set of good citizens who happen to be concerned about the fate of rain forests and caribou. We are that and we are more than that. As Unitarian Universalists, we represent a liberating force that has expressed itself in history in a variety of ways. Our open, self-governing, noncreedal congregations still stand for something that seems revolutionary in the world of religion. We have fought for racial justice, for the rights of women, for the rights of homosexuals, for religious freedom, and for the principles of democracy. At a time when the religious right would like to tinker a bit with the Constitution of the United States—perhaps adding school prayer to classrooms now, perhaps dropping Charles Darwin later—we are still engaged in some important larger environmental struggles.

When Unitarian Universalists enter environmental work, we are to embody seven principles, not only one. Our seventh principle is particularly popular nowadays. We have covenanted to affirm and promote, "respect for the interdependent web of all existence of which we are a part." Beyond that principle, the Unitarian Universalists have six more, all equally important for environmental justice. Our first principle recognizes, "the inherent worth and dignity of every person." Our second principle recognizes the need for "justice, equity, and compassion in human relations." This takes us beyond rainforests and caribou to a much broader agenda than that of either Earth First! or Deep Ecology.

Adams said, "A faith that is not the sister of justice is bound to bring us to grief." This is one of the most important messages Unitarian Universalists can bring to the green spirituality movement. In their rush to save our planet's wild spaces, some environmentalists have run with blinders, focusing attention on "the environment" while ignoring patterns of racism, sexism, and economic exploitation that frequently determine how people relate to their surroundings and to each other. There has been much talk of a supposed need for earth-centered spirituality. Justice-centered spirituality is what the world needs. Third World peasants are destroying tropical forests at an alarming rate. This is reason for global concern, but it is irresponsible and racist to blame the peasants while

ignoring the poverty and the neocolonialism push-
ing families into the wilderness.

James Luther Adams would caution Unitarian
Universalists of "idolatries of the mind and spirit," to
borrow another phrase from our Unitarian Universalist statement of principles and purposes. And, at
this point, Adams would comment on the irony in
certain features of creation spirituality. Advocates of
creation spirituality frequently rush to condemn
harshly Isaac Newton, Francis Bacon, and all of the
iconoclasts who swept away doctrinal restraints to lay
the foundations of modern science. The old humanists, we are told, took all of the spirit, all of the holiness, and all of the fun, out of nature to give us cold
and deadly materialism. At the next moment, cre-
ation/spirituality offers a cure: What we need is more
science. Only, this time, we need mystical theoretical
physicists and headline-grabbing biologists who will
give us works to help reestablish the tenants and teachings of thirteenth-century Christendom.

Something very odd is happening here, and I
suspect Adams would recognize new idolatries in the
making. God, for most religious liberals, is not an
object to be quantified or a theorem to be presented
in Nature Studies 101. And yet, today some Unitarian
Universalists listen to theologians who claim the existence of God the Creator has recently been "proven"
by laboratory tests and computer calculations. Richard Ostling suggests this new kind of religious think-

ing will provide the theological basis for the World Soul Movement of the future. Is the "new" a revived relic from the past?

The long shadow of Thomas Aquinas falls across much of creation spirituality and its variations. This may bother some Unitarian Universalists who recall our fourth principle with its call to "a free and responsible search for truth and meaning." In Thomas Aquinas's day, naturalists were expected to follow the established laws of the church. Much was said about "truths which are above nature," revealed by God. Any respect for nature on its own terms seemed pointless and even dangerous. Nature had to serve a particular purpose, already determined. It was "the Creator" and not "the creation" that really mattered. Scholars twisted and trimmed their arguments, closing their eyes and mouths at the right moments, to keep their science within the bounds set by church authorities. Heretics soon learned about the rack and the stake. We have named this time the Dark Ages, an age of religion, certainly, but not a time for today's environmentalists.

I suspect that James Luther Adams would offer two concerns, carefully balanced, for any Unitarian Universalists who may be interested in the spiritual side of the environmental movement. Adams would be concerned about some of the Earth Day activists in our congregations who have devoted their religious energy and attention to community projects. Somehow, these good people, all of their good works notwithstanding, seem to be missing something in their engagement on behalf of the environment. Call it reflection, meditation, or contemplation. Thoreau, who wanted to approach nature on nature's terms, had something to say on this theme. And some brilliant nature writers have followed on Thoreau's path. Right now, while working around New Bedford and Martha's Vineyard, I am rediscovering Rachel Carson, who was writing about her experiences on the Atlantic long before she wrote *Silent Spring*. When I read Rachel Carson, I connected with the energy of salt marshes and the powerful, fecund currents pressing through Buzzards Bay in April.

We need these personal moments of reconnection with something grander than ourselves, with something as intimate and as magnificent as Thoreau's Walden pond or John Muir's Sierra forests. At these moments, we may be reminded of who we are and how our relationships have developed with others. These are important times, and yet they are not the only times. The pastor, the healer, and the prophet, to fulfill their rolls, must return from the wilderness. Adams was concerned about what happens when we neglect spiritual renewal. He was also concerned about what has happened when people have wandered away to live in private gardens.

"The 'holy' thing in life," said Adams, "is the participation in those processes that give body and form to universal justice." "The faith of a church or of a nation is an adequate faith only when it inspires and enables people to give of their time and energy to shape the various institutions—social, economic, and political—of the common life." Anything less is simply a sedative, a painkiller faith, that in Adams's words, only "enables history to crush humanity." Look for this sort of thing in the New Age centers that only honor "the inner self," Visa, and Mastercard.

If tomorrow's version of the World Soul Movement only brings us to Marie Antoinette playing in a Versailles park while the Third World starves, it will be a sorry cause. An ecological theology turned inwards, fussing over its creeds and slogans, rolling about in its self-care and self-love and sneering at the unwashed masses, is something to avoid. It may carry Unitarian Universalists into the next century. It will not carry us there safely, nor beyond it at all.

> Be ye doers of the word, and not merely hearers who deceive themselves. For if any are hearers of the words and not doers, they are like those who look at themselves in a mirror, for they look at themselves and, on going away, immediately forget what they were like. But those who look into the perfect law, the law of liberty, and persevere, being not hearers who forget but doers who act—they will be blessed in their doing. (James 1:22-25)

Developing Theology

A Theology for Phenomenal Women

Dianne E. Arakawa

———————◆———————

The word "phenomenal" can be understood in at least two ways. It can mean "fantastic" or "unbelievably good." It is used commonly in our day to express awe and accolade. Our teens say, "I met this phenomenal person," or "I went to this phenomenal show." The word can also mean "experiential" or "sensuous." Kant, in his *Religion within the Limits of Reason Alone*, posited a system for understanding religion during the Enlightenment. There is, he wrote, a "noumenal" world of God beyond human understanding, and a "phenomenal" world of rational, moral human beings.[1] We here are presumably of this latter order.

Maya Angelou, contemporary writer and actress, wrote a poem entitled "Phenomenal Woman." As with much of her oeuvre, this piece gives physical shape and form to the strong and resilient inner spirit of its muse. In "Phenomenal Woman," Angelou makes both uses of the word "phenomenal." Women for her are "phenomenal," as in "fantastic" and "unbelievable." And women are also loci of individual "phenomenal" sense experience and "inner mystery."[2]

I want us to keep these two meanings in mind as we take a look at feminist/womanist theology. Women are phenomenal: wonderful and deserving of attention, no less than men or the stars. Also, women are diverse centers of particular and unrepeatable experience.

Feminist/Womanist Theology

I come to this project convinced of the importance of feminist/womanist theology in our day and age. My "conversion" occurred during my years at a small women's college in New England. Visiting professors of religion, such as Rosemary Radford Ruether and Mary Daly, lectured from time to time. A coterie of female divinity school students, graduates from our school, used to return to tell us what it was like in the field. My evolution to this perspective was gradual. Having experienced a fair amount of change in my early years, I grew up to be a rather cautious and careful person, not inclined to rash moves. Nonetheless, I was eventually convinced and won over to this way of looking at my own strong theistic faith, criticizing the present world and envisioning a new one.

In the last ten years I have gone through changes in how I understand feminist/womanist theology. But I am still persuaded by the tenets of this theological project, its power to alter the patterns of individual lives and its intention to transform the world. Beyond the "consciousness–raising groups" in the sixties, the development of women's studies programs on university campuses in the seventies, and the influence of feminist theology in most aspects of church life in the eighties, the girl has grown up. She has become a woman, a "phenomenally, phenomenal woman."

From Pre-Modern to Modernism

What is feminist/womanist theology? To answer, let me first say what I think theology is and then how theology has developed.

Theology is not a primarily sensate experience, felt by each of us in our own way, and at first ineffable, to be put into words. Rather, it is a secondary response to original experience, which attempts to articulate and communicate its knowledge to a community of faith. Theology is critical. Its task is to be self-critical about our initial experiences in relation to the contemporary situation in which we find ourselves. Finally, its task is to conceptualize what can be known universally. Theology is a mode of understanding our world and our place in it through a methodology of dialectical hermeneutics including deconstruction, reconstruction, and universalization.

Having defined theology, let us now turn to how it has developed. I think it is crucial for us to place our feminist/womanist project in its Western European historical context. We would not be talking about what we are had it not been for the foundation of the philosophical and theological structure earlier established.

In the middle of the eighteenth century, the most significant philosophical discussion was about whether the traditional Christian theism of revelation or the emerging Natural Religion was superior. In his *Dialogues Concerning Natural Religion*, David Hume, the Scottish philosophical skeptic, teased out through dialogues between three protagonists the strengths of their respective positions.[3] First, Demea offered a belief in the necessary and *a priori* knowledge of God. Second, Cleanthes advanced the Argument from Design that God's nature could be elicited *a posteriori* from an understanding of nature itself. And finally Philo maintained skepticism about both the necessary and rational arguments of his peers.

Hume's purpose was to criticize traditional theology as well as the so-called enlightened deism of his time. He claimed that although theology is indeed rational discourse, it cannot follow that God is also bound by reason and completely knowable; on the contrary, God is ultimately a mystery. "I admit of the absolute incomprehensibility of the Divine Nature...."[4] Hume introduced a new mode of philosophical and theological thinking that pointed out the limitations of rationalism and scientific empiricism.

At the beginning of the nineteenth century the philosopher Immanuel Kant purposely drew two distinctions in order to overcome Hume's criticisms. He said theology and knowledge about God belonged to a "phenomenal" world of senses, experience, observation, action, and morality different from a "noumenal" world of supersensibility, religion, transcendence, and God. The German philosopher sought to demonstrate the limits of the field in which we can talk about religion, to stress the importance of human duty, morality, and virtue, and to let God be God. The problem was that in so doing he set up a bifurcated system of the human and the divine, and advanced the supremacy of an unduly rational and moralistic form of Christianity.

A couple of decades later another German, G.W.F. Hegel, sought to invigorate theology by doing away with Kant's dualism. He advanced a dialectic of *Allgeinheit, Besonderheit,* and *Einzelheit*—being, non-being, and becoming. Hegel tried to show that God was "an absolute actuality," "an absolute spirit," not separated from the world, but intimately involved in its processes. His philosophical and theological system demonstrated a dynamic relationship between each of its parts.

At about the same time, Freiderich Schleiermacher was espousing his system. In his book *On Religion: Speeches to Its Cultured Despisers* the philosophertheologian made an important move. Instead of starting with a Kantian dualistic schema that separated God from humankind or a Hegelian dialectical system that related God to the rest of the system, Schleiermacher talked about human experience. He said religion was a sense of "absolute dependence on God," that there is in the human natural longing and propensity to give oneself to the Whole. He said, "Whoever utters anything of it, must necessarily have had it, for nowhere could he have heard it.... I would conduct you into the profoundest depths whence every feeling and conception receives its form."[5]

Schleiermacher lodged religion inside the human heart. He moved theology from supernatural systematics to a phenomenology of human consciousness and self-awareness. The founder of modern theology, he initiated a new mode of understanding the world and our place in it. And he helped lay the foundation for twentieth-century North American feminist/womanist theology.

This is a brief description of how British and Continental theology developed from the mid-eighteenth century to the beginning of the nineteenth century, making the transition from Enlightenment philosophy into "modern theology." This was a Western European endeavor, and the philosophers and theologians were all men. Their systematics were patriarchal, hierarchical, androcentric, and mysogynist. The God in whom they expressed their faith was conceived as a male God. Even so, through theological dialogue and debate an important conceptual transformation occurred at the beginning of the nineteenth century, which ushered in modern theology.

This involved what theologian David Tracy has called "a turn to the self." It is identified by a shift of foci from grand narratives to individual autobiographies, from comprehensive systematics to phenomenological studies, and from broad theories to expressions of concern for individual human experience with its attendant characteristics of imperfection, fragility, cruelty, guilt, shame, compassion, playfulness, nobility, and transcendence.

When we cross the Atlantic, we observe the development of modern theology on our shores and over the course of time. In the nineteenth century we see it in the individual pietism of the Great Awakening; in the early twentieth century in the psychology and pragmatism of William James; and in the last two decades in the Black theology of James Cone, the feminist theology of Rosemary Radford Ruether, and the womanist theology of Katie Geneva Cannon.

The "turning inwards" and exploration of the inner self in all of its complexity has not been without its own deep problems. In fact, some have been insisting for quite a while that we have crossed another threshold and entered a new phase in theology called "post-modernism." I would insist post-modern theology does indict the impoverishment of modern theology—its primary criterion of rationalism, its too easy generalization, its belief that things just need to be fixed to be made better, and its confidence in human evolutionism and progress.

The physicist-historian, Stephen Toulmin, has just brought out a fine book on this issue, entitled *Cosmopolis; the Hidden Agenda of Modernity*. He asks of the growing suspicion about modernism: "Given so problematic an agenda, what are philosophers to do? Must they now regard all philosophy as a kind of autobiography; or can they piece together an alternative program, out of the wreckage left by their parents and grandparents' demolition work?"[6]

Having thus traced the arc of the development of theology from premodernism through modernism and to postmodernism, I can now locate feminist/womanist theology on the cusp between modern theology and post-modern theology. This is not the same form of feminist theology I encountered many years ago as a young woman. Feminist/womanist theology has evolved significantly. Phenomenally.

In 1960 theologian Valerie Saiving wrote an article entitled "The Human Situation: A Feminine View." Today it might not sound earth-shattering, but then it was. It was the first explicitly theological article to criticize modern theology, specifically the work of Reinhold Niebuhr and Anders Nygren, for its failure to deal with women's experience. These theologies dealt only with the experience of men, said Saiving, and they left undeniably androcentric imprints.

We have come quite a distance from Saiving's critique of theology. But her observation about women's experience is still the basis upon which we develop feminist/womanist theology. Let us now turn to some of the enduring characteristics of this kind of theology as I see them.

The feminist/womanist project is based on nothing less than women's experience. It is founded on women's feelings, her feelings about herself, her body, those around her; what is her economic status; her race, ethnicity, and culture; her religious tradition; what is important to her; how she thinks and relates to, say, God, Jesus, and the Holy Spirit; how she is perceived and received by others.

Toni Morrison, in her powerful book *Beloved,* describes how her main character, a woman slave named Secthe, was physically free for twenty-eight days but had to learn to be truly free.

> Sethe had had twenty-eight days—the travel of one whole moon—of unslaved life. Days of healing, ease and real-talk. Days of company: knowing the names of forty, fifty other Negroes, their views, habits; where they had

been and what done; of feeling their fun and sorrow along with her own, which made it better. One taught her the alphabet; another a stitch. All taught her how it felt to wake up at dawn and decide what to do with the day. That's how she got through the waiting.... Bit by bit...along with the others, she had claimed herself. Freeing herself was one thing; claiming ownership of that freed self was another.[7]

Feminist/womanist theology starts with intense attention to the experience of women, all kinds of women. By encouraging women to speak, we give them rightful freedom. By hearing their stories, we are invited into their phenomenal worlds, to be transformed by the power of their images and ideas.

Feminist/womanist theology is critical and prophetic. By this I mean it does not accept the premise, the liberal fallacy, that we can believe anything we want or that we can do anything we choose. On the contrary, it is critical of its own premises as well as the larger context in which it operates. Feminist/womanist theology is deconstructive of destructive patriarchal patterns, reconstructive of inclusive feminist paradigms and creative of a larger world vision.

Roman Catholic theologian Anne Carr asserts in her systematics entitled *Transforming Grace:*

Interpretation includes two essential moments: an unmasking of regressive meanings or demystification, and a restoration of meaning. An adequate feminist interpretation is dialectical: It is suspicious as it unmasks the illusory or ideological aspects of symbols that denigrate the humanity of women, and it is restorative as it attempts to retrieve the genuinely transcendent meaning of symbols as affirming the authentic selfhood and self-transcendence of women.[8]

Feminist/womanist theology is dialogical because it revolves around ongoing conversation, through speech and also through the written word. As such, it is not an example of privatized and narcissistic experience, but the expression of communal and inclusive exchange.

Take, for example, *God's Fierce Whimsey*, the cooperative work of the Mud Flower Collective, an interracial group of Christian feminists/womanists, ordained and lay, based in Cambridge, Massachusetts. The entire book is an attempt at sustained theological conversation. Feminism is not only one kind of phenomenon. The women of the Mud Flower Collective know better.

> *Mary:* I think it's simply the struggle against sexism.
>
> *Carter:* I agree, but I'd have to add that this

involves a stubborn insistence, a refusal to compromise the well-being of women.

Kate: For me it doesn't have anything to do with women; it's the commitment to end white supremacy, male domination and economic exploitation.

Ada: For me feminism and feminist are different. Only the person can say if she's feminist; but feminism has to do with understanding sexism as the paradigm of all oppression. And I agree with the refusal to compromise women's welfare—both women's rights and well-being.

Bev: I'd have to say that it begins in a woman's assertion of her power. It's not, in the first instance, a theory, but a very personal act.

Bess: For me it always has to be preceded by the word black, and it means the creation of inclusivity and mutuality, which involves struggle against what I call the trinity of sexism, racism and classism....

Nancy: I believe it begins with the "experiencing of your experience" and that it means insisting on the well-being of women, all women, which is why racism must be examined in any feminist analysis.[9]

Futurist Riane Eisler in her book, *The Chalice and the Blade,* makes the point that a paradigmatic transformation from patriarch to partnership in society is needed and is indeed occurring.

> During the 19th and into the 20th century...
> (humanist ideologies)...failed to address the
> fact that at its heart lies a male-dominator,
> female-dominated model of the human spe-
> cies. The only ideology that frontally chal-
> lenges this model of human relations, as well
> as the principle of human ranking based on
> violence is, of course, feminism. For this rea-
> son it occupies a unique position both in
> modern history and in the history of our cul-
> tural revolution.[10]

Feminist/womanist theology tries to remember the one forgotten or intentionally left out, and recovering her memory, to celebrate her life and our common life. The goddesses, Tamar, Hagar, the Unnamed Woman, the Daughter of Jephthah, the Women of the Early Church, the Women at Jesus' tomb, the mystics, the women in the nineteenth and twentieth centuries of our own church tradition, Frances Ellen Watkins-Harper, the Unsung Heroes, our mothers, the Stranger, the Other, "the madwoman in the attic": These and more we memorialize.

Phyllis Trible, scholar of the Hebrew Bible, writes of this rhetorical hermeneutical approach in *Texts of Terror:*

As a critique of culture and faith in light of misogyny, feminism is a prophetic movement, examining the status quo, pronouncing judgement, and calling for repentance. The hermeneutic engages scripture in various ways. One approach documents the case against women.... By contrast a second approach discerns within the Bible critiques of patriarchy. It upholds forgotten texts and reinterprets familiar ones to shape a remnant theology that challenges the sexism of scripture. Yet a third approach incorporates the other two. It recounts tales of terror in memoriam to offer sympathetic readings of abused women.... In telling sad stories, a feminist hermeneutic seeks to redeem the time.[11]

In sum, feminist/womanist theology can be characterized by the following adjectives: experiential, critical, dialogical, relational, and redemptive. It starts with women's feelings and experience. It is self-critical and socially prophetic. It uses dialogue and conversation. It emphasizes unity and relationship. And it seeks to retrieve in order to redeem. Phenomenally.

From Modernism to Post-Modernism

I locate feminist/womanist theology on the cusp between modern theology and post-modern theology.

By this I mean that it displays characteristics of both. But it holds within itself the capacity for its own self-critique. Although the feminist/womanist project has been critical of patriarchy and androcentrism since its inception, it is becoming as critical of its very self. For as it seeks its own identity in the marketplace of ideas, it comes to face the realization that there exists an even greater pluralism of human experience than once imagined.

As Toulmin points out, it was John Donne who wrote, "'Tis all in pieces, all coherence gone, All just supply and all Relation...." Then William Butler Yeats wrote between the World Wars of our century: "Things fall apart; the center cannot hold; Mere anarchy is loosed upon the world." Feminist theology may soon be discovering—is already realizing—that even its center cannot hold. Or, as Julia Kristeva, post-modernist French feminist, declared, "We are all subjects in process on trial now."

This notion is driven home to me concerning the feminism of our own denomination. What has been happening up until quite recently, it seems to me, is rather uncritical celebration of middle-class white feminism with its attendant worship of the great white goddess. As Rosemary Ruether, Katie Cannon, and women of color have pointed out, we need to be perceptively aware of the interstructuring of feminism, racism, and classism. We need to be poised against racist feminism and classist feminism.

Let us look to the projects of the Mud Flower Collective, the Third World Feminists who recently produced the book *Inheriting Our Mother's Gardens,* and to Susan Thistlewaites's *Sex, Race and God* for more inclusive models for feminist/womanist theology.

I have tried to show how our feminist/womanist theology emerged from European premodern philosophy and theology and North American modern theology, and how it presently wavers on the cusp between modernism and post-modernism.

What happens next, it seems to me, will depend in large measure on our continuing and tenacious engagement in feminist/womanist theology and on inclusion in our conversation of other people of faith, both women and men, who have been marginalized or excluded. I have confidence, as does the "phenomenal woman" of Angelou's poem, that what we need is already in our midst. A theology for phenomenal women has within itself the capacity for withstanding critical self-scrutiny and for creating a wider horizon of freedom and justice in our world. May it be so.

In Generations to Come

Wayne B. Arnason

———————◆———————

My eleven–year–old daughter and I were driving back to Virginia from a summer vacation in New England and fishing in the back seat for a tape to play. My hands fell on the soundtrack for the movie "The Doors." When we popped it into the stereo, out came the ominous and hypnotic organ prelude to "When the Music's Over."

I have a special relationship with this song. I used the lyrics as the text for my 1969 Valedictory Address to the graduating seniors of Daniel McIntyre High School. I avoided quoting the more Freudian sections that deal with killing your father and sleeping with your mother, but I did quote the environmental kaddish-like wail "What have they done to the earth? What have they done to our fair sister?" I concluded with Morrison's bellowing demand: "WE WANT THE WORLD AND WE WANT IT NOW!" My valedictory address was not popular with the school administration.

I led my daughter on a tour of the song and its meaning for me as we rolled along the New Jersey Turnpike. She was not impressed: "It's weird, Dad," was all she had to say.

She's right. It *is* weird. It's nihilistic, arrogant, demanding. That doesn't mean I don't still love it, twenty-five years later, but it's hard to explain to my daughter why the song meant so much to me then. The adolescents and young adults of the 1960s did want the world—NOW! They (we!) were arrogant enough to believe that their idealism, correct thinking, and youthful energy could change the world forever. Maybe our energy has changed the world, but certainly not forever. The coming generations will make sure of that.

My daughter was born on a cusp between generations. She is likely on the leading edge of the next wave coming after the reactive "Generation X," a member of the millennial generation that will come of age in the first decade of the twenty-first century. In their 1991 book *Generations: The History of America's Future 1584-2069*, William Strauss and Neil Howe suggest that the children born in the late eighties and nineties will have much more in common with older grandparents or great–grandparents than with the generations immediately preceding them.

Their generation will have a "personality" Strauss and Howe describe as "Civic." They claim that not only do generations have distinct personalities (a theory important in the social sciences throughout much of the twentieth century), but also that these personalities recur in a discernible four-part cycle of generational styles that has an impact on politics, economics, culture, and, of course, religion.

This cycle of generations is driven by a recurring rhythm of "social moments" alternating between secular crises and spiritual awakenings. Secular crises involve a reordering of the public world of institutions and public behavior. In periods of spiritual awakening, society focuses on the inner world of values and private behavior. Going all the way back to 1584, Strauss and Howe boldly trace and define this cycle of "social moments" and the generational personalities arising from them through more than four hundred years of Western history. The cycle of generations is described as follows:

1. A dominant, inner–fixated *idealist generation* grows up as increasingly indulged youths after a secular crisis; comes of age inspiring a spiritual awakening; fragments into narcissistic, rising adults; cultivates principle as moralistic mid-lifers; and emerges as visionary elders guiding the next secular crisis.

2. A recessive *reactive generation* grows up as

underprotected and criticized youths during a spiritual awakening; matures into risk-taking, alienated rising adults; mellows into pragmatic mid-life leaders during a secular crisis; and maintains respect (but less affluence) as reclusive elders.

3. A dominant outer-fixated *civic generation* grows up as increasingly protected youths after a spiritual awakening; comes of age overcoming a secular crisis; unites into a heroic and achieving cadre of rising adults; sustains that image while building institutions as powerful mid-lifers; and emerges as busy elders attacked by the next spiritual awakening.

4. A recessive *adaptive generation* grows up as overprotected and suffocated youths during a secular crisis; matures into risk-adverse, conformist rising adults; produces indecisive mid-life arbitrator-leaders during a spiritual awakening; and maintains influence (but less respect) as sensitive elders.[1]

As each of these generations come of age, the era they bring to our social history is one that matches their personalities and that compensates for the deficiencies or repressions of their youth. The four eras are:

- An *awakening era* (Idealists coming of age)—triggers cultural creativity and the emergence of new ideals, as institutions built around old values are challenged by the emergence of a spiritual awakening.

- An *inner driven era* (Reactives coming of age)—individualism flourishes, new ideals are cultivated in separate camps, confidence in institutions declines, and secular problems are deferred.
- A *crisis era* (Civics coming of age)—opens with growing collective unity in the face of perceived social peril and culminates in a secular crisis in which danger is overcome and one set of new ideals triumphs.
- An *outer-driven era* (Adaptives coming of age)—society turns towards conformity and stability, triumphant ideals are secularized, and spiritual discontent is deferred.[2]

Where are we in this cycle now? Strauss and Howe suggest that 1961 through 1981 was an awakening era, and that we are now moving through the second half of an inner-driven era, with a crisis era on the horizon. In our Association, we are seeing a large group of retiring ministers from the adaptive generation, and many adapters who are concluding brief careers begun in mid-life. The ministerial leaders of our movement come from the idealist "boomer" generation and are quite concerned about having recruited so few younger ministers from the reactive generation following. Meanwhile, locally, the leadership and financial control of many of our congregations, especially the smaller ones, is only now moving out of the hands of the civic ("GI") generation which came of age in and fought World War II.

So, what has all this to do with the transient and the permanent in liberal religion, and with the ministry at the heart of liberal religion? Our faith and the ministries who serve it are part and parcel of the larger social and historical patterns of our culture. We have become aware of how the demographic changes of the past half century have affected the fortunes of our generations. We routinely hear twenty-five-year speakers at our annual UUMA services trace their careers in terms of larger social changes during their careers. Scholars have searched for a single, overarching cause or dynamic behind dramatic social changes. In his book *Man and Crisis,* José Ortega y Gasset declared that "the generation...is the most important conception in history. (It) is a dynamic compromise between mass and individual."

The possibility that generational personalities might make the biggest difference in the ways our social institutions and private lives change is an idea difficult to test and verify. Nevertheless, the Strauss and Howe theory of generational personalities makes sense to me, and it is backed up by enough research and data that it deserves a serious look. Liberal ministers ought to be interested in a generational theory of history; ministry is a profession practiced in multigenerational communities of memory and hope, which take very seriously the heritage passed on by previous generations and which look to renew and pass on that heritage to future generations.

Ministry is also lived on the boundary between the individual and the mass. Ministers in our pastoral roles live day to day with the joys and sorrows, triumphs and tribulations of individual church members. We interact and counsel with people at all stages of life, and we usually work in leadership teams with people from our own and from two other generations. However, in our prophetic roles, in the community and in the pulpit, we continually try to understand the spirit of the age, the problems of the present day, and what bearing the wisdom of the ages can have on these problems. When we consider whether the whole of liberal religion, the institutions of the church, and the roles of ministry will change as we enter the next millennium, the generational theory set forth by Strauss and Howe may bring us cause both for concern and hope.

Some cause for concern has to do with where their theory suggests we are headed in terms of recurring eras. Strauss and Howe say we are headed into a crisis era, with issues and events that define the crisis coming in the 2020s, when the boomer generation will be in senior roles of social "endowment" and anxious to secure their legacy to the future before passing from the scene.

The stereotype of the boomer generation, linked with sixties images of hippies and personal freedom, is somewhat deceptive when it comes to speculation about the boomer character as elder participants in our society. Oliver North is as much a baby boomer as Al Gore. They have in common, as they age, a profound sense of the moral stakes at issue in our society. Elder boomers will likely exercise considerable political control and do political battle well into the 2020s. The current alarm in our congregations about the rise of the religious right may well be only the beginning of a lengthy and fierce political and social fight over who will define the moral vision and the civil religion of Western society for the next half century.

Strauss and Howe do not specify the content of the crisis they foresee. I believe one scenario might involve growing social power and control by the religious right. A parallel crisis era in American history was that of the Civil War, when the idealist generation of the Transcendentalists grew up to confront a battle for the soul of the country. Such a future crisis would be something far more engaging than watching Senate votes on C-span.

The escalation of tactics in the battle over abortion rights is a harbinger of violence in future struggles in many areas of social concern for Unitarian Universalists. The next few decades look to be times of major social turmoil. The self-understanding of our society and the values that will guide and govern will be on the line. It may well be that the role of the "Generation X," as they move through their fifties, will be to deflect the self-righteous destructiveness of aging boomers as boomers foment the crisis of 2020 and square off for their last battle across ideological lines in the sand.

The position of Unitarian Universalism with respect to these generational shifts is problematic. For all their youthful sneering at institutions, the boomer generation has come and will continue to come back to institutions. They may find as they age, however, that their life experiences have brought them to firm ideological ground and that the openness and pluralism of Unitarian Universalism is ultimately not what they are looking for. Generation X is more ethnically diverse and much less cerebral than the boomers, perhaps not a good omen for growing UU membership.

Generation X can be expected to settle into much more stable patterns of family life than did boomers at comparable ages. Thus, religious education programs may well prove a bigger draw for this generation than for the boomers, rescuing the population base of our churches as we await the children of Generation X. According to the Strauss and Howe theory, these children, now in cradles and elementary schools, will be the next civic generation, a group that was very good for Unitarian Universalism last time around. The civic generation of the middle twenty-first century may well be good for us again, if we can weather the crisis of 2020 and are not meanwhile marginalized by a dominant religious right.

There is cause for hope in this generational theory of history when we reflect on the more intimate sides of pastoral and leadership roles our ministers will play in the next century. Religious institutions are quite durable. Even in the most secular of today's societies, they survive and resurge when spiritual awakenings again occur.

Within the churches, however, each new generation of ministers struggles with its place in the cycle. Ministers must effectively lead and comfort and inspire members of their own and other generations who are part of the church. It is not just your MBTI type or which school you went to that has an impact on your style of ministry and on the conflicts you encounter with some constituencies of the congregation. It can be a great asset to be aware of the personalities and skills of the generational groups in your congregation.

Today's civic "GI" generation of elders can put on a capital fund drive and build a new church without blinking an eye. The Young Adult Group of the reactive generation may well run a very satisfying program for themselves, but have little interest in tying it to the larger goals of the church. Because most UU church profiles tilt toward the older generations, many ministers strain to accommodate the leadership personalities and spiritual needs of the generation immediately ahead of them.

The next reactive and civic generations of ministers may find that dealing with congregations full of spiritual idealists in their seventies and eighties will be a challenging chore. Balancing these differences in generational style may be quite difficult in the short run, but to remember that in the long-term life of the congregation these generational cycles can be a source of strength rather than division is to find a source of consolation and hope.

Transience may be the only thing permanent in liberal religion and the liberal ministry. However, the perception of transience with which we live the course of careers and lifetimes, the changing cycle of the generations, and the frustrations we encounter with conflicting generational styles and priorities may have more to do with the limited range of our vision than with the enduring patterns truly there. As in chaos theory, the seemingly unrelated and random events that can shape the life of our congregations and Association may fall into perceivable patterns when viewed over a longer span.

Unitarian Universalism has sustained a place in North American culture through a full two and a half generational cycles. Will the message we proclaim— of the worth and dignity of all human beings, of the unending and diverse nature of spiritual insight, of the primacy of reason unfettered by dogmatic institutional forms—survive in North America through another cycle? It will if we can anticipate and respect the ways our message will be understood and interpreted and lived by succeeding generations with different personalities. It will if we are able to communicate across generational lines the significance of our message for the future of the human enterprise.

From the Earth to the Moon

Roger Brewin

> *"Soon it will be that people can live and work wherever they would, and be connected with the whole world."*
>
> Robert Heldman, *Future Telecommunications*

In the densely interconnected "Global Information Society" envisioned by the president of technology giant US West, physical distance and location become irrelevant. Heldman's statement is true, in so far as it accurately predicts what will soon be possible. The question it begs is whether we will choose to do so. Will the ability to telecommute mean that we will freely choose to live in an electronic global village? Will we largely abandon our present communities and driving patterns in doing so? What happens to the local church in such a world? My fascination lies not with the ultimate answer, but with the transitional ones: what choices do we make now and in the near future, about the impact we will allow technology to have on our lives, our society, and in particular, our ministry.

This utopian vision, that it is possible to do almost anything over almost unlimited distances, has been growing in our culture for a quarter century now. In 1970, when the Apollo 13 moon mission was endangered by an oxygen tank explosion, much was made of the ability to save the lives of the three astronauts by computing mid-course corrections on earth, transmitting them across distances approaching a quarter million miles. The computations had to be made on the ground because the on-board computing power of the Apollo craft was significantly less than that of a modern day automobile.[1]

In fact, the total computing power available to NASA was significantly less than can today be found on the home desktop of millions of Americans. Films of the Apollo 13 mission reveal a ground control crew frantically calculating last–minute solutions with pencils and slide rules! The immense (and largely unpredicted) advances in telecommunications and computers since then have had, and likely will continue to have, a far-reaching impact on both individuals and society. It is the ability of persons to talk and information to travel, not once over interplanetary distances, but rather repeatedly over the more mun-

238

dane distances of daily life, that has been the real revolution of the past quarter century.

In general, those who pursue the parish ministry are not likely to see the immediate benefit of the coming "information superhighway." This vast network of cable and telephone lines, connecting millions of terminals and televisions, will focus on the delivery of information, primarily, and goods secondarily. Its promoters see 500 channels of programming, with dozens dedicated to home shopping. They see first-run movies on demand and have instant access to huge private and government data banks.[2]

Although there may be benefits for church administration and sermon writing in all of this, it will not focus on bringing people closer together. In fact, by eliminating the need for many face-to-face encounters, it will do just the opposite and be somewhat antithetical to the needs of congregations and ministers. The informal discussions of more structured support groups in people's homes or church offices can be replaced with video conferencing, but such a substitution ignores that much of the value of these activities lies in the feel and presence and touch of people in the group and in the private exchanges before and after.

The biggest advantage touted for all this globalization is the elimination of travel. We are told we will no longer need to go in person to get our needs met. But the primary needs met by churches and ministers are those for person–to–person encounters. In twenty years of ministry, I have driven a distance roughly equal to the one–way journey of Apollo, some 230,000 miles, the distance from the earth to the moon. Almost all of that travel was in pursuit of the face–to–face encounter, with a person in a hospital bed, a family in their dining room, a board around their conference table, or a congregation in their sanctuary. Unlike services and businesses that deliver information or goods, we deliver ourselves; and no substitute for that presence, even on the ubiquitous telephone, is satisfactory for very long.

Ministers don't need technology to eliminate travel. Whether far from their parishes or in the weekly driving necessary to stay in touch with even the most local of congregations, ministers and congregations need technologies that reduce the isolation in the miles that separate our various activities. The communications technology that was in its infancy on those early space flights has served to answer many of those time and distance problems. That same technology creates a whole new set of difficulties, as its capabilities tend to dictate how we work and a whole new set of expectations, some unwelcome, among us.

Despite the miles, answering machines, call-forwarding, and various other technological wonders can serve to keep us "in the neighborhood" and able to respond to both institutional and personal situations. Whenever we "telecommute" back to our congregations, because of a church crisis or a pastoral need, that is the opening step of a process that is completed only with personal contact. If we allow the phone call or the fax to become a substitute for engaging people directly, then we break the basic covenant in our form of community, namely that we will be with one another in all things.

If a technological advance allows a minister to initiate or continue contact with a person under circumstances that would otherwise be impossible, then we should embrace it. If it makes our administrative and sermon preparation duties more efficient, then we should welcome it. If it can reach us in a distant emergency and precede our arrival with contact that feels like it is coming from just down the street, then we should count it a providential instrument!

The feeling that we are "just down the street," from one another is vital to the daily practice of our profession. After personal trust, no other issue affects the relationship between minister and parishioner as much as "availability." It may be expressed in search committee packets as "warmth," in ministerial evaluations as "openness," and in conversations when the minister is not present as anything from friendliness to caring, but it comes down to the question of whether the minister is "there" for people, emotionally and physically. In a society perceived as increasingly impersonal, both emotional and physical presence are and will continue to be central to the tasks set for ministers.

Ministers are allowed inside the normal barriers that persons and families set up. We visit when others might be kept at bay and are told things that others never know. It is our physical presence that is usually the sticking point. "Can you see me now?" they ask. "Can you stay as long as this might take?" they wonder. "Are you in the office? In town? Close enough to get here soon?" Distance matters.

For most of this century, those issues have not been a barrier. Our standard model has been the parish church—a congregation identified by their concentration and location in one town or neighborhood, usually including a resident minister living as part of the primary community. With the wiring of American life into a near universal telephone system, parishioners' access to their minister was limited only by social convention, such as not calling during dinner, and by the driving time across town.

But the boundaries of the parish are expanding. Commuting distances from central cities increase. Congregations take on a regional flavor, servicing several scattered communities. The ranks of interim and extension pastorates swell, increasing the likelihood that the minister has little permanent connection to the community. Church members seem to be less concerned about which church is closest, and travel farther to find one that meets their needs.

My own experience comes from serving five parishes by commuting hundreds of miles each month rather than frequently moving my home. Between September and May, I spend at least 100 days at home, four hours' travel away from my principal church. With a growing number of UU ministers seeking pulpits, and a growing number of congregations (many too small to support full-time ministry) seeking professional leadership, I believe that settlements served by long–range commutes—what the Universalist tradition refers to as circuit riding—will have an increasing popularity, as small congregations link themselves together to afford the shared services of a single minister.

That feeling that the minister is just down the street is also threatened by the increasing mobility of our lives and complexity of our commitments. Conferences, collegial activities, continuing education, and the growing popularity of both second homes and shorter vacations spread throughout the year mean that both minister and member will find themselves frequently absent from the physical setting of the parish, yet still needing to be in touch. The increasing use of what is now considered relatively esoteric communications equipment will render that form of ministry more practical, more acceptable, and more fun. It will also bring us new problems to solve.

Theory is wonderful stuff, but the proof is in the application. So I offer you first three vignettes in which distance presents a problem for ministry, and in which technology plays a role in providing an answer. (We'll get to the ones in which technology is the problem later.) The first of these three is from real life—it occurred in my ministry this past summer. The other two are composites. All of what is described has occurred in my ministry or in the ministry of a colleague. Only the particular sequencing of some events is fictional.

◆ ◆ ◆

The grandparents live in Bowling Green, Ohio, their grandchild in Toronto, Ontario. They wish to have him named and dedicated before a small family gathering, during the summer, on a date when the two families can both be in the same place. The difficulty comes with the minister, who will be four hours away most of the time until Labor Day, and who is unlikely to be in either place at the same time as all the other participants. The family is cool to the suggestion that another minister, "a stranger," could substitute.

On the basis of a casual suggestion, a hand–held camera records the minister reading a fifteen–minute service, with appropriate pauses for the giving of the child's name, the responses to questions asked of godparents, the presentation of a flower, and the repeating of the individual lines of blessing by the entire family. An overnight delivery service brings the videotape from the minister's summer residence to Ohio.

Whether it is the awkwardness of paying such solemn attention to a television set, or the simple inadequacy of the videotape presence, the ceremony does not occur. But the resulting conversation among three generations as to how to properly welcome this new member into their family produces a plan for a future ceremony, prepared and conducted by family members, using some of the words and format on the videotape.

The tape is returned to the minister with thanks for both the effort and the inspiration.

At 2:00 P.M. a church member calls her minister's office in a nearby suburb. The answering machine provides her with the minister's schedule and invites her to call back during her office hours or to leave a message. She leaves a message. At 5:30 P.M. the minister, from an out-of-town conference site, calls her machine and retrieves her messages. The congregant is called at 6:00 P.M. Her call-forwarding service sends the inquiry to a friend's home, who informs the minister that she will return after 9:00 P.M. from the funeral home.

At 9:30 that evening the minister calls again, and after a few minutes' discussion the changes are agreed to in the memorial service. The minister recalls her office machine, and changes the message tape to reflect the new schedule. The following morning, before the flight back to the church, two faxes are sent; one to the funeral home director with text to give to a relative to look over before the service, the other to the church member who has volunteered to produce an order of service for the memorial on her home computer.

A minister serving two congregations some two hundred miles apart is driving from one parish to the other and takes a call on her car phone. The office manager at the church she has just left has been contacted by a local reporter, looking for the minister's opinion for a story to be printed the following day. She takes the paper's number and places a call. The reporter is out on a story and will be back at his desk at a time when the minister is committed to a board meeting at the other church.

During the last fifty miles of her drive, she dictates into a hand-held recorder several statements. Upon arriving at the church she asks the secretary to enter the comments into the computer and send them by e-mail to the reporter. The following day, the office manager calls back to say that the afternoon edition carried two of her quotes. She asks if she was quoted accurately. "Word for word," she replies.

◆ ◆ ◆

In each of these instances of pastoral service or professional expertise, distances (the 150 miles from the minister's office to his beachside cottage, the 200 miles between her parishes, the 400 miles to the conference site) all faded into insignificance. The technology simply meant that interactions that once could have taken place only within the same neighborhood or across town can now be accomplished over much greater distances. Even a televised image of the minister (which does not replace a personal presence) provides an alternative in the case of typical vacation arrangements to no presence at all.

This is not a hymn of blind praise to technology. These stories are told by one who does not own a personal computer, nor use one except on a borrowed basis. (The e-mail story comes from a former parish with a "tcchie" for an office manager. Otherwise, though, I do own and use the items mentioned.) Neither of the congregations I currently serve owns a computer either, and since neither has paid secretarial services, that circumstance will probably not change soon. "Why not?" some of you will ask, especially those taking notes on a laptop. "You'll be able to do so much more," you'll say. "If you've got spread sheets and data bases and all of the wonderful office software."

The first answer, the easy one, is that I don't need to. Both my congregations have volunteers with PCs that put out very professional–looking newsletters, keep an up-dated mailing list, keep the books and produce a very readable monthly statement, and print attractive Sunday bulletins. The harder answer is that I don't want to. My ethical stance toward technological innovation is that I will embrace it only if and when it truly enhances what I want or, in the case of my congregations, need to accomplish.

I get by with a simple dedicated word processor—printer, screen, and software all in one unit, complete with carrying handle. It prints slowly, but otherwise handles sermons and letters as well as anything costing ten times as much. I don't want to center any more of my ministry than that on a keyboard.

I've had an answering machine since my days as a draft counselor, when they cost a fortune and took up a third of a desk top. I've been dictating sermons as I commute (I live 240 miles from my principal parish) for about a decade. I enthusiastically embrace these two devices. I gained some comfort in front of a camera by hosting a televised panel show for the past four years. The personal fax machine and the car phone are relatively new; a falling price curve and improving capabilities finally crossing on that chart that plots my resistance to any new purchase. The jury is still out on these two.

Let me now give you the scenarios in which technology is the problem.

At my last interim congregation I had only one significant argument with the Board through the whole year. It came over the issue of call waiting—

those little clicks on the line that "allow" you to answer another call by putting the first on hold.

Board members, frustrated by busy signals in a church with a high volume of telephone traffic, wanted to be able to get through to me or the secretary whenever they called, and to not have to return calls several times.

I objected strenuously. "Busy means busy," I told them. "If the call I'm on is in any sense a pastoral matter, I do not want to be breaking away, breaking the flow of that conversation." I offered them the alternative of a second line (I told them I did not want it to ring in my office, and that I would strongly prefer not to answer it, but they would be able to put a message on the answering machine.) They liked the compromise, but not the cost. They got call waiting after I left.

Like many people I have a strong aversion to paging devices. The idea that someone can "summon" me, and expect an instantaneous reply, simply goes against the grain personally and professionally. The idea that a beeper would be worn every waking hour (which is what the expectation quickly escalates to) would destroy the vital concept that there are portions of my life where I am not a minister and times when I am not, no matter what the circumstances, on call.

But as I have said, I own a cellular phone. It makes the fifteen hours I spend each month commuting and driving to church functions and appointments more efficient. I don't give out the number. It is not possible to intrude on my expressway reverie. You could pry it out of my wife in an emergency, but even then, you probably wouldn't get through. Because I do not usually expect to receive calls, I seldom have the phone turned on. It is, by my choice, a send only device. Its designer might be horrified that I am "wasting" half of its capabilities, but the truth is, I have adapted a potentially annoying piece of technology to my needs.

I suggest to my congregation that if they need to reach me on the road, they call the office and leave a message on that answering machine. I can and do call in from the car to retrieve messages—and I'll get back to them quicker than if they wait "til he gets back."

Technological capability creates expectations as readily as it meets them. I recall vividly a conversation with a parishioner, angry because an August request, left casually on my office answering machine, had not been responded to (from her perspective) until September. She felt ignored, she said, unimportant. It hadn't been urgent, but she had nevertheless expected a more prompt response.

This occurred before the means to retrieve messages remotely was widely available. She said that she thought I "might have been" on vacation in August. "Couldn't somebody have picked up the messages and returned my call?" she inquired. It was a telling point.

I thought I was improving my level of service by leaving the machine on during a two–week absence, because folks would not have to call back repeatedly and get no answer. In fact, I had created an expectation that some live contact would shortly follow the recorded message. The impression of a physical presence had been created—an invitation from a recognizable voice to leave a message implies that same person will soon be getting back to you—and then not lived up to.

In fact, I had called back within two weeks, on three separate occasions. There had been no answer each time. She did not have an answering machine and was therefore exempt from the very expectation mine had placed me under.

That was more than ten years ago. Today, one of my expectations as a minister is that most of my parishioners will have answering machines. I accept that some choose not to for good personal reasons (and that quite a few own one, but leave it turned off much of the time—like my cellular phone—so as not to have to live up to unwelcome expectations). There is frustration in calling someone back and simply having the phone ring, but the frustration is my problem.

How should ministers and churches approach technological advances in the future? By insisting that their needs drive the devices, and not the other way around. Not every church needs a fax machine, or at least not the "high incoming volume" model recently promoted by the denomination. That may serve the needs of our headquarters (which is not a bad thing) but would probably be detrimental to a small congregation's office if it results in a blitz of arriving faxes.

Not every minister needs a car phone, though some may benefit from a "universal phone number," allowing a call to find you at any phone. Very promising for churches with small staffs or limited phone volunteer pools are upcoming devices that automatically call your membership, or a selected group within it, and deliver a prerecorded message (reminding folks of the new time for the Wednesday discussion group or telling them that someone is in the hospital). In this case, the down side is the impersonal quality of the communication, but that is outweighed by the interactions it can generate.

The best advice is this: Unless you absolutely love gadgets, go slowly with any new technology. Or old technology for that matter. Don't be pressured into buying something just because it is becoming popular. Borrow or rent it for a while. See what it does for you and your approach to ministry. If it annoys you, or forces you to do things in a way that makes you uncomfortable, don't make it permanent. If you like it, but it doesn't advance the cause of bringing you closer to one another, then just think of it as a toy. Enjoy it, but be ready to lay it aside and get back to ministry.

In the quarter century since Apollo, we have not ventured very far beyond the surface of our planet.

But ever since we caught that first glimpse of earth, as seen by those who had traveled to another world, we have seen our travels here differently. It is the connections we can discover and make between ourselves that seem more important now, rather than the distances we can put between us. Our technology has not taken us beyond the moon, or even back there. It has given us many opportunities to go beyond our geographic boundaries here and still remain connected to one another.

"We are what we know," says James Burke, host of the PBS series "The Day the Universe Changed." The world *is* a much smaller place than we had ever previously known or imagined. Distances no longer make nations strangers to one another, nor do they keep any of us from being "just down the street."

Recreating Religious History

William Dean

———————◆———————

An earlier version of this essay was published as "The Importance of Retelling our Story" in Regaining Historical Consciousness: Proceedings of the Earl Morse Wilbur History Colloquium *(Starr King School for the Ministry, 1994).*

Roman Catholics in the 1960s, Mormons in the 1980s, and mainline Protestants off and on for the past 100 years have learned the hard way that historical criticism brings unanticipated consequences.

For Catholics, Vatican II opened the door to historical understandings of scripture and tradition. Although this allowed the church to enter into more direct interaction with the biblical critics and church historians of the secular university, it also took away from the church its uncomplicated confidence in the divine inspiration of scripture and in the divine source of the church's rites and pronouncements. For many individual Catholics, a comforting naiveté was taken away.

When the Mormons opened themselves to critical historical understandings, they were especially vulnerable. By the 1980s, committed Mormons could read learned biographies of the sainted Joseph Smith and his wives, which quietly questioned not only the literal accuracy of his visions and claims, but the morality of the man himself.

The Protestant submission to historical inquiry began much earlier. The opening of higher criticism of the Bible annulled the marriage of literalistic religious history to serious natural history. Historical analysis meant that religious people could no longer carry on guiltlessly with miracles and dreams of eternal life, and that the history of the church no longer inspired the earlier glowing admiration.

Religious liberals need not anticipate the specific catastrophes that beset Catholics and Protestants. These liberals have accepted the importance of historical criticism for 100 years. They have embraced natural history, just as they have typically seen in the workings of the secular mind something of spiritual importance. But even if liberals have avoided some consequences of the literalism that made Christian denominations so vulnerable to historical criticism, they have not escaped all of its consequences.

To explain why, let me define three forms of historical criticism: (1) historical objectivism, (2) historical relativism, and (3) historicism, sometimes called constructivism. *Objectivism* assumes not only that things can be known as they actually happened, but also that past history has its own structure. The objective interpreter of history is one who discovers the structure of the settled past, knowing that structure does not lie at the surface but believing that with the right methods it can be unearthed. *Relativism* typically assumes that there is a given structure, but goes on to acknowledge that this structure looks different from every angle and that there is no one angle all observers share. The third form of historical criticism, *historicism*, has risen to prominence in the postmodern era. It claims that history has no structure until it is interpreted and that interpretation gives history much of the structure it has. In effect, it claims not only that things are not simply what they are discovered to be, but also that in large part they are what they are now seen to be, as a past stream of history mingles with the present stream of history. The historicist assumes that there simply is no given structure, and in that respect is postmodern rather than modern.

Now why should religious communities undertake this last and most radical form of historical criticism? Only for practical reasons. Increasingly, arguments for fixed and universal structures in history seem insupportable. The objectivists and relativists seem to be staking their religious lives on something they cannot demonstrate and that has no practical importance.

Thus it has become time-wasting to be religious in a nonhistoricist way. To be a historicist, on the other hand, allows one to constructively interpret what is affirmed, and then move on to more important things. This is a revolution of historical criticism that the religious liberals have not yet undergone, but should undergo. Let me suggest what that might mean more specifically.

Like other religious people, liberals have had to yield some claims in the face of the criticisms of history. Sometimes their claims to know the truth have fallen before critics who demonstrate that all experience—even religious experience—is qualified by the circumstances of the history in which it occurs.

Postmodern historicism makes religious liberals vulnerable to further criticism, but it may also give them new opportunities and mandates.

Like other religious people, liberals believe in realities that transcend historical process. Even when they acknowledge that their truths are not supernatural or miraculous, that their truths may be known only in and for their social and cultural circumstance, religious liberals still claim that these truths are about *realities* that are eternal and universal, that are magisterial precisely because they are unaffected by historical change and circumstance.

Historicism, as I understand it, claims that such history-transcending realities do not exist. It claims that everything is historical, that everything lives within natural and cultural processes, and that nothing is known to transcend those processes. Historicism can be understood as the claim that everything begins through some historical gesture and lives only as long as other historical gestures allow it to live. To elaborate this idea using the evolutionary metaphor, every interpretation begins as a spontaneous variation of some historical creature; every interpretation is accepted or rejected through environmental selection, and every interpretation will perish when the environment finds it no longer useful.

Historicism as a postmodern, or poststructural, cosmology can do much for a people's humility—but also, as we shall see, for a people's legitimate sense of its own importance. It is humbling to recognize that a people's truth cannot be authorized as a truth that utterly transcends that people. Historicism contends that the deepest wisdom we hold is not a wisdom that transcends us, but a truth that has grown up around us and will perish when our truth is forgotten.

But how can historicism contribute to a people's legitimate sense of its own importance? Precisely by arguing that it is people, after all, who construct history. The deepest truths we hold, the highest values we cherish, the moral mandates under which we live, the beauties we hold before our eyes, are all realities humans have originally imagined and thrust forth for consideration by the historical environment. Or to put it urgently: if the world is to be redeemed, then it is historical entities, including ones we have imagined, who will redeem it. In making that claim, historicism puts before us as historical creatures the deepest conceivable responsibility.

To place God so thoroughly in history is not to deny God's existence. It is only to affirm that God exists as a historical reality. The historicist perspective makes it possible to acknowledge that traditions of moral and religious value are imagined and, thereby, literally created by human beings—and, at the same time, to call upon people to honor and obey these traditions as realities that stand over against themselves.

Such an acceptance of religious history is still not common for religious liberals. Like virtually everyone else, they prefer to believe that the spirit they venerate is venerable because it is, in the words of Henry Nelson Wieman, a "good not our own," because it is eternal and infinite while they are temporal and finite. They prefer to organize their moral lives around rights and virtues that ought never be denied by anyone, anywhere, whereas I am arguing that God or any ultimate reality arises as a historical convention and lives on as a tradition, yet is to be treated as utterly real.

My intent is to note not the problems of an ahistorical religious cosmology, but the advantages of a historicist religious cosmology.

A religious cosmology that is thoroughly historicist has this practical advantage: It leads religious people to set their eyes on historical circumstances rather than on ahistorical "realities", and this prepares them to interact constructively with their environment. This can be illustrated, at least negatively, by reference to theological education. Theological or ministerial students are sometimes ill-equipped to find anything practical to say—at least anything based on their graduate education—to those who will surround them after they leave graduate school. Often, their best hope lies in first convincing people that they must involve themselves in theology before they can be religious, and then switch the conversation to theology. The point is that these students are typically given very little help by their graduate education in addressing with any particular authority people's religious problems in society.

In short, religious understandings that are thoroughly historical incline religious people to think about the religious meaning of their historical circumstances. Religious understandings derived from history do not need to ask, as most religious understandings typically do, how they can be related to society. Rather, they arise from attention to historical developments in society, and thus already relate to society.

The historicists begin their work discussing broad historical conditions—not theories, not extrahistorical realities, not private and subjective feelings, but broad social and cultural practices. Students of religion, ministers, priests, and religious people generally should see how their religious questions arise from a spiritual analysis of both contemporary and earlier history. Using these two historical resources, religious thinkers will generate religious ideas that speak to history.

Let me apply these concepts to liberal religious thought. Even as they turn outward to public history rather than to private history, liberal religious thinkers are involved in a quite specific form of criticism. Their prime commitment is not to social criticism of the material and political culture, nor to cultural criticism of the aesthetic and artistic culture, but to religious criticism of their spiritual culture. They ask, primarily, what is there in the historical texture of the society that harmonizes it, that reconciles its divergent strains, that makes their society a whole society rather than a mere plurality of societies? How can this source of reconciliation and purpose be discerned in their historic tradition? How is it to be understood, expressed, and acted on?

Religious critics ask this question in two quite different ways. First, they inquire into their historical tradition. What, they ask, has given them as a people a public sense of the whole, and as persons a private sense of the whole, as they have attempted to become whole people in a whole society? Second, they ask: What now gives us a sense of whole? Without question, John Dewey argued, these two answers will diverge. Sometimes our present sense of the historical whole will stand indicted by the spiritual reality that once unified the society in its earlier phases. Conversely, sometimes the spiritual history received from the past will stand indicted by the spiritual history that gives coherence and meaning to the present society.

Of one thing Dewey was certain: The problem of finding wholeness in the spiritual culture is always changing, just as the biological world is always changing. Just as the biological process is always a struggle between the organism that results from a spontaneous variation and the environment that decides whether to accept that organism, so the religious process is a struggle between the spiritual culture that results from new spiritual variations and the environment of old religious traditions. Thus, our personal and our societal meanings arise from historical streams and must be revised when those streams rush against each other. Equally, the answers to religious questions, like the answers to evolutionary problems, are always changing, evolving, undergoing revision.

This can be borne out through a brief look at the development of religious theories. Unitarians, for example, have had to revise their understandings continually. At one moment they accepted a transcendentalist idealism that seemed to make sense of their received historical tradition. At other times they accepted a left-of-center moral system or a religious cosmology with a bias toward process philosophy. At still later moments they felt called upon to reevaluate those traditions in the light of new circumstances that called them into question. Transcendental reason began to seem, say, more like the projection of temporary wishes than like eternal answers; socialist moral systems began to seem unworkable when confronted by twentieth-century European experience; any grand cosmology—let alone the cosmology of process philosophy—began to look as if it had outreached its true evidence when it attempted to describe timeless and universal structures.

In each instance, new historical experiences arose that challenged earlier religious traditions. New spiritual insight and the knowledge of historic traditions had to be reconciled, and nothing better than the human imagination was available as the source of the reconciling ideas.

I assume that a religious sense of the whole is at work—a largely noncognitive apprehension of the harmonizing ideals that have driven our culture religiously, followed by a new apprehension of the whole in the contemporary culture, followed by a struggle toward the reconciliation of these conflicting apprehensions. This spiral of development is unrelenting; it leads us either to revise our inherited answers, or to spurn our new answers in the name of inherited answers, or—as is usually the case—to introduce a third answer that harmonizes the two. It is this dialogue, said Dewey, that should orient our religious talk and work. We are constantly required to imagine how, by what sacred ideals, we might reconcile our received spiritual history with our contemporary history. This continual revision, led by the unrelenting religious imagination, will yield new religious conventions and, in effect, yield new gods or new spiritual realities. The task of religious liberals, therefore, is to overcome the dissonance between received history and contemporaneous history by introducing an imaginative reconciliation and thus to *create* history. Therein lies the moral consequence of historical interpretation.

Let me illustrate this constructivist contention by reference to Garry Wills's recent *Lincoln at Gettysburg*. The book is a study of the Gettysburg address and of the events and people surrounding it. By writing the book, Wills changed history as a discipline. He argued that Lincoln's principal aim in giving the address was "not emancipation but the preservation of self-government."[1] Second, Wills changed the discipline of history by explaining, by reference to one speech, the power of rhetoric; his 313-page book on the three-paragraph Gettysburg address is subtitled, "The Words that Remade America." But while this would have been reason enough to publish the book, this is not the genius of the book.

The genius of the book is a comment on how Lincoln created history—changed the reality of history. The result, Wills said, was that, at the completion of the Gettysburg address, the crowd "walked off from those curving graves on the hillside under a changed sky, into a different America."[2] The Gettysburg address, in its new appreciation of the importance of equality and self-government, reinterpreted the Declaration of Independence so that it, in turn, reinterpreted the Constitution so that it, in turn, reinterpreted—literally changed—America itself.

To heighten the drama, let me add that Lincoln's act of conjuring a new past was effected by a man who, as a Transcendentalist, would have denied its possibility. After all, Lincoln, as what Wills calls a "theological Unitarian," saw historical change as illusory and believed that history's so-called change is the slave to unchanging ideas beyond history. History for Lincoln is only a moving window on static ideas. History does not innovate, but only copies into practice the permanent rational ideas that stand well beyond practice.[3] And yet, ironically, Lincoln himself changed America through a nation-making and historical act of speech.

Once you accept this much about Wills's argument, you cannot help but entertain the further question: did Wills's interpretation of Lincoln and of the Gettysburg address, in fact, create a new Lincoln and a new address? Lincoln, the Declaration creator, who became a Constitution creator, who became a creator of a new America, may not have existed before Wills's book quite as he existed after Wills's book. The book, it becomes apparent, is the first link in the chain of literary interpretations—the link from which all other links are suspended—and is instrumental in creating new historical realities.

Liberal religious people can retell their story with some of the same dramatic, reality-creating effects that Garry Wills achieved. This point makes more sense if one accepts the new power of history-making as it lies implicit in post-structuralist historicism. I am not here discussing the importance of the past, or the importance of appreciating the impact of the past on the present. I take it for granted that any religious group should be deeply familiar with its own history. I am discussing not the power of the past on the present, but the power of the present on the past. I am talking about the power of historical criticism: it is not only an instrument for discerning the traditions of the past; it is an instrument for interpreting and thereby re-creating the past.

There is a choice about how to interpret the past. Liberal religious people can exercise real discretion in deciding what the past will be seen as, and thus, to some extent, in determining what it will be. Finally, and most importantly, how they choose to interpret the past will have something to do not only with what the past is but with how it will become a force in the future.

Liberal religious people are very closely tied to the history of America, particularly to the history of its religious and philosophical culture. In telling their story as a denomination or as two denominations, they tell a story about America. What they choose to emphasize in those stories can both interpret and create the past. By telling these stories they can lift out of the past certain otherwise neglected episodes or sequences, see them in a light that would not otherwise be cast, connect them with the present in ways they would otherwise never be connected. These stories can elicit from the past a set of possibilities that might otherwise never have been elicited.

Out of this process not only a new past but new orientations for the present can be created. The old story about the past is remembered because it speaks religiously to a sense of the whole. The new and imagined story about the past can become an effort to harmonize the divergent pulls of an old and a present sense of the whole. What first appears to be only a new construction of the past turns out to be a way to change the future. If a religious group such as wants to change itself and then change the world in ways never before imagined, then the first thing is to recreate its religious history by telling a new story about its past.

Whatever Happened to
Liberal Christianity?

Earl K. Holt III

In 1822, toward the end of his life, Thomas Jefferson penned two letters containing sentences probably quoted more often from the pulpits of our liberal churches than anything else he ever wrote. The first reads, "I trust that there is not a young man now living in the United States who will not die a Unitarian." The second, "I confidently expect that the present generation will see Unitarianism become the general religion of the United States."

It would seem from these statements that Jefferson hardly qualifies as a prophet, yet I believe there is a sense in which he was correct. Certainly, Unitarianism (and in the last three decades Unitarian Universalism) has never been a popular movement in terms of adherents. Even during the best of times the membership of Unitarian churches never numbered more than about one-tenth of one percent of the general population, and now some thirty years after merger with the Universalists we fall far short of even that modest figure. Furthermore, if religions were rated by pollsters in the same way political candidates are measured, our so-called "negative numbers" would be pretty high. By many we are looked upon as a collection of loony religious misfits, atheists, and infidels. It's not hard to see where these misperceptions come from. We do tolerate a lot of flakiness—that is in the nature of any place that strives toward openness, tolerance, and freedom—and unfortunately the more bizarre issues and events among us are those most likely to get noticed and publicized.

But if Unitarianism as an institution never even came close to fulfilling Jefferson's expectation, the story is quite different when we consider the influence of Unitarian ideas. In the generation for which Jefferson made his prediction, those who came of age in the middle years of the nineteenth century, Unitarians and Unitarian ideas were at the very heart and center of the developing American culture. It was in this time that Boston earned its nickname of the Athens of America, and with some twenty-four Unitarian congregations in the city, in them a significant number of its leading citizens, Unitarianism too earned a nickname: the Boston Religion. America's preeminent institution of higher learning, Harvard University, in the middle and late nineteenth century, was to all extents and purposes a Unitarian institution. Ralph Waldo Emerson left the Unitarian ministry after a brief stint at Second Church in Boston, but his historical significance lies at least as much in his influence on the development of Unitarian theology as on American literature. All his Transcendentalist associates were either Unitarians or fellow-travelers.

But even more than this, it could be said that in the initial religious conflict that gave rise to Unitarianism in this country, between Calvinist fatalism and Unitarian liberalism, the Unitarians won. Not, certainly, in the sense of building a huge denominational enterprise but by its influence in bringing the spirit of liberal Christianity to the fore in all the major Protestant bodies, which were and would remain for more than a century the dominant element in American religion and culture, the so-called mainline churches.

Our movement changed the whole tenor of mainstream religious thought in this country. It was with this in mind that the great Unitarian minister of this century, A. Powell Davies, once said that there are millions of Unitarians in America—not necessarily in Unitarian churches but in virtually all the churches and outside them as well, among the unchurched. It was Davies who perceived that for most Americans their "real religion" was not the stated doctrine of their church but faith in the underlying tenets of liberal democracy, a faith that was rooted in the same Enlightenment ideas that had inspired Unitarianism in its American origins: confidence in the human spirit and optimism about the human prospect.

Of course this is not the whole story. Religious conservatism, from early Calvinism through the periodic revivals known as Great Awakenings to the resurgent Fundamentalism of our own era, has also had a continuing and significant impact on American life. It was a phenomenon that greatly impressed de Tocqueville, and large parts of his classic book, *Democracy in America*, are devoted to a discussion of the peculiar attraction for the freedom-loving Americans of severely doctrinal religion. He hypothesized that the roots of this phenomenon might lie in a reaction to the challenge of freedom, a seeking for security and limits and community since their public and social life was so much characterized by possibility, openness, and individualism.

But by and large for a long time, at least until the middle years of this century and certainly in the years to which he referred, Jefferson was not so very wrong. What triumphed, or at least gained ascendancy, was not Unitarianism in a narrow or institutional sense, but liberal Christianity, which is what he meant by the word. Read the letters, written in 1822, from which those two familiar quotations are drawn: "Had the doctrines of Jesus been preached always as pure as they came from his lips, the whole civilized world would now have been Christian. I rejoice that in this blessed country of free inquiry and belief, which has surrendered its conscience to neither kings nor priests, the genuine doctrine of only one God is reviving, and I trust that there is not a young man now living in the United States who will not die a Unitarian."

For Jefferson, Unitarianism was simply the religion of Jesus. In his second letter he equates Unitarianism with what he called "primitive Christianity," meaning the faith of the early church before the adoption of the first creeds. "No historical fact is better established," he wrote, "than that the doctrine of one God, pure and uncompounded, was that of the early ages of Christianity; and was among the efficacious doctrines which gave it triumph over the polytheism of the ancients, sickened with the absurdities of their own theology....The pure and simple unity of the Creator of the Universe, is now all but ascendant in the Eastern States, it is dawning in the West, and advancing toward the South; and I confidently expect that the present generation will see Unitarianism become the general religion of the United States...."

Until perhaps a half-century ago, then, it is arguable that liberal Christianity was indeed the dominant religion of the United States. What happened to it? In the mainline churches of our time it no longer has notable champions, certainly none to compare with preachers like Harry Emerson Fosdick who a half-century ago was preaching sermons that today would be considered rank heresy in many of even the more liberal mainline churches. I should be clear that I am talking about theological liberalism. Fosdick and his ilk were also by and large "Social Gospel" preachers, and there's no shortage of social gospel and social witness in many churches (conservative as well as liberal) today. But theological liberalism is in short supply. Institutionally, most churches are moving away from liberal Christianity, in response to the activity of their more conservative members, who are frequently the most active and vocal of their constituents. Conservatives have even formed whole new denominations made up of formerly mainline Presbyterian and other churches.

And what is the situation among us Unitarian Universalists? Liberal Christianity, I would say, has been marginalized, to the point now where Christianity is widely considered at best just one possible option on a kind of religious smorgasbord. Within our little household of faith, we have a tiny minority of churches and persons who identify themselves as explicitly Christian. They are looked upon, and for the most part regard themselves, as a fringe group, even as they witness to what was once the center and indeed virtually the whole substance of our faith. Liberal Christianity, which could still be a most powerful expression of religion in our culture generally, for many present-day Unitarian Universalists seems to be an embarrassment. This is understandable to some degree. Christianity (or at least those who claim the label Christian for themselves) has done a lot of things to give Christianity a bad name.

But ironically, even tragically, our relationship to this tradition is more than just strained. Christianity is the only religion toward which some Unitarian Universalists routinely exhibit outright intolerance, hostility, and derision. Some seem to suppose that all Christians are and always have been mindless, antediluvian, biblical literalists. This is not simply a misunderstanding of others, but of our own past. It is simple ignorance of those who have gone before and what they believed, the biblical foundation of their—of our—faith. It is a failure to recognize that the values we cherish in common—reason, freedom, tolerance, justice for the oppressed, the worth and dignity of every human soul—derive from the particular history and concrete experience of those who lived as liberal Christians.

Yet after all is said and done, we retain, if not a consciously Christian identity, then at least a Christian ethos. We meet on Sunday mornings. We refer to our places of worship as churches. And the worship within them most commonly uses forms deriving from centuries of liberal Christian practice. An enduring issue for our movement is the relationship to its Christian roots. Hardly a minister has not preached more than once on the subject, "Are Unitarians Christian?"

And one of the things that has defined us as a people is the tension implied in that question. We would be a very different church if we ever got to a place where this question was definitively answered and the tension disappeared. But it is true that our general theological movement has been not only away from any form of orthodox Christian exclusivity, but even away from our own liberal Christian roots.

Unquestionably good intentions inform and underlie this movement, a genuine desire to embrace diversity and pluralism and build a universal church in which, as Channing put it, none could be excluded except by the death of goodness within themselves. Consistent and noble is the desire among us to draw the circle of religious fellowship ever more widely, to accept ever-increasing theological diversity. Historically, our American movement has embraced first the non-Christian, then the non-theist. Most recently some entertain (with how much depth it remains to be seen) polytheistic traditions. Yeats wondered whether the center could hold. Our question might be whether we can find any center at all.

We know that we cannot seek a center in commonality of creed. Our congregational polity supports wide diversity in congregational styles and practices. What we do have in common is a history and a tradition. Our common ground is liberal Christianity. This is the soil in which our movement was nourished, and in which it has flourished when it flourished. It is our tap root. A root does not limit how broadly we may grow or dictate the directions we may take from it, but if cut ourselves off from it, we will wither. Quite arguably, there is a missing dimension in the liberal religion of our era. Among us, too, is evidence of thinness or emptiness. The evidence shows in the pursuit of theological and social fads—spiritual trendiness. But we move powerfully into the new only out of a profound sense of integrity, not through aimlessly trying out this and that.

T. S. Eliot once remarked that a tradition cannot be inherited, it must be earned by great labor. In this task we have patently failed. Beyond thoughtless namedropping, we do little to honor our past; for the most part we don't even teach it very well. Eliot was trying to say that tradition is not a gift but an achievement, not something we are given but something we must struggle to gain. Tradition is not imitation, not blind or timid adherence to the ways of the past. It entails judgement as well as knowledge of what has been, and a connection not only to the temporal but the timeless. To earn a tradition is to achieve a context for our life, to achieve a basis for moral judgement and a means for comparing its measure and meaning with other values in other times. To earn a tradition is to find our place in time and in eternity, which is surely a significant aspect of what a church is for, a religious endeavor.

It is a very basic but vitally important human task

to come to terms with one's past. I believe it is a religious task as well, for institutions as well as individuals. Earning a tradition for us means coming to terms with our liberal Christian roots, and as we do I believe we will open the way to a significant future. As Eliot wrote, in summarizing the religious pilgrimage, at the end of all our exploring, we will arrive at where we started and know the place for the first time.

What Has Been Kept

Ronald Knapp

———————◆———————

It was thirty years ago, in 1964, after eleven years of serving Methodist churches, that I was received into fellowship in the Unitarian Universalist ministry. Over the decades I have looked out at the Unitarian Universalist world, always with love, sometimes with amusement, and not infrequently with chagrin and consternation.

For all my years in the Unitarian Universalist ministry, it seems to me we have been a movement inundated by wave after wave of fads: human potential fads, fads of social concern, theological fads. All have been seen as having some cosmic significance, some ultimate value, before they fizzled and disappeared.

Unitarians were said in the last century to be

"God's frozen people." In this last quarter of the twentieth century, it seems to me we have thawed out, at least theologically, and are flowing, willy–nilly, all over the place. To mix metaphors—and to quote one of my father's favorite expressions—"We are like the person who climbed on a horse and rode off in all four directions at once."

A century and a half ago Theodore Parker challenged the Unitarian world with his sermon, "The Transient and Permanent in Christianity." As we approach the twenty-first century, we must ask, "What is permanent in Unitarian Universalism?" Borrowing from William Butler Yeats, we could ask whether "mere anarchy is loosed upon" the Unitarian Universalist world. Will "things fly apart?" Will "the center hold?" Is there a center? Or have we now only the transient? Has there been an enduring center of our collective faith?

I name four elements I believe are, and ought to be, permanent elements of our Unitarian Universalist faith. They are ideas with a long history among us, ideas found in actual or incipient form throughout our history.

The first two permanent elements I cite will not, I think, occasion any controversy. They are named in a phrase valued among us, universally affirmed if not universally practiced. The phrase is the "*free and disciplined* search for truth."

At the heart of Unitarian Universalist faith lies

the idea of *radical freedom of belief.* No one—no minister, no church, no officer of our Association—has the authority to tell individual Unitarian Universalists what they must believe. Individuals must work out matters of belief for themselves. For more than a century that idea, in the form of "liberty clauses," has been a part of any corporate affirmations we have devised. The doctrine of radical freedom of belief is permanent in Unitarian Universalism.

But liberty can lead to license. Freedom of belief can lead to all kinds of absurdities unless it has a powerful corrective. In US history there have been those who believed—believed religiously—that African Americans were an inferior race who, therefore, could and should in the name of God be subjected to slavery. In our own day there are those who believe it is God's will that they should shoot and kill doctors who perform abortions. Contemporary Unitarian Universalists may not hold these particular views. But it is easy, if we focus only on individual freedom of belief, to believe, like Alice's White Queen, "six impossible things before breakfast." It is even easy to arrive at the absurd notion that "it doesn't matter what you believe as long as you believe it." Well, it does matter. And this is where discipline must come into the picture.

Every once in a while I overhear some Unitarian Universalist say, "In this church you can believe what you want to believe." I always wince when I hear that.

That is exactly the opposite of what is *vital* in liberal religion. That shallow understanding of our freedom is the cardinal sin of liberal religion, the sin against the holy spirit. Unitarian Universalists are not called to believe what they want to believe, but what they are *required* by the careful deliberations of their own minds to believe. By discipline is meant careful deliberation.

A few years ago I was to officiate at a wedding in the Strategic Air Command Chapel at Offut Air Force Base. I was assigned a young airman to help me around the chapel. A fundamentalist, who had never heard of Unitarian Universalism, he wanted to know something about my religion. As I was explaining, he said, "I understand. You believe whatever it is you want to believe."

"No. No, that is not it," I replied. "We believe what we are required to believe by the dictates of our own active and critical minds."

It occurred to me, as I reflected on that conversation with the young airman, that "believing what one wants to believe" is the essence of fundamentalism. One does not believe in the virgin birth, or the immaculate conception, or the literal resurrection of Christ from the tomb because there is any evidence that persuades. One believes in spite of evidence. One believes because in one's heart one wants to believe.

The free and disciplined search for truth is at the very heart of our faith. It is not an easy faith. Ours is not a shortcut religion. It requires no less than a life-long commitment to the disciplined search. John Locke, the English philosopher whose writing had a profound effect on the shape and character of Unitarian Universalism, said it as well as it can be said: "One unerring mark of the love of truth," said Locke, "is not entertaining any proposition with greater assurance than the proofs it is built upon will warrant."

The third and fourth permanent elements in Unitarian Universalism have a very long history among us and have been percolating in our movement ever since the beginning, but appear to be controversial in our time. I shall name them the *authority of reason* and *the unity of truth.*

Sometimes when I talk about reason, people want to know what I mean, expecting some esoteric answer. But there is nothing difficult about what is meant by reason in the context of Unitarian Universalist history. It is as simple as asking questions regarding any belief. "Is it reasonable to believe this?" and "Does what I believe square with what else I know about the world and about the universe?" There is also a communal aspect to a reasonable approach. In the context of liberal faith, reason asks, "Does what I believe, individually and personally, resonate with what we know communally and collectively to be true?"

This concept and use of reason permeates our entire religious heritage, but it appears now to be under great attack from within our movement itself. "Reason" seems at times in contemporary Unitarian

Universalist usage almost like a dirty word. Some seem at times almost to echo Martin Luther who said, "Reason is an ass." Yet it is very important that reason be understood as a crucial and permanent element in Unitarian Universalism. It is important because it represents the only collective authority we as a faith community can turn to in our theological diversity.

In the religions of this part of the world, in the Jewish and Christian traditions, there have been two primary sources of communal religious authority. For Roman Catholics the primary source of authority is the church's tradition. For Jews and Protestants it is scripture, the Torah and the Bible. When people of the dominant faith in our culture argue or debate matters of faith, they turn to such sources of authority to evaluate beliefs. Unitarian Universalists, who have by and large rejected scripture and the church as authoritative, have turned to reason as the authority. I can think of no other alternative short of philosophical solipsism or intellectual anarchy. Without reason we have no common basis for evaluating what we believe individually in the context of community.

Some of what I have just written about reason can also be said of the fourth permanent element in Unitarian Universalism, *the unity of truth*. Throughout our history Unitarian Universalists have attempted to build bridges between the sacred and the profane. Throughout our history we have been in the forefront of those insisting on a reconciliation between science and religion. One of my predecessors in the pulpit of First Unitarian Church in Omaha, for example, is notable for having been the first minister in North America to embrace Darwin's theory of evolution.

In spite of this long history, however, there is a strain in current Unitarian Universalism toward dualism. I, for one, am thankful that we are not talking so much about "my truth" and "your truth," as we did a decade or so ago, as if everything were subjective. But it seems to me more and more Unitarian Universalists are talking as if truth were divisible, as if religious truth was of a different substance, of a different world, than scientific or secular truth.

My own guide in this matter has long been Walt Whitman. In "Song of Myself" Whitman has his poet/prophet say to the scientist, "My house is not your house, but I must go through your house to get to my house." In our world we must be willing to go through the world of science, through the world of accumulated knowledge, to arrive at an authentic religion and an authentic spirituality for our time. The experience of religion and the study of science are not the same, but they deal with the same truth. "Truth is truth to the end of reckoning," wrote the poet Robert Browning. Such a spirit and the search for that truth has always been and must continue to be a permanent feature of liberal religious faith.

The free and disciplined search for truth, the authority of reason, and the unity of truth together make up the torch of liberal religion. They are permanent aspects of Unitarian Universalism that must not be sacrificed to the transient. If we are to leave a vital and living heritage for those who will follow us in the next century, they must be affirmed, strengthened, and renewed here now at the end of this century.

Present day Unitarian Universalists, it seems to me, are far too inclined to get locked into contemporaneity, locked into the idea that the only important things are our time, our world, or our thoughts. We need to remember consistently that we are part of a historical movement extending from far back in the distant past and far forward, we hope, into the distant future.

We are the spiritual children of Michael Servetus, who died in flames, and of Francis David, who died in prison. They died because they proclaimed Unitarian faith. We are the children of Channing and Emerson and Parker and Murray and Ballou who shaped the faith in America. We are the children of Susan B. Anthony and Olympia Brown and a whole host of others—women and men—who spread the gospel of human rights, of civil rights, of equality for all throughout this part of the world. We are the children of John Locke and of Thomas Jefferson and of that whole historic period called the Enlightenment.

> We drink from a well we did not dig.
> We worship in a temple we did not build.

And yet we are also building for the future, building not alone for ourselves, but for those who will come after. The words of wisdom from Havelock Ellis' *The New Spirit* come as close to being scripture for me as any I know.

> In every age the present is merely the shifting point at which past and future meet, and we can have no quarrel with either. There can be no world without traditions; neither can there be any life without movement. There is never a moment when the new dawn is not breaking over the earth, and never a moment when the sunset ceases to die....
>
> In the moral world we are ourselves the light-bearers, and the cosmic process is in us made flesh. For a brief space it is granted to us, if we will, to enlighten the darkness that surrounds our path. As in the ancient torch-races, which seemed to Lucretius to be the symbol of all life, we press forward torch in hand along the course. Soon from behind comes the runner who will outpace us. All our skill lies in giving into that hand the living torch, bright and unflickering, as we ourselves disappear in the darkness.

Into the Woods: In Search of Our Stories

Susan Pangerl

———————◆———————

The mythic figures of my childhood have revisited me several times in the last few years through the guise of Stephen Sondheim's play *Into the Woods*.[1] Some twenty-two fairy tale characters come to life, each yearning for something "more." The first act sets the stage, revealing each character's belief of where this "more," this source of happiness, would be found, what the conditions for its fulfillment would be. The omniscient narrator removes any ambiguity as to the characters' motives and desires, or the anticipated outcome for each character.

With the second act, the rules change. Forces intervene. Life takes unexpected turns. Wishes are (seemingly) granted, even as other losses occur. The disquieting desire for something other, something not yet known, persists. In the words of Cinderella's Prince, "no frustration is more keen . . . [than] when the one thing you want is a thing that you've not yet seen."

As I first knew them, these figures were harbingers of good and evil, right and wrong, justice and injustice. I could trust that their purpose in life, if not self consciously known, was indubitably known by the omniscient narrator—the knower of all things. This narrator explains that these are people unfamiliar with, and ill equipped for, making decisions. Filled with arrogant, self certainty, he proclaims the necessity of his place as objective observer, his essential function of always remaining outside, never part, of the story. Anticipating the growing desperation of his fellow characters, this narrator warns that if he is "dragged into this mess . . . [they'll] never know how your story ends." In other words, it will become a world of chaos; they will have to tell their own stories.

The ever–present narrator outlives his usefulness, and by communal decision, becomes the sacrificial offering to the murdered giant's enraged wife. Now these characters are clothed in ambiguity, their motives are mixed; even their plot lines, neatly set out as self contained vignettes in the beginning, become intertwined, even jumbled by the end.

This play provokes laughter. It scrambles the mythical topography of my childhood and leaves its ending unfinished. Yet, it is strangely comforting. How can this be? Sondheim has captured a particular slice of American cultural reality. Through the use of stories, known virtually to all generations in our culture, he reveals a dimension of our postmodern world[2]—namely, the future isn't what it used to be! Within our moment in history, ambiguity looms large; the sources from which we have drawn meaning and sustenance are fraying and even threadbare.[3]

Into the Woods provides for its audience a visual and auditory feast, the sounds and sights of which linger long after its performance has concluded, precisely because it is a kind of visual and musical metaphor for the condition of what William Dean has termed our spiritual culture.[4] Spiritual culture incorporates all those public dimensions of thought, behavior, emotion, and language that express the most basic *raison d'etre* of a society. It is the contextual whole out of which pragmatic guides and motivations for action are drawn.

In this understanding, the religious is a people's sense of the whole of the world and their place within this whole; it offers a mythic standpoint from which to gain a sense of the whole. Of relevance for Unitarian Universalist theology is Dean's conviction that interpretations of the whole contribute to, that is, change our experience of the whole. Interpretation does not simply reflect what is "out there"; it bears a dynamic relationship to the reality it attempts to describe.

The spiritual culture to which Sondheim and Dean address themselves is that shifting, even vanishing, consensually experienced sense of the whole that also haunts liberal religionists. We grapple with the absence of shared visions, the mounting sense of anomie and pessimism, the suspicion of intellectual elitism, and the despair over building community in the midst of profound difference and otherness. Those of us who are inclined to find solace in theological and philosophical languages interpret American spiritual culture as postmodern. Such a term suggests the fragmenting and fracturing character of this period, in which reliance on the traditional voices of authority (whether scientific or theological) is dying or already deceased. The very possibility of speaking of "the whole" is itself suspect. Yet as religious people we do, albeit in what sounds at times more like a cacophony of voices.

We are a religious community of searchers and seekers; questing for some truth, some vision of the whole of life that will sustain us in our journey. We are thoroughly historical; our truths are discovered in history. There is no final, transhistorical arbiter standing outside of history to whom we can appeal. Truths about ourselves, about people, about the world evolve out of our engagement with each other and the world. The purposiveness of our human community is known only through our immersion in the daily ambiguities of living.

Most of us tread cautiously in the realm of "God language," often as much out of a fear of being identified with the conservative edge of Christianity as out of a well articulated understanding of what is lacking for us in such language. We have, for all intents and purposes, given over to the conservative (and even moderate) sectors of Christianity the domain of theological language, opting instead for languages taken from secular disciplines. In reaction to the sometimes deafening chorus of (the postmodern, post-structural, post-feminist, post Christian) voices, many American religious traditions have sought security in the return to tradition, attempting to resurrect solid foundations capable of weathering the "post" storm whirling through our cultural landscape. At best, this is a dubious project of wanting to return to the idealized safety of home.

Unitarian Universalism is an unabashedly American movement: a hybrid species rather than a transplant from a foreign soil. Our movement has been inextricably intertwined with the tumultuous development of this country. Our religious character is indubitably American. By this I mean that there is a kind of optimism, an attitude of unlimited possibilities even in the face of contrary realities. The risk of this attitude is vertigo (the dizzying reality of too many choices and not enough structure or limits). Less dramatically put, it can lead to the absence of content in our allegiance to process and our fear of premature foreclosure. Our principle of free inquiry in matters religious provides an ever evolving meeting ground on which we come together. It is our movement's burden, as well as its strength, to hold in creative tension the ambiguities of our differences and otherness.[5]

Whereas other religious movements, as largely immigrant populations, have struggled over the seeming contradiction of being American and religious,[6] our story has been different. Our history[7] has been more that of the carrier of significant American myths, both those that have encouraged exclusivity and exceptionalism as well as democratizing myths. We have been, in microcosm, a mirror of the dominant American myths and how they have been told.[8] There are irresolvable ironies in our historical stance as a religious movement. We frequently stand at the social, political, and cultural margins; and yet, as a largely white, educated, middle-class movement, we stand squarely in the American socio-political-cultural center, benefiting from this position in untold ways.

Unitarian Universalism as a religious movement is, par excellence, a creature of modernity. Modern theology's search for the universal across histories and cultures, for a wisdom untainted by particularities, has characterized the elan of our movement. Theodore Parker, in his sermon, "The Transient and Permanent in Christianity," embodies this modernist theological quest. This pursuit is driven by the desire to discover what is universal within history, with the aim of moral improvement in accordance with universal truths. This search for universals can be a refusal to live in the particulars of one's life. There has been, for Unitarian Universalists, a kind of searching for absolutes as if they are simply out there to be unearthed, (e.g., looking to foreign lands as if wisdom is better discerned on distant shores).

Our movement's public history bears the imprint of this rational pursuit of religious truth, a venture analogous to the intellectual pursuit of scientific knowledge. Its tenor and tone is distinctively formed by the lingering impact of the Enlightenment, particularly in its conferring of sacrality to the autonomy of the individual, its deep faith in reason,[9] its abiding belief in human goodness, and its nearly visceral distrust of authority (especially as it is externally imposed). Also inherited from our Enlightenment legacy is a discomfort with the chaotic and ambiguous. We prefer light over darkness, clarity and singularity of purpose over an inductive meandering toward understanding. Our ways of knowing and perceiving what is real continue to reflect these Enlightenment sensibilities.

Subtly excluded in this inherited Enlightenment legacy are ways of knowing and being identified as characteristic of women's experiencing, in their cultural associations with embodiment, nurturance, physicality, and relationality. Our movement continues to struggle, as does the larger culture in which it is rooted, with the patriarchal ordering of reality: a reality determined through separation, division, and dominance.

Parker's question was one of what was worthy of reclaiming; in sifting through the transient, the particulars, what remained to guide our future? Elsewhere, Parker voiced his own exasperation with Unitarianism as having a history of failed opportunities to open itself as a mass movement. This failure is, I believe, linked to our resistance to grapple with particulars, our aversion to getting messy in the muddy ambiguities of immediate struggles. We are inclined to hold out, instead, for pristine truths known in their clarity and to rely on an overly narrow understanding of reason, to the exclusion of other modes of knowing grounded in relationality.

This moment in history provokes a different question, not that of what are the universals to be retrieved. The quest for universals has run aground in its inability to embrace otherness, difference that is not just a mirror image of oneself. One sees signs of its demise in the bankruptcy of a humanism, uncorrected for sexism, racism, and homophobia, and in the crumbling of modern and neo-orthodox theologies in their return to universals. Now the questions are of particulars, of what is transformational. What frees individuals in community for that which is life-giving? What facilitates the building of communities that are prototypes, not archetypes, in a world that is desperate for care, sustenance, relationality, and physicality? What sources of theological understanding carry the seeds for "communities that bless specificity, difference, solidarity, embodiment, anticipation, and transformation"[10] and yet engage postmodern sensibilities.

Having set out some of the tangled threads of our spiritual culture, I'm tempted to follow Sondheim's lead and rest, without offering guides with which to sift through this maze. Sondheim, in his theatrical mode, does offer a path to follow. It is a path grounded in the urgent necessities of the life crises of his characters. In the dynamic encounters between the desires and choices of these characters and the intervening forces of circumstance and nature, new understandings unfold. Likewise, our survival and flourishing as an American religious movement requires our willingness to publicly reclaim our constructive task of the continuous revisioning of theology. This task of revisioning must corporately engage the very postmodern sensibilities that cause us to question our future as a religious movement.[11] We cannot afford the laziness of denial, the leisure of naiveté, nor the pessimism of nihilism.

Our public theology, if it is transformational, needs to listen closely to the creative and critical voices of feminist and womanist theologies. Their many contributions to cultural analysis as well as their contemporary efforts to articulate the diversity of women's experience has not yet made its way into the canons of our denomination. The task of developing a public theology, while building on the historical currents that gave form to our religious movement, requires us to articulate a theology whose evolving authority rests within the relational matrices of meaning which underlie our communities of discourse. These relational realities compose our religious identity.

I believe that the legacies we choose to nurture are discovered by delving deeply and mindfully into the relational processes that hold us together. It is our task to find the metaphors, the sacred language, adequate to gently hold our stories. May we, with our unfinished stories, be able to patiently listen, confidently tell, and graciously hold the sacred whole that rests in the space between us.

After the Apocalypse

Rebecca Parker

In 1841 Theodore Parker saw that things pass away, and new things arise. In the midst of the flux of things religious—theological doctrine, polity, ritual practices—he felt confident there was something that was permanent, something that did not pass away. This Eternal Truth might manifest itself in particular and transient guises within time and place, but its essence was permanent.

He wrote in "The Transient and Permanent in Christianity": "The words of Christianity have come down to us from the lips of that Hebrew youth, gentle and beautiful as the light of a star, not spent by their journey through time and through space. . . . Through centuries of wasting, these words have flown on, like a dove in the storm, and now wait to descend on hearts pure and earnest. . . ."

Parker claimed that what endures, received as a gift, and sanctioned by the intuitions and instincts of the human heart, is this one, simple truth: God is. "The great truth which springs up spontaneous in the holy heart—there is a God."

From the perspective of the late twentieth century, Parker's confidence in absolute truth is one of the things that has passed away. Even as early as 1859, the great Unitarian institutionalist Henry Whitney Bellows in his address *The Suspense of Faith* characterized his time as a season of doubt, "despondency, self-questioning, and anxiety." And, in 1867 Matthew Arnold would write in *Dover Beach*,

> . . . the world, which seems
> To lie before us like a land of dreams. . . .
> Hath really neither joy, nor love, nor light,
> Nor certitude, nor peace, nor help for pain….

Our time is skeptical of absolute truth claims. We politely allow another to hold whatever views are held, not out of tolerance or humility, but because our basic faith is that there is no truth with a capital "T".

Universal, eternal truths, have been scuttled in post-modern, post-structuralist intellectual circles. The dominant understanding of our time is radically historical. The Greek image of eternal essences that appear in accidental guises within the flux of history has been abandoned. In its place is a vivid relativism, which insists that attention be on the particulars of time, place, gender, race, culture, social placement, and land. Difference, particularity, uniqueness—these are the foci of scholarly research and reflection in religious studies and theology.

In a radically historical understanding of existence, we are responsible for what abides and what is lost. There are no eternal givens. Even "human nature" is a construct, shaped by history and place. In other words, Parker's "truth which springs up spontaneous in the heart" is not an eternally given quality of the human soul, it is a gift of human history and culture. Whether it abides depends on whether and how we receive this gift, and whether and how we pass it on.

Surprisingly, Parker's exploration of the transient and the permanent is not altogether incompatible with this point. The most startling claim Parker makes is not his confidence that God exists, but his view of how this truth is sanctioned. It is sanctioned by instinct and intuition—not by the rational mind considering evidence, not by the authority of Jesus as the Revelation of God, not by the authority of the church's doctrine handed down generation to generation, and not by the authority of scripture. The light comes from human beings.

Perhaps Parker can be interpreted as one who is less interested in defending an Aristotelian concept of essence and accident, than he is in presenting human beings as creators of religion. What is "eternal" is the religion-making activity—its products (doctrine, ritual, church structures, etc.) vary from place to place and time to time. The activity of religion-making persistently appears in every time and place—just as does the making of language, the making of music and dance and art, the making of economic systems, the making of educational systems, and the making of family.

Whereas "Parkerism" tended toward an ahistorical, non-contextual understanding of religious experience that cut Unitarians loose from acknowledging a link between religious experience and tradition/body/place/community, one can also read Parker as pointing toward an affirmation that religious experience arises within the body—the realm of instinct, emotion, and felt intuitions, rather than the realm of mind in some elevated, abstract, or dryly rational functioning. He turns our attention to desire, longing, love, fear, the experience of being moved. I think we would do well to take from Parker this sense of "givenness" and "embeddedness" in feeling and this recognition of ourselves as creators of religion from *our felt experience.*

It is in our hands to shape the liberal tradition. The heritage will be influenced by our reflection and our active commitment to the ideas, ideals, and values we choose to receive, salvage, forge, and pass on.

It matters that we attend critically to our tradition and seek to discern consciously what is at stake in the conflicts, cross-currents, and challenges of our time. It matters that we make religion out of the "givenness" and "embeddedness" of our experience. We must move by feel, move in our bodies, taking seriously our longings, passions, sentiments, intuitions, fears, and desires.

Among the various cross–currents of this moment in history are two that capture my full attention. One is the deep conflict between the religious left and the religious right in North America. What is at stake here? The second is a deeper reality this split points to: the breakdown of modernity in the West and the post-apocalyptic character of the present age. What is the religious task for us, in our time?

Theodore Parker said the words of Jesus "reveal to us the presence of God, which else we might not have seen so clearly in the first wind-flower of spring, in the falling of a sparrow, in the distress of a nation; in the sorrow or the rapture of the world." Parker was confident that this sense of the presence of God was the essence of human religious feeling, the permanent pulse of Christianity. But what Parker felt was permanent is what, in my mind, is most fragile within Unitarian Universalism and the most under attack within current American Christianity.

The present American religious scene is characterized by deep conflicts between the religious left and the religious right. The conflict has been character-ized in the language of religious war by Patrick Buchanan. Robert Wuthnow calls it "The Struggle for America's Soul" in a book of that title. Others are speaking of culture wars.

This conflict is not a matter of abstract ideas, politely debated in academic classrooms, town halls, and church meetings. It is a matter of flesh and blood. Lives are threatened, and some have been lost. Power is being wielded with a heavy hand, and fear is rising. In Pensacola, Florida, a Unitarian Universalist was shot to death while serving as a protective escort for a doc-tor who performs abortions in a Florida abortion clinic. The religious right opposes abortion, the reli-gious left affirms it. Religious liberals have risked their lives to defend the sacredness of women's bodies, and women's right to self-determination. The sacredness of the unborn and a woman's duty to fulfill her God-ordained vocation of motherhood is being fought for violently by religious conservatives.

In the Midwest an in-the-closet lesbian clergywoman in the United Methodist Church is tailed by members of the conservative Good News Caucus. They photograph her activities, follow her into book-stores and snoop out the titles of books she has pur-chased. They bring charges against her, calling for her dismissal from the ministry. A week after the denomi-nation votes to reaffirm its ban on the ordination of out-of-the-closet lesbians and gays, she puts a gun in her own mouth and pulls the trigger.

Two thousand people, mostly women, gather in Minneapolis, called together in response to the World Council of Churches Ecumenical Decade in Solidarity with Women. They re-imagine God, Christ, and Church. The keynote speakers are women of color: Mercy Ouduye from Africa, Hyung-Kyung Chung from Korea, Rita Nakashima Brock and Bernice Johnson Reagon from the United States. Women's bodies are celebrated as the dwelling place of the divine. A ritual is performed with these words,

> *Our mother Sophia, we are women in your image:*
> *With the milk of our breasts we suckle the children;*
> *With the knowledge of our hearts we feed*
> *humanity. . .*
> *With nectar between our thighs we invite a lover,*
> *we birth a child;*
> *With our warm body fluids we remind the world of*
> *its pleasures and sensations.*
> *With our moist mouths we kiss away a tear,*
> *we smile encouragement.*
> *With the honey of wisdom in our mouths,*
> *we prophesy a full humanity to all the peoples.*
> (from the re-imagining conference publication
> November 4-7, 1993)

After the conference, leaders of the religious right within the United Methodist Church and the

Presbyterian Church call the event heretical and advocate the mass withholding of financial contributions to the denomination. Several million dollars are withheld in the Presbyterian church. Mary Ann Lundy, Director of the Women's Ministry unit for the Presbyterian Church (USA) and co-chair of the US Committee on the Ecumenical Decade, is fired by the Presbyterian church.

These conflicts, according to Robert Wuthnow, represent something new in the American religious scene. Although the nineteenth century saw splits develop over slavery, over the power of the laity and the rights of women, and over fine points of doctrine, and although the end of the nineteenth century saw the rise of fundamentalism as a protest against modernity, the nineteenth century was predominantly marked by a theological consensus which was evangelical Christianity.

Evangelical Christianity was liberal: progressive, activist, reform oriented, supportive of women's rights, Arminian not Calvinist in its view of human nature. Revivalism was liberal. Liberalism was the mainstream. Reactions to the dominant liberal mainstream began in the late nineteenth century with the rise of fundamentalism and its reactions to modernity. Fundamentalism was matched by its sophisticated cousin, neo-orthodoxy, which protested the confidence in human beings sported by evangelical/liberal Christianity with its do-good/can-do, reform-oriented optimism.

By the mid-twentieth century, liberal Protestantism had been chastened by neo-orthodoxy, but a progressive left wing remained. Liberal Protestantism was healthy enough to contribute to the civil rights movement. White liberals responded to the leadership of Martin Luther King, Jr., who himself found some of his inspiration in the liberal theology of Walter Rauchenbusch, Boston Personalism, and Henry Nelson Wieman.

In the 1950s the lines of religious conflict in America were described by Will Herberg to be between Protestant, Catholic, and Jew; but by 1970 this was no longer the case. What has emerged is a new split that cuts through the heart of American Protestantism, American Catholicism, and possibly American Judaism. The split is between the religious left and the religious right. Between the two sides, there are deep hostilities and misgivings. National Council of Churches official Peggy L. Shriver characterizes the split this way: "Liberals abhor the smugness, the self-righteousness, the absolute certainty, the judgmentalism, the lovelessness of a narrow, dogmatic faith. [Conservatives] scorn the fuzziness, the marshmallow convictions, the inclusiveness that makes membership meaningless—the 'anything goes' attitude that views even Scripture as relative."

Sociologist of religion Robert Wuthnow reports that the categories "religious liberal" and "religious conservative" are familiar enough to Americans that most people were willing to identify themselves as one or the other in a 1984 national survey by Gallup. In that poll 43 percent characterized themselves as liberal (with 19 percent as "very liberal") and 41 percent characterized themselves as conservative (with 18 percent "very conservative").

On the right we have fundamentalists, evangelicals, and religious conservatives. On the left we have religious liberals and radicals, humanists, and secularists. The conflicts between these two camps are fierce, and they center on homosexuality, the rights of women, and the authority of the Bible.

What to make of this conflict? Harvey Cox says it represents competing responses to the collapse of modernity. Religious radicals and religious conservatives, according to Cox in *Beyond the Secular City*, are each struggling to bring the resources of religious tradition to bear in the face of the collapse of modernity.

Liberation theology interprets the movements of our time as God's liberating work to dismantle structures of oppression and injustice and bring about new possibilities for human communities of justice and love. This interpretation is at the heart of the radical left: gay liberation theology, feminist theology, black, womanist, mujerista, miyung, and Latin American liberation theology. God is the divine disturber/trickster/liberator who disrupts and deconstructs the established world and breaks through into new life and new justice.

Neo-evangelical theology and fundamentalism interpret the chaos of the present time as an escalating threat to traditional values, already threatened by the nineteenth-century developments in American religion. To those on the right, the religious task in the midst of cultural breakdown is to preserve a remnant of faithfulness to what was threatened by modernity (a religion of dependence, trust, receptivity, and obedience) and is being threatened afresh by the breakdown of modernity, which is modernity in the extreme. Post-modernity, from the conservative perspective, is hyper-modernity: relativism, secularism, valuelessness, change for the sake of change, loss of tradition and roots.

The rise of the religious right is interpreted by the religious left as a backlash against progress: resistance to feminists and womanists; people of color; lesbians, gays, and bisexual people; and an effort to preserve the old world order. The rise of the religious right is interpreted by itself as a bid to preserve human values of family, connection to land and tradition, obedience to something greater than oneself, intuition, feeling, emotion, and trust, in the face of a dominant culture that assaults these values in an increasingly chaotic way.

What I have learned through sustained engagement with the religious right in church battles over homosexuality, women, and biblical interpretation is that in each arena of conflict what is at issue is religious authority. For the conservatives authority is derived from the transcendent God, revealed in Scripture. For the liberals, authority emerges from human experience, both individual witness to religious experience, and communal experience in the immediate life of the church and in the experience of the religious community over time.

There is a contrasting religious sensibility at work. For the liberals, the deep religiosity is that God is present in human life. Liberalism is grounded in a spirituality of incarnation: "God is with us." This is the foundation for asserting that the human experience of homosexual practice as loving, committed, and life-enhancing should have authority in the church—that what we know from our experience should take precedence over any rigid reading of the letter of the law. This is the foundation for asserting the ordination of women: that God is present in human life regardless of gender, and women and men can testify to this presence and witness it in their lives.

The spirituality grounded in a sense of God's presence in life as an active, intimate, free Spirit within us is what is being fiercely battled by the religious right. Claim to religious authority that derives from a confidence in human religious experience of God's action in history is what is been strategically denied. The religious experience of women; people of color; and lesbians, gays, and bisexuals is being contested.

Parker's claim that a sense of God's presence is a permanent and universal religious sensibility is belied by the events of our time: It is a sensibility that can be neglected and a sensibility that can be actively attacked.

In the present context of mainstream American religion, those who operate out of this sensibility are under attack. Unitarian Universalists, for the most part, align themselves in support of lesbians and gays and women and men of color who are claiming their power to speak out of their religious experience. But are we willing to align ourselves religiously? Do we share their faith that God is, and that God is with us? Do we claim Parker's faith that the word of God is written in the human heart? Has Parker's confidence passed away in our Association? Are we willing to savor and sustain in our religious communities a faith we may have neglected? Should we?

Do we have this faith? Or, are we, as my colleague Ron Cook has so tenderly articulated it, the people who are, at heart, deeply conflicted over whether or not we can say the everlasting yea, can rest trustfully in the arms of God's love?

Is faith in part a gift of heritage and tradition that might be lost? To what extent does its power in the world depend on the sustenance of religious solidarity and community when its individual prophets are martyred? To what extent does it require faithful embodiment in institutional forms to be a transforming and blessing sensibility in human society? Where are Unitarian Universalists in this struggle? Are we willing to be active in a society that is deeply torn over the liberating presence of God?

Are we willing to lay claim to our roots in an incarnational and prophetic faith as James Luther Adams has called us to do? Or do we cling to faith in universal human religiosity that ignores its own best insight: human beings are the dwelling place of God, and this is the foundation of our freedom.

Given Harvey Cox's analysis that the deep conflict between the left and the right represents competing responses to the breakdown of modernity, what is the religious task in our time? On the one hand, I would suggest that we see clearly the way in which the experience of the holy in the midst of human experience is being asserted in our time by women, women and men of color, sexual minorities, and the poor. I believe we should align ourselves religiously with these movements—supporting them by what we teach in our theological schools, with our financial resources, with ecumenical efforts in local situations, with hospitality to the battle-weary in our communities, and with an evangelistic clarity that our faith affirms the presence of the divine in human experience.

Let me be more specific: If the gay Lutheran pastor in your town is forced to resign by the synod, organize your congregation to serve a meal to the congregation in grief. Invite the defrocked pastor to speak. If Mary Ann Lundy is fired for her leadership in the Ecumenical Decade, write a letter of support to her. Resist the temptation to bash Christians when you preach or speak out against the religious right. Discriminate between the Christian Right and the liberal or radical Christians who are being actively opposed. Communicate our common religious faith with people who are affirming in their lives and their theology that God is with us, in the flesh and blood of this life. Be presumptuous enough to speak for radical and liberal Christianity as *our faith*, and defend it.

I believe we need to let go of the religious myth that imagines a new world coming and face more honestly the conditions of cultural breakdown that we are in the midst of. As we face the new millennium, I believe we would be wise to draw on the apocalyptic myth to locate ourselves in time, not as people waiting for the overthrow of the present world order and the birth of the new, but as people living in the aftermath of apocalypse. I think our attention needs to be on seeing the marks of past violence in our personal and collective experience, and recognizing the degree of breakdown of "old world orders" around us.

In the aftermath of apocalypse, what is the religious enterprise? I think it can be imagined as a kind of salvage work. If we see ourselves as scavengers among the ruins of a collapsing civilization, our task becomes recognizing the resources that sustain and restore life that are in our midst and ready to hand.

We accept our dependence on sources of life greater than ourselves and open our hearts to receive survival knowledge from those who have found restoration. We know ourselves to be living in a time of breakdown and breakthrough, chaos and creativity, fragmentation and resourcefulness, pain and grace. Our task includes tending to injury in ourselves and others, collecting resources buried in the rubble and ruin, and constructing shelters for body and spirit, family and community.

I believe we face a new millennium from the context of a dominant culture in collapse. Ours is a time of chaos and creativity. Modern, Western society is a decadent, failing culture whose gestures in the throes of breakdown include backlash against the forces of its demise (women, people of color, sexual minorities); genocidal performances to assert control and dominance (the Persian Gulf War); reactionary efforts to respond to chaos, fear, confusion, and despair in major institutions (public education, the criminal justice system); nostalgia and denial (the Reagan years). The standard litany of our present crisis laments rising crime and violence, changing patterns of family life that leave many children in poverty, the sense of economic stagnation, personal despair and spiritual hunger, lack of commitment to the common good, the persistence of racism, and the anxiety created by an unsustainable global economic system that involves severe discrepancies between the rich minority and the poor majority along with exploitation of the environment.

At the same time that some things are breaking down in our society, there are arenas of great vitality and freshness. Creativity in the arts—film, music, poetry, drama—is flourishing. New movements in religion and spirituality (the recovery movements and women's spirituality movements come to mind) seem to be blossoming. Academic scholarship is bursting with the freshness and power of contributions from women and men of color and white feminists. Computer technology, advancing at breathtaking speed, characterized often by a spirit of whimsy and play, is opening up new patterns of human connection in hyper-space. Cross-cultural encounters and counterculture movements are moving new possibilities into the mainstream in medicine, business practices, religion, and the arts.

Efforts to feel and see our time whole are overwhelming and intoxicating. Living in these times I feel the simultaneous presence of violence, chaos, breakdown, loss, creativity, liberation, new possibilities, recovery, hope, isolation, despair, connection, empowerment. While some things are being actively dismantled, others are being actively created. While some things seem to be self-destructing on their own, proving Whitehead's claim that evil is finally always unsustainable, others seem to be evolving in an effulgence of creativity (MTV, virtual reality, genetic engineering, special effects cartoon violence in the movies) without planning, intentionality, or adequate ethical reflection.

Generally, the present culture overwhelms one with a sense of tremendous speed and out–of–controlness. The culture feels like it is on a binge, on a manic, wild ride. "Stop the world; I want to get off" seems more and more like a sane response, and the search for manageability leads many to smaller and smaller spheres of activity. Tribal enclaves become increasingly attractive, and when you venture downtown you enter a public square filled with mass media displays, garbage, boarded-up storefronts, newspaper headlines reporting violence, rap music booming high-energy despair, blockbuster movies trading on murder sprees, and homeless people asking for handouts.

Our ability to move in an engaged and creative way in our current context may be hampered or enhanced by our religious myths. It has been typical of liberals to live from the perspective of an apocalyptic myth that imagines that the world as it is known will come to an end and a new age will dawn. In the most vivid forms of this religious myth, the end of the old world comes violently, a cataclysm wrought by God, or God's angels. Evil is vanquished, and from the rubble of destruction a new creation materializes. The liberal version of apocalyptic imagination skips the violent parts—death comes naturally, an organic, acceptable process of transformation, an inevitable by-product of evolutionary progress, as life unfolds into greater forms of beauty and justice.

That the old evil will pass away and the new world will be born remains hope's favorite scenario. Apocalyptic imagination sees breakdown in the future and lives in a present that is dominated by an existing world order that is in the way of what one hopes for. In our time, apocalyptic imagination in the liberal mode has identified the dangerous Dominant World Order, the Evil Empire, in various ways: patriarchy, capitalism, institutional racism, fundamentalist Christianity, Western civilization, heterosexism, etc. I have done my share of positing Evil Empires and feeling that hope is to be found in an exodus from this oppressive empire, or a dismantling assault on this empire.

I am coming to feel that apocalyptic imagination is hindering our ability to see the world we are actually in. Apocalypse may not be ahead of us. It may, instead, be behind us, and happening around us and within us now.

We are living now in a post-slavery, post-holocaust, post-Vietnam, post-Hiroshima, post-communist world. We are living in the aftermath of collective violence that has been severe, massive, and traumatic. The scars from the sufferings of slavery, genocide, and meaningless war mark our bodies and the bodies of our families. We are living in the midst of rain forest burning, the rapid death of species, the growing pollution of the air and water.

After the Apocalypse

What happens if we stop imagining that there is a cataclysm ahead of us? And turn and see the apocalypse now?

The way I see it, an apocalypse has already occurred. We stand, at present, in a civilization's ruins. The rubble of broken institutions, and maimed lives—including our own—is with us. In my dreams over the past twenty years, the recurring images of the world are post-war images: a city in smoking ruins at twilight, fire-bombed to ashes, and scavengers or resistance conspirators move among the ruins.

There are also waking images of apocalypse: The pictures of slashed and burned forests; gulls drowning in oil, Los Angeles on fire, anguished faces of children orphaned in Rwanda, the fields of genocide in Cambodia and Vietnam, napalmed rice fields, Europe's Jews piled in mass graves, wounded Iranian soldiers buried alive in the sand, the rubble of Nagasaki and Hiroshima.

These are snapshots of apocalypse. They picture a civilization that is dissembling in violence. We are living in the aftermath of violence: What I encounter on a daily basis in my neighborhood is the aftermath of the violence of white supremacy, the violence of economic greed; the violence of lost values; the violence of environmental devastation.

In the traditional religious myth of exodus, one lives within an oppressive dominant order and is called by God to depart on a journey to the promised land.

Salvation comes through departure. The departure may be apocalyptic: The plagues visited upon Egypt eased the escape. The death of Jesus on the Cross, prelude to the dawn of new life, was violent and anguished. The religious person is a pilgrim on the way to another land, a come-outer on a search for God in the wilderness.

But if we alter our religious imagination to place the apocalypse behind us, our religious task shifts. In a city in ruins the task is to walk among the ruins and salvage what can be saved, and gather what resources may be found to reconstruct the city.

This is where I think we should imaginatively situate ourselves. It means imagining the American continent not as a place of frontier and opportunity, but as a land scarred by the tragedy of slavery, home to exiles and refugees who know intimately the price of leaving and the complexity of creating a new life that holds something of the past. These exiles have been in conflict with one another and with those their adventures have displaced, in an ongoing struggle to be a place of liberty, equality, and abundance.

In a post-apocalypse world our religious tasks are threefold.

Truth-telling. We must commit ourselves to paying attention and saying what we see. The religious community, through our preaching, speaking, and writing, must provide a clear-eyed description of the world. We are to be reporters. We are to refuse to close our eyes, we are to resist distracting ourselves with imagined future worlds, or an optimistic religion that places hope in quick-fix sentiments like "we are all one" when what we are actually doing is killing each other.

Salvaging. We must become conservators of history and tradition, identifying those resources for the spirit contained in the wisdom of the world's religious that we can use and making them available to people who have lost them. In the rubble of Descartes and Kant collapsing, and the ruin created by the compulsive duplicity of government, in the confusion of higher education locked into narrow disciplines and competing agendas, we need the Sabbath candles, the house of study, the bread of communion, the silence of sitting, the teachings of Jesus, the poetry of Rumi, the dance of Sufis, the water of baptism, the body-rhythm of gospel singing, the word of prayer, the images of hell, the narratives of the soul's dark night, the cross, the ox-herding pictures.

We must find what needs to be saved, what can be used, and tend to these resources as stewards entrusted with gifts. We must resist stealing them, and learn what gives us the right in any religious tradition to embrace the practice. We must resist squandering them, relinquish being spiritual consumers, or users, who take for selfish reasons, and give nothing back. In the mix of beauty and injustice that marks any religious tradition, we must judge what gives life and what oppresses. We must take our place as appraisers and stewards of religious value. We must see that the work of salvaging involves creating communities that shelter and protect religious tradition, and with generous hospitality make these resources available to a world in ruins.

Choosing our guides. In a post-apocalyptic world guidance is needed from those who have moved beyond victimization and the paralysis of grief or denial into survival. We must look to the voices of those who have found a way to live lives of dignity, depth, honesty, creativity, and activism in the midst of the world's disrespect, superficiality, duplicity, violent redundancy, and passivity. We must take counsel from survivors, resistors, and truth tellers. Here, I think of sources such as African-American women's literature, the experiences of lesbians and gays, the people who have experienced recovery from addiction through twelve-step practices. The guides we need are what William James called the twice-born: people who have grappled with loss and denial, with lies and injustices, and found a way to survive.

A predominant sense that loss has already occurred is what colors the tone of Adrienne Rich's poetry—she is a truth-teller. Tragedy is the starting point in Alice Walker's novel, *The Color Purple,* and Toni Morrison's *Beloved.* These writers create in a context of loss, suffering, marginalization. Their narratives are narratives of survival, restoration, and the attainment of peace.

In a post-apocalyptic world we cannot locate hope in "things not seen," but need tangible witness to survival, just as the disciples did of old. We find it in the lives of those who are present with us, bearing the scars of suffering and survival.

My friend Will Brown survived being a prisoner of war during the Korean war. In the winter, it snowed. At night the prisoners slept on the icy ground, outdoors, with blankets but no other shelter over them. The guards would light a fire and keep watch. Will says you could recognize the prisoners who lost hope. They would go and sleep by the fire. Something about the weakened state they were in, from cold and lack of food, made it impossible for the body to be warmed by the fire and retain its resistance to illness. Those who slept by the fire got sick and died. The ones who had hope slept in the snow and stayed away from the fire. They survived.

In our time, hope means not running away from the icy, hard ground of suffering, violence, injustice, deceit. It also means not walking past the color purple, it means savoring the sweetness of human love, lighting the Sabbath candles, smelling the spices, and opening your heart to the sources of refreshment and grace that are given to us. Survival means working to reconstruct from the ruins we are in, a world of hospitality and peace. It means having to reconstitute the world with no apparent power.

Born of Woman, Born of Earth

Shirley Ann Ranck

———————◆———————

Out of all the thea/ological discussions and debates in liberal religion in the latter half of the twentieth century, I see at least two permanent insights emerging. One is that we are all born of woman. The other is that we are all born of earth. Women have reclaimed the female half of our human religious history and have discovered that it is pagan: It honors woman, and it honors the earth. I am very proud of the fact that Unitarian Universalism has accepted these pagan roots as an important and growing part of our theological diversity and our understanding of who we are as Unitarian Universalists.

As a woman, my religious history is rooted in the ancient pre-patriarchal world when the divine was imaged as a Great Goddess who gave birth to all of creation. Archeologists such as Raphael Patai[1], Rachel Levy[2], and Marija Gimbutas[3] tell us that for many thousands of years human beings worshipped this divine mother. In the words of Joseph Campbell, the Goddess was "a metaphysical symbol: the arch personification of the power of Space, Time and Matter, within whose bounds all beings arise and die.... And everything having form or name...was Her child within Her womb."[4] In Campbell's opinion, "there can be no doubt that in the very earliest ages of human history, the magical force and wonder of the female was no less a marvel than the universe itself and this gave to women a prodigious power."[5]

The male consort of the Goddess, her son-lover, gradually became more and more important and powerful. Mythology tells us that in early historic times Goddesses and Gods reigned together with varying amounts of power. Eventually the male deities became the chief deities. In Judaism and Christianity, the male God became the only deity. I was raised in a culture that assumed that this male monotheism was superior to polytheism. What a marvelous smoke screen to hide the real issue, which was the demise of female divinity!

It is difficult to describe the intense shock of recognition and anger that I felt as a woman at the moment when I realized that in contrast to Christians, who worship a divine father and son, the pilgrims who made their way to Eleusis for 2,000 or more years worshipped a divine mother and daughter. The medium is indeed the message. All the teachings of love and justice in the world could not erase or make up for the stark and overwhelming absence of the divine female in my Protestant Christian upbringing.

Another moment of shock occurred when I came upon a painting of the towering Athena as she may have looked inside the Parthenon. The Parthenon! The most famous temple of all time! Built for the Goddess! Somehow that fact had not registered with me, perhaps had never been emphasized. A tame and patriarchal Goddess, but a Goddess nonetheless, presiding over the glory of ancient Greece.

Pagans they were called, those Greeks and Romans, Minoans and Canaanites, Egyptians and Old Europeans who worshipped Goddesses. As a woman, I need to claim that heritage. I need to know that great civilizations were created by people who worshipped the divine as female. If the myths of a culture reflect its social arrangements, women must have had power and respect. The myths tell us that in very early times the Goddess reigned.

In later times, male deities waged battles against her, tricked her into giving up her power or, if she was very powerful, married her. If the myths of a culture reflect its social arrangements, women must have suffered an overall loss of power and respect. And yet, in the old pagan religions, even after all the battles and the exalting of male deities to the most powerful positions, the Goddesses were still there. Zeus had to ask Themis to convene the deities. Hera married Zeus, but fought him all the way. And it was Athena who stood in the Parthenon. As a woman, I need very much to reclaim my pagan religious roots. I also believe that men as well as women need to know that for many thousands of years of our human heritage God was female.

In Judaism and Christianity there is only the father or the father and son. According to Raphael Patai,[6] Yahweh had a female partner for many centuries, but she has been very effectively edited out of the scriptures. Christianity exalted Mary for a while, but never in Protestantism. If the myths of a culture reflect its social arrangements, we should not be surprised that no woman has been elected president and only six women presently serve in the United States Senate.

There is another reason for all of us to embrace pagan traditions. The earth is in a severe crisis. Our water is polluted, our cities are choking on poisonous smog, the ozone layer has huge holes in it, and our forests are disappearing. Something is terribly wrong with our attitudes toward these life-giving ecosystems. What is the source of such attitudes? Some say the industrial revolution, which cut us off from our agricultural roots, is causing the pollution. But I think that the problem has much deeper, long-standing origins.

Patriarchal societies all over the world have for

centuries promulgated a world view that can be imagined in the form of a ladder. God is at the top, below God are the angels, below them is man, below him is woman, below her are children and below them is the earth, and its other creatures. In this scheme, higher is better, more important and in control of what is below. The material world, the earth, and even our own bodies have been seen as inferior to an imaginary supernatural realm where some nonmaterial part of us may go after death if we will just obey the authority above us. The divine in this view resides in the supernatural realm, not in the material world.

The biblical tradition gave man dominion over the earth as well as over women and children. Humanists lopped off God and the angels from the top of the ladder, but left the rest of the image in place. We have all learned to look upon the earth as a bundle of resources at the bottom of the ladder, resources to be exploited. Such a world view undergirds the development of industries that pollute and human relationships that degrade and exploit. It condones and encourages the use of force. It generates resentment, hatred, and war. How? Those at the top of the ladder are raised to believe that they have to fight to control everyone and everything below them on the ladder. Those below feel resentment or participate in their own degradation by believing themselves to be inferior.

The old religions revered the earth, just as they revered a woman's body as the giver and sustainer of life. The most ancient Greek deity was Gaia, or Earth. The world view was more of a cycle or spiral. Death was a natural part of life, and the material bodies of the dead, as well as their spirits, were thought to become part of the stones, the hills, the wind. As the song "Breaths" says, "The dead are not under the earth, they are in the rustling trees, they are in the groaning woods, they are in the crying grass, they are in the moaning rocks.... They are in the woman's breast, they are in the wailing child, they are with us in the home, they are with us in the crowd."[7] Such a concept of death seems more and more appealing as we reject the supernaturalism of our Western religions.

In the pagan religions the divine was immanent as well as transcendent. Rocks and hills and rivers and trees were understood to be alive with energy. Sophia Fahs pointed out many years ago that our scientists have now learned that "the dividing line between the living and the nonliving is no longer clear. Matter, once thought to be something to be touched and seen, is now believed to be energy at rest. Energy is found to be matter in excessive motion. Energy-matter is electrical. In every area of research we soon get to the intangible and the invisible, which is nevertheless part of the material world.... The universe as a whole may be alive."[8] As human beings, we need to climb down from the ladder and join in the circle—not only of all humans, but of all life.

Paganism offers us a world view that is in keeping with another aspect of our scientific knowledge: the universe as "self-governed and self-regulating, interrelated and interacting to the farthest reaches of space-time."[9] Western religion has instead seen the cosmos as controlled by an almighty personal being. Even the concept of world community has been one of conquest and dominion—the "good" winning out over and destroying the "bad" and establishing a kingdom of righteousness. In the words of Sophia Fahs, "The natural order resembles a democracy more than a kingdom, a balanced interdependence better described as cooperation."[10] Starhawk points out that scientists now have conferences on the Gaia hypothesis (that the Earth is alive) without acknowledging that this is what witches and shamans have been saying for thousands of years."[11]

Paganism also suggests a different story of our origins and of our future. Brian Swimme[12] points out that twentieth-century physicists have actually discovered the very origin of all things. Then he compares the responses of scientists with the response of a pagan. The scientists called the theory "Big Bang" and found it "abhorrent." They used images of exploding bombs to describe the process. Faced with the same information, Starhawk, a pagan, writes: "Out of the point, the swelling, out of the swelling, the egg, out of the egg, the fire, out of the fire, the stars."[13] Swimme comments, "Not bombs, not explosions, not abhorrence; rather, she sees the event for what it is, a birthing moment, the Great Birth. The elementary particles rushed apart in their trillion degree heat, yes, and became stars, yes, and all of this is a swelling, an egg, a mysterious engendering that is the root reality behind all the various facts. To miss the reality of birth in these scientific facts is to miss everything."

In considering the myths of the future that inform our society, Catherine Keller[14] quotes from the book of Revelations: "Then the seventh angel poured his bowl on the air; and out of the sanctuary came a loud voice from the throne, which said 'It is over!' And there followed flashes of lightening and peals of thunder, and a violent earthquake, like none before it in human history, so violent it was." (Rev. 16:17)

Keller points out that the nuclear and ecological threats are manifestations of "the unchecked power of the military/industrial establishment, subliminally inspired and justified by apocalyptic assumptions of an end of history." She comments that we have been "pre-programmed by ancient visions to expect that when the going gets rough, the world will go." She goes on to say that we need a new vision, a spirituality that imagines an open and sustainable future.[15] Keller then suggests that we need a new full concept of time, a helical time, and that we might look to earth-centered sources for such a concept. We do not need a new heaven and earth. We need to come home to our own bodies and our own earth.

I believe that the most significant thea/ological

change in our liberal religion in the latter part of the twentieth century was the addition of a new principle to our agreed-upon Unitarian Universalist Principles and Purposes. It is the one that says that we affirm "the interdependent web of all existence of which we are a part." If we do indeed act upon that principle, we will be subverting every form of arrogance and oppression and exploitation of human beings and the earth. I hope we will also add earth-based traditions to the list of our sources of inspiration.

People often ask me why it is necessary to use the word pagan. Why not just say earth-based religion or some other nonthreatening term? My answer is that pagan makes a larger demand and holds forth a larger vision. We could stay up there on the ladder with all of our hierarchies in place and plead the cause of caring for the earth, of being better, if just as arrogant stewards of our resources. We might improve our environment that way for a while, but the arrogance and the model of dominance and submission as a way of life would be untouched. The real source of our problem, the patriarchal model of obedience to authority, would remain to trouble us again and again.

Paganism offers us something more. That more flows from the notion of the divine as immanent, and it has implications for human relationships as well as for our relationship to the earth. "Thou art Goddess," the pagan says, "Thou art God." The divine resides in female and in male, in the earth itself, and in both sides of all the splits and barriers we have erected. Unitarian Universalist pagans meet in circles that include the ancestors and the elements of nature. Pagans share leadership, teaching each other the necessary skills. Paganism offers us power—not dominance as we have learned to define power, but personal strength.

Reclaiming the ancient pagan myths of female power is absolutely necessary if we are to look with clear eyes at our own society with its male dominance and its authoritarian structure. The very ancient forms of power appear not to have been matriarchal, that is, a reverse of the patriarchal system, but rather more of a sharing of power and responsibility. Today we know that a healthy sense of one's own power causes a person to have less need for domination over others. We know that the patriarchal need to dominate is a symptom of insecurity and a lack of healthy personal power. In the pre-patriarchal world where power apparently was shared, peace reigned.

Paganism offers us more than an imperative to clean up the mess we have made of the earth. It offers us personal power, a circle of shared power, a deep sense of respect and connectedness with the earth and its creatures, and the prospect of real peace, within and among us.

Ideas That Can Save the World

Roy Reynolds

During my seminary days a professor replied to some issues I was raising in a class by saying, "Roy, we're not trying to save the world."

My response was quick. "Speak for yourself. You may not be, but I am." That was why I had left another profession to study for the ministry. I felt at the time that the earth was tugging me into her service. The passion that burned in me was, literally, to help save the world.

The needs of the earth remain the larger context for ministry and continue to shape my ministry. They may not be the framing context for every clergyperson's ministry. Many needs call us into service. But the larger context of the earth is the lens through which we must look if we are to address the issues our children will have to face. Now is the time to take seriously the questions of survival of life on this planet, while we can still do something significant to help.

I believe that the threat to nature posed by our modern civilization is the primary problem facing humanity. We are consuming energy and natural resources at increasing rates. Our desires continue unabated, to control nature for our purposes. We are destroying the atmosphere and our water supply. The costs of environmental damage are not acknowledged in our economic accounts. Interest in addressing such concerns in the national forum remains peripheral.

I hope we, as Unitarian Universalists, will rise to the challenge. Over the next decade our faith will be tested. We will have to face some difficult questions. Are we willing to adopt an ethic giving priority to environmental justice? Will we embrace nature as a full partner and include other species of animals and plants in our understanding of community? Will we change our beliefs radically enough to critique our foundational Enlightenment heritage? And critique as well our naive faith in the primacy of "objective knowledge?" Can we acknowledge and own the whole of our humanness, including our unconscious? Can we affirm Heisenberg's paradox of uncertainty? Are we willing to envision our faith as a gift to the world, with its lived ideals of multicultural diversity, empowerment through partnership, social justice, authentic community, and, most urgently, ecological sustainability?

How we ministers respond matters extremely. We are listened to by, and in dialogue with, some of the key leaders of our society. Among our children are many future leaders. We must match the challenge with vision and prophetic passion. Recall from your studies the power in the messages of the Hebrew prophets. Who among us is Amos? Elijah? Jeremiah? We need that kind of passionate preaching on the fundamental threats to our survival, naming the culprits, calling for changes, and stirring our people to action. If we preach so from our pulpits and follow up with community involvement, provide parallel programs of education for adults and children, and model our concerns in the ways we do our church business and build and maintain our properties, we shall make a significant difference. If we do these things, we can change ourselves, our congregations, and society in ways that will move us toward saving the world.

That is my apocalyptic message and call to action. But no apocalypse is worth its salt unless it contains a message of hope. I do detect some promising signs on the horizon, powerful ideas reshaping science and the human imagination. Ideas are powerful. Think of the influence of the ideas of freedom, justice, and love, not only on our liberal faith, but on much of humanity. But Western civilization has lacked comparably powerful ideas linking humanity with nature's processes. As a result we view ourselves as separate from nature and somehow ruling it.

Links are now being made. Ideas emerging over the past few decades in science and philosophy show considerable promise. In recent years they have begun to bear fruit. These ideas have the potential to reframe human experience into a more benign relationship with nature. I offer to the conversation shaping the future of Unitarian Universalist ministry a summary of some key ideas pregnant with promise.

Ideas emerging in science and philosophy since the 1920s amount to a reimaging of nature. Quantum physics was the first big one. It opened up to science the realm of subatomic, or particle physics, and began to replace the billiard ball mechanics of classical physics as an explanation of the basic structure of nature. Quantum reality defies our commonsense notions. It reveals no solid matter. Atoms and particles are vibrations of energy in enormous, empty spaces. The hard edges of any object are an illusion resulting from the limitations of our sight. Quantum physics is making real to us an invisible world of mystery and paradox, transforming our understanding of space-time reality.

From the same impulse for discovery and understanding in the 1920s came Alfred North Whitehead's philosophy of organicism. Whitehead articulated a sophisticated description of how the web of nature creatively unfolds. Charles Hartshorne, Henry Nelson

Wieman, and others saw in Whitehead's thought tremendous implications for liberal theology and gave birth to process theology. They depict a universe alive with experience. All occasions of experience relate to all others in a process of becoming, moving toward beauty, truth, and harmony. God in this picture is more like a verb, acting on and acted upon by all occasions past and present in the universe. As Wieman termed it, the universe is best understood as "creative interchange."

Process theology, in an amazing way, repudiates scientific materialism. Following Whitehead, Hartshorne articulated a metaphysical panpsychism, the view that all things have subjective experience. All things are atoms of conscious experience, having qualities not unrelated to human mental experience. Whitehead preferred the word "feeling"; all things experience feeling. We are a long way from Newtonian mechanics now!

Along came general systems theory in the 1950s. It grew from an overlay of biology, cybernetics, and information theory. The fundamental idea is that living systems exist in open exchange with an environment, taking in, processing, and giving off energy, information, and matter. Using positive and negative feedback, living systems grow and counteract the forces of entropy as they become more complex and differentiated. Living systems are biased toward their own maintenance and renewal, or autopoiesis. They evolve through a sequence of structures, yet maintain their integrity as discrete systems. This process is known as "self-organization."

Literally all living things are a self-organizing system: cells, humans, social institutions, whatever. In recent decades, a convincing theory has been proposed, by an atmospheric chemist and a biologist working as a team, that the earth itself is a living system. This is the Gaia hypothesis. This idea alone, its implications understood, may transform liberal religious thought.

In his last years Gregory Bateson, anthropologist and systems theorist, proposed that mind is immanent in nature, not in a solid, spatial structure, but in the processes in which systems organize and renew themselves and evolve. In this conception mind is not simply located in a discrete place or ego, in a brain or body or personality. It is a process immanent in the pathways coupling organisms with their environments. Cognition and life are inseparable. Impressive theoretical research is ongoing in the field of cognitive science, furthering this understanding.

It may be appropriate to think that the interdependent web is conscious. If we need in our theologies an understanding of God, we might more properly think of God, rather than as Creator, as the Mind of the universe and the physical universe as God's body.

All these ideas reinforce one another and help

us to understand much better what we mean by the "interdependent web of all existence of which we are a part." That image is already the most powerful symbol of our faith. If other ideas and images implicit in this new intellectual wave take hold in our congregations, as I hope they do, and if they interweave with a profound spiritual and ethical longing in the hearts of our members, already manifesting, then the interdependent web will take on much richer and deeper meaning for Unitarian Universalists. The web already symbolizes the fact and mystery of all life on earth and the connectedness of all of nature, human and otherwise, on this planet and throughout the universe. For many of us, though, the idea that mental processes and conscious, purposive intelligence resides anywhere other than in the brains of humans and the "higher animals" is highly suspect. Yet the new "sciences of becoming" and process philosophy are affirming that the Web of Life is intelligent. Nature is once again enchanted.

If we can overcome our fearful misconception that to follow this richer meaning would betray reason and science, Sunday worship and all other expressions of our faith can be transformed. These new and powerful ideas would open us up to exploring the implications of a new theology and to practicing a spirituality of the interdependent web. This orientation of liberal faith will motivate us to save the world.

Unitarian Universalism and Religious Purpose

Michael Werner

"Every time people go down the relativist road the path darkens and the light recedes." [1]

My voice in this series of essays is that of a serious layperson and a humanist and is, in some measure, meant to illuminate our tradition from within rather than from the top of that tradition. As Marx and Engels said, "Ruling ideas are those of the ruling class." [2] I hope to show that the professional ministerial perspective has limited Unitarian Universalism and that religion's enduring traits are now ignored. I hope to show that we have abandoned our religious calling in an age when our strengths are needed more than ever. Let me start by viewing our tradition through the long lens of history and then using that lens to focus on the present and the future.

Religion began not in a church, but around a campfire. In the ancient glow of flames and embers, stone-age parents confronted the eternal questions of existence. Who are we? What is our purpose? What happens when we die? How should we live? Why is there suffering? Why be good?

They did what any parent would do. They answered the best they could with what they knew or simply made up the rest. Those questions around the campfire have been voiced in millions of ways since, but the questions persist. It is our humanity speaking.

Definitions of religion, as we all know, cast a net around a large amorphous subject. Simplistic, Neoplatonic, exact definitions never really capture all the nuances. For example, Tillich's "that which is our ultimate concern" definition covers too broad a landscape. Theoretically, it could cover a football fanatic's concerns. But religion is something more.

Wittgenstein showed how some words like beauty, culture, and religion have no exact definition and are best understood by "family traits."[3] Some of those "family traits" for religion might include belief/disbelief in God, a moral code, an account of evil, prayer, ritual, religious experience, revealed truth, an account of our purpose, belief in experience after death, social bonding, political bonding, sacred places, and rituals. Not all religions have all traits, and no trait is definitive. Both ideological and functional aspects of religion seem to be part of that campfire scene. Yet, liberal religion in the last few decades has stressed, almost to exclusion, the functional or process aspects of religion with the focus on the social and the psychological.

I maintain that our fundamental religious needs have never progressed beyond those discussions at the campfire, but Unitarian Universalism has neglected some of these concerns to embrace others. At its heart, religion is trying to give answers to the old metaphysical, epistimological, and ethical questions. The permanence in religion is that integrated whole story about our world and lives. I believe we have lost touch with our ancient need for these answers at the insistence of the demands of our transitory historical period.

We are immersed in a neoromantic age.[4] Ours is the postmodern age dominated by subjectivity and by a distrust of science and technology. This cultural loss of faith in reason, progress, the intellectual tradition, and the political process has been filled with a renewed interest in mysticism, neoromantic pursuits, and social alienation.

Postmodernism provides the assumptive, unchallenged premises that permeate all our thinking in culture and, indeed, in Unitarian Universalism. It looks at all our ideas of truth and our basic sense of reality as merely social constructions. There are no ultimate foundations for anything one believes, the postmodernist argues. Postmodernism emerged out of the growing awareness of the cultural basis for beliefs. Postmodernism stresses how the subconscious needs for power and control can use reason as an instrumental tool for rationalizing dominating behavior. These ideas, merged with a profound philosophical skepticism, have ultimately led to the postmodernist malaise in which we are immersed.

Unitarian Universalism has evolved into the paradigmic, postmodern religion. Its inherent relativism is uniquely suited to the times. UU theological schools today strive not to provide the content of religion, but merely to provide tools for the minister to facilitate the functional aspects of religion. A minister is to become only a process tool so that laypersons can arrive at their own religious beliefs in a supportive, nurturing atmosphere. Khoren Arisian observes, "Unitarian Universalism consequently remains cognitively empty at its center."[5]

My own experience bears this out. I was already comfortable "coming out" of traditional religion before becoming a UU. I found a nurturing community, but, sadly, no real support to fill the metaphysical void. An arduous religious quest to define my own humanism was not helped by Unitarian Universalism. It was only because of my own persistence that I gained a world view that maintained my intellectual integrity and was intuitionally satisfying. My experience has shown that many Unitarian Universalists are not so persistent and settle for a less satisfying grounding.

Why has this occurred? Certainly the noncreedal aspects of our religion have an important role. Our heritage of free thought demands that we not coerce others in their thinking. Still, something has changed in our UU tradition that seems to have deified relativism, pluralism, and uncritical acceptance at the expense of our long–held tradition of rational religion.

If there is one thing that postmodernism has taught us, it is that we need to look at people's hidden motives for clues to what is really going on. Our ministers, like any others, must try to hold on to the affections of their congregations. They must show membership growth if they want to stay in their positions or advance. The pecuniary and psychological incentives of attracting the largest possible audience can sway the most prophetic voice. Money talks, and truth can be the victim. How much of the religious redefinition game is played to manipulatively obfuscate, rather than to illuminate, our religious lives? How much of the deification of mystery and the unknown (the so-called "God of the gaps") evades the job of truth making? How much of theological vagueness is merely fear of confrontation, lack of answers, or at worst laziness?

At one time the Unitarians were resigned to being a small, but prophetic minority. In 1830 it was said, "Our object is not to convert men to our party, but to our principles."[6] Some of our greatest leaders, such as Channing, Parker, Emerson, and Wilson, had to stand up to conservative reactionaries outside and within in our religion. Only in time have we embraced the radical message that they preached. For all our liberal talk, the conservative nature of our tradition is all too evident in retrospect. Today, in our eagerness to expand our membership, we embrace a simplistic pluralism that parallels the mediocrity of television, seeking larger audiences while dismantling what our tradition has historically and uniquely offered, that is, reason in liberal religion. Neoconservatives find unchallenged acceptance under a banner of pluralism.

The marketing of a cognitively vague religion certainly fits the tenor of the times. It also fits the basic capabilities of our ministry, who generally do not have a solid educational grounding in philosophy including humanism. Humanism, as generally conceived by most ministers, is cast from a simplistic 1930s Humanist Manifesto snapshot, rather than seen as an evolving, vital tradition. If a minister does not have the knowledge, she or he certainly can't teach it. The majority of our ministers now come out of nondenominational schools, and even the ones that attend denominational schools receive what is basically a liberal Christian education. Even though approximately 75 percent of Unitarian Universalists consider themselves to be humanists, atheists, or agnostics,[7] ministers depend on traditions that most of us have long since left. We don't invent our own religion, but cling to decrepit models of the past.

What I call for is a renewed interest in our religious foundations. Going against the grain in an age of and religion of anti-foundationalism, I call for a religion that takes the philosophical quest seriously again. We have done an excellent job on such functional aspects of religion as building nurturing, supportive communities. But religion must answer the questions by the campfire. Our duty resides not just in the process, but also in providing content. Ministers should reassume their rabbinic duty, that is, their duty as teachers. Ministers should give up the illusion that they are empty vessels attempting to facilitate others' growth and enter again into a dialogue of truth seeking.

There are many arguments against active theological leadership; space does not permit complete answers. First, the postmodern epistomological crises is one of extremism. Even Richard Rorty, the leading postmodernist, has stood on the nihilistic abyss and stepped back saying, "We should not become so openminded that our brains fall out." The intellectual trend is now moderating to a "neopragmatism." Many are saying that John Dewey had it right all along. He held that truth is instrumental, evolutionary, and probablistic. We can look at the world relativistically without looking at it arbitrarily. Most humanists believed that all along.

Humanism may be the horizon that cannot be surpassed. The active support and teaching of humanist foundations is consistent with our UU heritage and morally demanded by the intellectually honest. For example, at the 1994 Parliament of World Religions in Chicago, the global ethics statement was a basic primer in humanist ethics.

We fail in our promise of religion if we do not seek to provide foundational knowledge concerning the workings of the world, however tentative, to the best of our abilities. We become only a social and psychological support club if we do not. A "copout" around the campfire leads to alienated, foundationless lives. Many observers have noted a "spiritual vacuum" that has led to an amoral and alienated society. We may be, in part, to blame.

Studies have shown that society has become increasingly secular while covered with a thin veneer of God talk.[8] Note that a secular society is not necessarily an ethically humanist one. The existential void has largely been left unfilled as people think they have only two choices, fundamentalism or a nihilistic relativism. There is a middle way, and that is humanism, but the whole message is not even known by our own clergy. People yearn for foundations, and the religious right have targeted and been successful in attracting the "unchurched." The transitory UU interest in an emotionally manipulative "spirituality" will fade in time as people reach for deeper roots.

Wilfred Cantwell Smith sees religion as that in which we ultimately place our faith.[9] It is that to which we are ultimately committed. Religious pluralism is an important value, but not one that ultimately grounds our lives. Religion must provide answers about the depths and wholeness of what this world is about and develop an integrated story. One should be able to answer the question, Why be moral?

Religion must become more like science by employing a communal search using critical reason. Realistically, truth building is more a negative process than a positive one, and this may seem at odds with some who place highest value on supportive community building. In fact, it is part of any healthy community. In the process, we can still maintain freedom of thought, while not playing dumb. The metaphysically crippled are not helped by our exceptional pastoral skills. An absolutism of the subjective does not provide an ethical base.

There is a spiritual crisis today. There is a crisis of intellectual nerve. Although history shows alternate cycles of rational thinking and myth thinking in domination, there is no guarantee our own irrational age will moderate. If liberal religion is to be prophetic, it must stand up to the dominating irrationalities. If liberal religion is to be humane, we must heal the wounded, metaphysical soul as well as the wounded psyche. If liberal religion is to be relevant, we must heal the sick society using the best tools of heart and mind. If liberal religion is to be religious, it must seek the truth. If liberal religion is to be liberal, it must advance against our own conservative bondage and be a voice of both reason and compassion.

Afterword

Alice Blair Wesley

———————◆———————

Look, they are one people, and they have one language; and this is only the beginning of what they will do; nothing they propose will be impossible for them. Come, let us go down and confuse their language there, so that they will not understand one another's speech.

Genesis 11: 6-7

Therefore, all scribes who have been trained for the kingdom of heaven are like householders who bring out of their treasures what is new and what is old.

Matthew 13:52

We speak of many worlds. We speak of the world of opera, the world of high finance, the world of sports, the world of computer nerds, the world of the church, and so on. There's a Unitarian Universalist world and the *World*. What can one say of all these worlds?

In our time devotees of the world of opera fear it can't reproduce itself for a new generation. The world of baseball is big, but then there's no World Series one year. As for the world of the church, who can figure what's happening there? Do those in the world of computer nerds care what's going or coming in the world of the church? Could they help if even some of them did care? Or do? What can one say of all these worlds?

Even worlds with huge armies and tons of archives can end almost overnight. One day there's a Soviet Union; the next day there's not. Other worlds, like the world of MTV, pop up like mushrooms, grow like Topsy, and subtly change all the rules of other worlds. Worlds weaken or shrink suddenly. Worlds take as long as the Roman Empire or the Vatican to fade. Worlds grow steadily or erratically or vanish, all the time. Rather as things do in Lewis Carroll's Wonderland or in any dream.

We in the late twentieth century are noticing this curious variability in how long worlds last, partly because of the speed-up in communications technology. Bosnia and Rwanda happen and we learn about it instantly. Hype also heightens our awareness of endings.

Every day TV journalists competing for our attention cry "Ruinous scandal!" and "Wolf!" Fund raisers on the right and on the left of every issue and competing for our money, all yell through mass mailings that "The sky will fall!" unless we send at once $10, $25, $50, or more if we possibly can.

False prophets cry "Peace, peace" when there is none, as Jeremiah said. False prophets also cry "The End! The End!" in such cacophony that there is more than a little hysteria.

We in the late twentieth century are hardly the first to notice that worlds end a lot. Hebrews of three and four millennia ago were probably nomadic mule drivers. Hebrew families moved with the caravans of commerce, threading their way among the varied and shifting societies and empires of ancient Egypt, Jordan, Syria, Iran, Iraq, Arabia, even India for generations. They noticed that worlds end often, and in a wondrous strange variety of ways. What we call the Bible came out of a long, long heritage of world watching, and great stories about worlds ending, some of them quite funny.

To ask why and how worlds end or endure and to formulate some answers is to set forth a theology of history. Some do so in prose essays. Authors and editors of The Book of Genesis were content to do it with a series of stories.

Scholars talk about the economy of some biblical authors. Some of them could just sketch characters and scenes, even epochs with such art that interpreters have amplified the evocative hints of short passages for centuries. Enduring art does that. It endures because it is fertile. It evokes varied interpretation and so provides the continuity of wide, long views of human destiny, of living, changing cultures.

Necessity must have been the mother of such efficient art as the Yahwist's (whenever he wrote or whoever she was). The unit labor cost of a piece of vellum in those days may have been about that of a few sound bites of network TV time in ours. The artist with the widest vision of worlds had to say it with marvelous brevity.

The Yahwist had already told the story of the passing of one world, Noah's. The people did wickedness. Radical wickedness won't long work. Sure, we all do some, both without intending to and on purpose. But if enough of the people do enough wickedness, their world, flooded with destructiveness, is destroyed. No need to spell out the details to state the worldwide principle: Common morality really matters.

Not that morality is the only variable in how long a world lasts. After the devastation of Noah's world, there were only Noah, Mrs. Noah, their three sons and three daughters-in-law to start civilization over again. Undismayed, they "knew" each other with good will. No doubt they enjoyed doing so, and the babies were born in consequence. In a few generations there were plenty of people again. Nice families all. In nine little verses of the eleventh chapter of Genesis, the Yahwist tells the story of their world.

They decided to live close, however many they got to be. They would build their brick city up to heaven. And they could do this because they had a name for themselves and a common language. The Yahwist tells us that if only they could have kept their common language, these folks would have found any common endeavor no challenge. They could have done anything, with no risk of corporate failure. *With no drama!* Can you feature that?

Yahweh couldn't feature it. Or wouldn't. Yahweh confused their language. So another world ended, this one in babble. With nothing but trivial gestures to share, the people left off making their city and wandered away. Afterwards, their abandoned effort was called the Tower of Babel, a monument to confusion.

It wasn't the end of the whole world. A world ended, not with a flood or a bang but with the diminishing whine of deflating high hopes. Not that the people did anything so bad, it's just that in the kind of world we have been given, we can only have a fine world with drama. Anything fine we propose to do will prove difficult or impossible, especially if we won't figure out how to make sense to one another. There's got to be a patient passion for precision and profundity, or corporate human enterprise will die. Another worldwide principle: Meaningless talk won't do.

Maybe you have thought the Yahwist was a

simple–minded person from a simple world long superseded. I think she was as sophisticated a student of world history as any in our day. I'm a little "d" democrat. I have no trouble believing that mule–driving Hebrews and their world–watching heirs, who settled in a part of the world crossed by all the major trade routes of empires, could develop a genius for theology of history and language.

It's not all that uncommon for a people to lose their common language. Nor is it all that uncommon for poets to understand that loss as an exceedingly serious threat to an entire world. Without a vision of where we are going, people cannot be a zesty, freely cooperating people. Nobody has yet figured out how to communicate a vision without using commonly understood figures of speech, words. And all words wear out. They get conflated and slide into other words, sometimes with flatly contrary meanings. After a while you can't even utter a simple message.

Come, let us reason together. Hear the voice of the data. All together they say: Thou shalt love. Is that Word not proved in our own best experience? Any time we together love life and our neighbors, we are in an up-and-coming, just neighborhood of good gladness. Glory be! It is here among us for the living all along! So God, our name for That which is greater than all yet present in each, our name for the creative, sustaining, community-forming, judging, re-creating Power, is love (my paraphrase of First Isaiah and

1 John). Say something like that and you get blank looks, a cynical shrug, or endlessly complicated, dull-as-dishwater prose argumentation.

"Woe is me! I am one of unclean lips and I live among a people of unclean lips. Our language is fouled. Therefore, they have eyes but cannot see; they have ears and cannot hear." So the poet Isaiah exclaimed. Such is the repeated cry, age after age, of the apocalyptic poet who sees a precious world under threat the people cannot even see approaching because without a common language, we are figuratively blind, deaf, dumb, and numb. Corporately, commonly, we can neither see, hear, speak, nor feel what truly matters.

The prescription for scribbling scribes in such a time? Go to your treasures, the laid up stores of the culture's literary heritage. Borrow from other cultures if they are available to you. Become a bricoleur. Reconstruct. Edit. Translate. Re-write. Mix and use what is new and what is old, whatever you need to get the job done—only paint a vision of a truly fair and just world the people will love and delight to make and live whatever the challenges!

It's the oldest advice to artists/theologians/preachers in the world. It's what the Yahwist did. It's what the prophets did. It's what the authors of the Gospels did. It's what all great scribes and painters and musicians and sculptors and dramatists and orators and statesmen do. So much for the novelty of "postmodernism."

A caveat: It's also what con artists and fakes and demagogues try to appear to be doing. So there's *no* let-up of the need for critical common sense.

◆ ◆ ◆

Reading the papers here collected as they arrived, I was surprised by the concentration of apocalyptic tenor. Writers say we've got to have a paradigm shift, that we have betrayed or are betraying our heritage, or that we've been looking at everything wrongly for a long time, since the composition of the first chapter of Genesis!

Not that the papers reflect a common view. Anything but. We're all over the map, most notably in our theologies of history. To use the term of the Noah story, some of our authors are concerned with our wickedness: with the destructive impact of our materialism on nature, with our cruel blindness to racism, to sexism, to gross economic injustice, and so on. These are proper concerns. It is possible that our churches and/or our culture could die from want of our attention and concerted action concerning just these matters. Surely, we ought to address these serious concerns together.

Yet a prior and larger factor of our weakness or strength and hope for our future as a Unitarian Universalist people may be the state of our common language. If we could get all our members to read all these papers, a number of them would prove incomprehensible to substantially sized groups of us. Theologies of history and languages are linked, because our access to and our evaluation of the worlds of the past have so much to do with *which* stored and new symbols are commonly available to us now. It is precisely our theologies of history that this collection of papers shows to be very far apart.

What do I mean when I say apocalyptic? We call the period of late Hellenistic literature from roughly 250 BCE to 350 CE the Age of Apocalyptic. That is because, in that time of rapidly mixing and changing cultures, a specific literary tradition developed that came to be called apocalyptic.

Apocalypse is a word derived from Greek. The Greek word meant vision. But in the specific literary tradition of apocalyptic writing, authors of the genre nearly always presented their vision as having been shown to them in a trance or a dream, all at once and complete with vast ramifications for their world. That was the literary convention. That is why the word apocalypse came to be translated into English as revelation. The best known now, of the many apocalypses written, is the Apocalypse of St. John, alternately called The Revelation of St. John, because "John's" book made it (thought not without challenge) into the biblical canon. All these apocalypses involved visions of a world ending because there was no other way to save any of the good from mighty evil rulers, sort of like in our Marvel comics and science fiction novels and films.

Technically, we ought not conflate the word apocalypse, a *vision* of a world's ending, with the *event* of a world's ending. But we do. Now we call apocalyptic any writing or speech that forecasts a world's ending, with or without reference to a vision.

Because we have already altered the meaning of the word apocalyptic, I suggest that we go ahead and alter it some more. We have called apocalyptic any writing or speech that *forecasts* a world's ending. Suppose we also extend the term to any writing or speech which *recasts* or assumes the ending of some world in the past.

If you would grant this liberty, then I think I could show that much of our liberal theology of history has been apocalyptic. Our theology has importantly been about some world's end. I'll show you what I mean with a couple of examples.

First take the second verse of one of our favorite hymns, "Faith of the Larger Liberty,"

> Heroes of faith in every age, far-seeing, self-denying
> wrought an increasing heritage, monarch and creed defying.
> Faith of the free! In thy dear name the costly heritage we claim:

their living and their dying.

Singing the Living Tradition, No. 287

The hymn refers to a world none of us has ever lived in. It was a world in which European monarchs legally mandated the creed everybody had to subscribe to or risk paying a horrible penalty. That world was ended by the grace of God and our spiritual ancestors working together. It happened a long time ago, but that doesn't mean we the heirs can just take it easy. "What e'er our plight"—we have the "plight" of "oppression" in our world, too—we are to take the inspiration of our ancestors' example, and, living "faith's confession," "make the world more fair." (v. 3)

"Monarch and creed defying." How easily we sing that! At the time of the "defying" *most* people reacted about as we would now if folks took to defying the US Constitution and the laws against child abuse and calling it the true religion. Most people thought the monarch was the only thing that stood between them and chaos and that the creed was as holy as we hold the Bill of Rights. What our spiritual ancestors did scared the bejeebers out of most people. They fought the Thirty Years War over it. Tens upon tens of thousands went hungry and got wounded and had their crops and houses burned and died. The suffering! The suffering!

Clearly, when we sing "Faith of a Larger Liberty," we are not urging one another on to bring again such a time, though I suppose it could be so misinterpreted. Nor do we mean, really, to demonize "monarchs," who surely as a class did more good on the whole than not, before people had widely conceived free churches, much less a republican form of government.

But much (I don't say all) apocalyptic theology grossly oversimplifies. My point here simply is that to appreciate and to use well an apocalyptic tradition is not so simple a thing to do. Oversimplification can be dangerous. To appreciate and use it well is to do a lot of qualifying and specifying, even when, after all is said, we affirm a text as we do this hymn.

Take Theodore Parker's sermon, "The Transient and Permanent in Christianity," as an example. Was it apocalyptic, either forecasting or recasting a world's end? Parker thought the world of conventional Christianity, pallid and superstitious, would end. It would end as soon as the results of the new German biblical criticism were widely understood. He meant to shorten the cultural lag in his New England world, at a time when very few people read German, even at Harvard. He didn't want to end Christianity, just the world of pallid and superstitious Christianity "of the Pulpit" and "of the People."

> But if error prevail for a time and grow old in the world, truth will triumph at last, and we shall see the Son of God as he is. Lifted up he shall draw all nations unto him. Then

will men understand the Word of Jesus, which shall not pass away.... His words judge the nations....They kindle anew the flame of devotion in hearts long cold. They are the Spirit and Life.

Without excusing his critics for their viciousness, we can say that Parker could have spent some more time trying to understand those he cavalierly labeled, in effect, jerks! That they retaliated with some distress and rather sharply does not seem in retrospect as though it should have been all that unexpected. It was and still is—to say the least—unfruitful to dismiss all who don't agree with us as either naive or callow.

I say again much of our liberal theology of history has been and is about some world's end, and therefore also hopeful for some better, more enduring world in the future. We can use a common interpretive key if we ask the same questions of each author of past historical papers.

Which world is this writer assuming, implicitly or explicitly, has already ended or will end? Or should end? Is that ending judged a good thing or terrible? If it is judged good that some world ended or will or should, what was or is wrong with it in the author's view? If it is judged a terrible thing that some world ended or is about to end, whose were or are the organizing principles of the opposition? So are we to celebrate or mourn? And *what* kind of action is now called for? Should we just proceed as we have been doing? Because everything is fine now? Stay calm and wait? Or be heartily courageous and work as we have never worked before? What about the future, is it dreaded or hoped for? Is a new world expected to come soon or slowly? Will it come no matter what we do, or will it require that we help it come with our exertions?

After we ask these questions, we can talk with more clarity about whether we find an author's vision credible and about which parts seem right on and which off the mark.

Another clarifying exercise: Underscore an author's use of all-embracing terms. Then ask who or what the author may illogically exclude from his or her own all-embracing terms. Too often what's excluded is the author. Watch out for the excluded author!

For example, Parker said in his sermon, "The Transient and Permanent," "One snatches one thing, another is pleased with another; there is *no dry, clear sight of anything. Everyone* plays philosopher out of the small treasures of his own fancy." [my italics][2]

"No dry, clear sight" embraced all sight but his own? Parker was not himself among the "everyone" playing philosopher out of "small treasures"? That is, indeed, what he claimed.

Theodore Parker was a brilliant saint. That one such as he could make so illogical and offensive a claim ought to make us wary of generalizations of our own time, in the papers here collected. And compassionate. It can be awfully hard to see illogical exclusions from our own all-embracing terms, which any theology of history *must* use.

To ask how and why worlds end or endure and to formulate some answers is to posit facts and principles in the world, the whole world embracing smaller worlds. To set forth a theology of history at all is to adopt as our own a larger view whose reach exceeds in time and space what is passing. But none of us has seen the whole thing, though we live in it. We dwell in a mystery exceeding our knowing but not our sense of its reality. In theologizing, what we do is lift up some facts and principles that appear to be relevant and pertinent in worlds we know something about. We then—we hope—logically extrapolate and apply these facts and principles to the whole. We infer what must be crucially true of the whole from our experience of a part. And this is a legitimate, necessary thing to do. The hard part is remembering that we always and only speak from the viewpoints of limited worlds within the whole.

Yet it is precisely our faith that our world is within the larger whole that rightly allows an abiding and staying confidence in our own most thoughtfully lived answers. If they have borne reasoning scrutiny and the weight of our own experience, then our answers are more than just human constructs. Our answers participate in the world. They are part of us, and we are part of the interdependent web of existence in which all things in *mutual* relations are acted upon and are acting. Our answers are not excluded from the embracing, interdependent web. Our answers really matter. And they can be right.

The issue is not whether our answers can be finally proved in our world. They cannot be. This issue is whether we will together think and live and work our answers through until we can say, Here we stand for we can do no other, so help us God. Let us walk together in the spirit of both humility and fidelity.

That the world is so much grander than our power to grasp and categorize it is more than enough to keep us humble and more than enough for sane rejoicing that we know well enough what a healthy religious community is and that we do have a vision of a just and fair world. These great gifts are summoning from us love, critical reason, courage, creativity, and also trust in the ground and source of all that gives us breath and history.

I began with an impressionistic view of the way the world may seem to many these days. This view of the world is related to how rapidly we are asked to integrate change in our time. Ours is not the first time this has happened. We can yet learn from treasures laid up how to put together the new and the old in such a way that many may see a vision of a fair and just world toward which we shall want to move in free covenant together.

To do so is to engage in high drama. It goes well with much singing. I want to be there with you for the singing. There's much to sing about, world without end!

About the Contributors

---◆---

Dianne E. Arakawa is a Unitarian Universalist minister. She earned her B.A. at Wheaton College in 1974, and her M.Div. at Harvard in 1978. Dianne currently serves on the Board of Directors for the Unitarian Universalist Christian Fellowship.

Wayne B. Arnason was elected President of the Unitarian Universalist Minister's Association in 1993. A fourth-generation UU from our Icelandic Canadian tradition, Arnason is a graduate of Harvard and served our congregations in San Francisco and Hayward, California, before becoming Youth Programs Director for the UUA in 1980. Since 1984 he has been parish minister of Thomas Jefferson Memorial Church, UU, in Charlottesville, Virginia. Wayne has authored and edited books, curricula, and essays on UU history, spirituality, and medical and professional ethics. In 1990 he was given the Angus Maclean Award for Excellence in Religious Education.

George Kimmich Beach is Senior Minister of the Unitarian Universalist Church of Arlington, Virginia, and a Member of the UUA Commission on Appraisal. He is the author of *If Yes Is the Answer, What Is the Question?* (Skinner House, 1995) and edited two volumes of essays by James Luther Adams (Beacon Press).

Roger Brewin has been a Unitarian Universalist minister since 1977. He currently serves as parish minister of the Maumee Valley UU Congregation in Perrysburg, Ohio.

John A. Buehrens was elected President of the Unitarian Universalist Association in 1993. As a minister since 1973 he has served congregations in Knoxville, Dallas, and New York.

John Alexie Crane has been a Unitarian minister for more than forty years and has repeatedly explored the questions of the essential nature of UU religion. In recent years, at UU leadership schools, Lex has refined his evolving understanding of this issue in discussion with groups of people from many diverse congregations.

William Dean is Professor of Religion, Gustavus Adolphus College. His last three books are: *American Religious Empiricism* (1986*), History Making History: The New Historicism in American Religious Thought* (1988), and *The Religious Critic in American Culture* (1994). He is a post-structural theological historicist now writing religious criticism of American culture.

Sandra Decker has been the Director of Religious Education at the First Unitarian Church of Berkeley, California, while completing her M.Div. at the Pacific School of Religion, with the goal of becoming a parish minister. She is currently working on her M.A. thesis on James Luther Adams and his contributions to Liberation Theology. She has done antiracism training for over five years, including three years with the Black Concerns Working Group, and she is on the core committee of UUs for a Just Economic Community.

Richard M. Fewkes has been minister of the First Parish, Unitarian, in Norwell, Massachusetts, since 1969. He has served as President of the Ballou Channing District and the BCD UU Minister's Association, is a member of the Board of the UU Urban Ministry in Boston, is vice president of the Partner Church Council, and has been editor of the *UU Psi Symposium Annual Journal* since 1975. Fewkes is a long-time student of Theodore Parker, and his sermons in the persona of Parker have been very popular.

James Ishmael Ford is Parish Minister of the Unitarian Church North, in Mequon, Wisconsin. A student of Zen for twenty-five years, he has formal permission to teach Zen meditation in the Soto tradition. He serves as secretary for the Unitarian Universalist Buddhist Fellowship and edits its newsletter, the *UU Sangha.*

Richard S. Gilbert has been Parish Minister of Rochester's First Unitarian Church since 1970. He chaired the UUA Task Force on Economic Justice and was on the Board of the Unitarian Universalist Service Committee. He is author of *How Much Do We Deserve? An Inquiry in Distributive Justice*, (University Press of America, 1991).

Earl K. Holt III has served since 1974 as minister of the historic First Unitarian Church of St. Louis. A graduate of Brown University and Starr King School for the Ministry, he is the author of *William Greenleaf Eliot, Conservative Radical* and of numerous articles on church history and congregational polity. Among a variety of community and denominational activities, he serves currently as vice chairman of the Board of Trustees at Starr King.

William Jones, religion professor, Black Studies Director at Florida State University, and Unitarian Universalist minister, has received degrees from Brown, Harvard, and Howard. His current research on global oppression and conflict resolution augments the nontheistic religion and philosophy he advanced in *Is God a White Racist?*, "The Legitimacy and Necessity of Counter-violence," and "African American Religious Humanism."

Ronald Knapp, who began his ministry with the United Methodist Church, has been a Unitarian Universalist minister for thirty-one years and has been minister of the First Unitarian Church of Omaha for the past twenty years. He holds degrees from Central Michigan University (B.S.), Drew University (M.Div.), and Dartmouth (M.A.L.S.)

Spencer Lavan has been Dean and CEO of Meadville/ Lombard Theological School in Chicago since 1988. A Unitarian Universalist minister who has devoted most of his thirty-two year ministry to higher education, he holds a Ph.D. in comparative religion from McGill University. Lavan previously taught Islam and Asian religions at Tufts University and medical humanities at the University of New England.

Colleen M. McDonald came into ministry with backgrounds in teaching and psychiatric occupational therapy. Ordained by the First Unitarian Society of Madison, Wisconsin, where she served two years, she's been Minister of Religious Education in Rockford, Illinois, since 1989. A graduate of the Independent Study Program, she's currently an advisor to M.R.E. students.

Fredric John Muir is parish minister of the Annapolis Unitarian Universalist Church. He has served the Unitarian Universalist Church of Sanford, Maine; was chaplain at a community hospital in Brooklyn, New York; and interned at Community Church, New York. He is the author of *A Reason for Hope: Liberation Theology Confronts a Liberal Faith.*

Robert Murphy has been active in environmental justice work for over twenty years. He managed the Sierra Club's Boston office during the 1970s and later served as a business agent for one of Boston's major labor unions. Bob now works as a parish ministry intern for the First Unitarian Church of New Bedford, Massachusetts.

About the Contributors

In addition to being the parish minister of the Unitarian Universalist Fellowship of Sonoma County in Santa Rosa, California, **Dan O'Neal** is a teacher, a Zen meditator, a workshop leader, and a writer. Dan is on the editorial team that produced this volume.

Susan Pangerl, Ph.D., is a Unitarian Universalist minister and a member of the clinical and training staff of the Center for Religion and Psychotherapy of Chicago. Her professional life challenges the traditional expectations of ministry in her weaving together of cultural and psychological roots for spiritual meaning in the American context. Her work expresses feminist revisioning of psychoanalysis and practical theology.

Elizabeth Parish was ordained a Unitarian Universalist minister in 1989. She earned her B.A. from Wake Forest University, and her M.Div. from Harvard Divinity School.

Rebecca Parker is president of Starr King School for the Ministry, a post she has held since 1990. A United Methodist minister in dual fellowship with the Unitarian Universalist Association, she served as a parish minister in the Pacific Northwest for ten years. Rebecca is also a teacher and an author. Her primary academic interests are process theology and feminist theology.

Shirley Ann Ranck is the author of the highly acclaimed UU adult curriculum, *Cakes for the Queen of Heaven*. She earned her Ph.D. from Fordham University and her M.Div. from Starr King.

Roy Reynolds is minister of Northwest Unitarian Universalist Congregation, Atlanta, Georgia. His visionary thinking extends over three decades, encompassing his previous career as an urban planner. Roy is Southeast UUMA Treasurer, board member of the UU Process Theology Network, active with the Atlanta Faith and Environment Connection, and a member of the UU Musicians Network.

Peter T. Richardson was ordained in 1965 in Kent, Ohio, and since 1992 has served the Unitarian Universalist Congregation in Andover, Massachusetts. He has traveled to seventeen countries on religious pilgrimage, published several hundred photographs, and authored *The Spiritual Founders of Our Constitution* and *Meditations in a Maine Meeting House.*

Carl Scoval earned his B.A. at Oberlin College and his S.T.B. from Harvard Divinity School. His first ten years of ministry were at the First Parish in Sudbury, Massachusetts. Since 1967 he has served as minister of King's Chapel in Boston.

Arvid Straube earned his D.Min. from Meadville/Lombard in 1979 and was ordained to the Unitarian Universalist ministry in the same year. Since 1991 he has served as minister of the Eno River Unitarian Universalist Fellowship in Durham, North Carolina.

Michael Werner is a lay Unitarian Universalist, president of the American Humanist Association, and treasurer of the Friends of Religious Humanism. His research interest is in rethinking liberal religion beyond the present postmodern malaise.

About the Contributors

Conrad Wright is one of the mostly highly respected living Unitarian Universalist scholars. He earned his doctorate at Harvard in 1947. Conrad is professor emeritus of American Church History at Harvard Divinity School. He is the author of numerous books, including *The Beginnings of Unitarianism in America* and *A Stream of Light*.

Pieces and papers by **Alice Blair Wesley** have appeared in the *JLM* (1975), *Faith and Freedom* (1979), *Kairos* (1980), the *UU Christian* (1982 and 1989), *First Days Record* (1985), the *UU Extension Manual* (1986), *UUMA Selected Essays* (1987, 1992, and 1994), and *Wellsprings: Sources in UU Feminism* (1992). Her book *Myths of Time and History* has been widely used by study groups in our congregations. She serves as Minister of the UU Fellowship of Harford County, Maryland.

Notes

---◆---

Introduction
1. Arnold J. Toynbee, quoted in Richard Tarnas, *The Passion of the Western Mind* (New York, NY: Ballantine Books,1991), p. 411.
2. Richard Tarnas, *The Passion of the Western Mind*, (New York, NY: Ballantine Books, 1991).
3. Charlene Spretnak, *States of Grace: The Recovery of Meaning in the Postmodern Age* (San Francisco: Harper, 1991), p. 224.
4. Robert Bellah, quoted in Alan Durning, *How Much is Enough?*, (New York, NY: Norton & Company, 1992), p. 88.
5. Angus MacLean, quoted in Sophia Fahs, *Today's Children and Yesterday's Heritage*, (Boston, MA: Beacon Press, 1952), p. 88.

The Passionate Enduring Center
1. William James, *Writings: 1878-1899*, ed., Gerald E. Myers (New York, NY: Library of America, 1992), p. 502.
2. Joseph Campbell, *Myths to Live By* (New York, NY: Bantam, 1973), p. 24.

Notes

3. Gilbert Murray, *Five Stages of Greek Religion* (New York, NY: Greenwood, 1955), pp. 166-167.
4. Glen Fisher, *Mindsets: The Role of Culture and Perception in International Relations* (Yarmouth, ME: Intercultural Press, 1988). Fisher defines mindsets as "set ways of perceiving, reasoning and viewing the world that govern...how events are evaluated and how decisions are made."
5. Joseph Campbell, *The Masks of God: Occidental Mythology* (New York, NY: Viking, 1964), p. 378.
6. From the article on worship in the *Encyclopedic Dictionary of Religion* (Washington, DC: 1979).
7. Alfred North Whitehead, *Process and Reality: An Essay on Cosmology* (New York, NY: Free Press, 1978), p. 342.
8. *Random House Dictionary* (New York, NY: Random House, 1966).
9. Robert B. Tapp, *Religion Among the Unitarian Universalists* (New York, NY: Seminar Press, 1973), p. 224.
10. Robert L'H. Miller, "The Religious Value System of Unitarian Universalists," *Review of Religious Research*, Spring, 1976.
11. *Ibid.*, pp. 207-208.
12. *Ibid.*, pp. 205-207.
13. *Ibid.*, pp 207-208.
14. *Ibid.*, p. 208.

The Lotus in the West

1. In fact this misattribution continues. For instance Rick Fields's delightful study, *How the Swans Came to the Lake: A Narrative History of Buddhism in America* (Boulder, CO: Shambhala Publications, 1986) makes this claim, as does Thomas Tweed's *The American Encounter with Buddhism 1844-1912: Victorian Culture and the Limits of Dissent* (Bloomington, IN: Indiana University Press, 1992).
2. A first-rate exploration of the Four Noble Truths is contained in Walpola Rahula's classic *What the Buddha Taught* (New York, NY: Grove Press, 1959 and 1974).
3. For more on the image of the interdependent web and the

Jeweled Net of Indra, and its source in *Hua-yen* Buddhism, see footnote nine.

4. Contemporary religious liberals who would like to explore these three interdependent aspects of the Buddhist way may find two books by the American Zen master Robert Aitken particularly helpful. His *Taking the Path of Zen* (San Francisco, CA: North Point Press, 1982) provides a lucid introduction to the practice of the Zen form of Buddhist meditation as well as a brief introduction to Buddhist morality. Aitken's *The Mind of Clover: Essays in Zen Buddhist Ethics* (San Francisco, CA: North Point Press, 1982) explores the depths of Buddhist morality at greater length, and as he goes on reveals much of just what Buddhist wisdom or insight might be.

5. In this light, a review of the many books by Thomas A.J. Altizer may be advantageous. Masao Abe's *Zen & Western Thought* (Honolulu, HI: University of Hawaii Press, 1989) offers, in part, an instructive look at the death of God movement from a Buddhist perspective. Indeed, the various authors of the Kyoto School have found much profit from comparisons of Buddhist and death of God Christian concepts.

6. In this regard a very interesting book to look at is Rita Gross, *Buddhism After Patriarchy: A Feminist History, Analysis, and Reconstruction of Buddhism* (Albany, NY: SUNY, 1993).

7. Mike Port, "Buddhists as Unitarian Universalists—What's Up?" in May 1994, *UU Sangha*, 1: 7.

8. I jokingly call myself an "atheist who prays." But the joke seems to reveal a deep emotional state, one I seem to share with many other Unitarian Universalists.

9. Derived from the practices of *Theravada* Buddhism, the moderately eclectic and lay-led Western *Vipassana* community offers a range of sophisticated practices but puts considerably less emphasis on the place of teachers than is found in Zen and other traditional Buddhist communities. This egalitarian style, while grounded in solid disciplines, may well become the strongest element in the evolution of a

Unitarian Universalist Buddhism. A particularly good introduction to this fascinating development in Western Buddhism is Jack Kornfield's *A Path With Heart: A Guide Through the Perils and Promises of Spiritual Life* (New York, NY: Bantam Books, 1993).

10. It is hard to recommend just one book for Thich Nhat Hanh, and it is almost insulting to attempt to do so for the field of *Vajrayana* Buddhism. However, one of Thich Nhat Hanh's perennially popular books is *Being Peace* (Berkeley, CA: Parallax Press, 1987). One good introduction to the *Vajrayana* is John Blofeld, *The Tantric Mysticism of Tibet* (London, England: George Allen and Unwin, 1970). Of the many writers on *Vajrayana* Buddhism, one of the continually most popular is the late tulku Chogyam Trungpa. His *Cutting Through Spiritual Materialism,* (Boulder, CO: Shambhala Publications, 1973) has become a Western Buddhist classic.

11. For a brief introduction see Heinrich Dumoulin, *Zen Buddhism: A History, Volume 1, India and China* (New York, NY: Macmillan, 1988), pp. 45-49. This "cosmotheism," sometimes and perhaps better called "totalism" is developed in the *Avatamsaka Sutra,* a core *Mahayana* text closely associated with Zen Buddhism. Called *Hua-yen* in Chinese and *Kegon* in Japanese, totalism may prove to be the most significant of the many contributions to Western religious life coming out of our contemporary interreligious dialogues.

At more depth, two very good introductions to the *Hua-yen* are Francis Cook, *Hua-yen Buddhism: The Jewel Net of Indra* (University Park, PA: The Pennsylvania State University Press, 1977) and Thomas Cleary, *Entry Into the Inconceivable: An Introduction to Hua-yen Buddhism* (Honolulu, HI: University of Hawaii Press, 1983). Cleary, who is rapidly becoming a modern day *Kumarajiva,* producing numerous English language versions of crucial Buddhist texts, has also produced a complete translation: *The Flower Ornament Scripture: A Translation of the Avatamsaka Sutra* (3 vols, Boulder, CO: Shambhala Books, 1984, 1986, and 1987).

12. It really seems many of us simply equate the universe and God. This view gives rise to a number of ethical and theological difficulties, many of which are resolved in the panentheism of process theology. A number of theologians have noticed similarities between the concepts of *Hua-yen* and the panentheism of Alfred Whitehead, Henry Wieman, and Charles Hartshorne. At the same time, I am not suggesting Buddhism proposes any form of theism as we generally understand the word—although I've found within this conversation a possible use for that old word "God" that has been helpful for me.

13. Another Western philosophical system of interest that may be further illuminated in the light of Buddhism is Systems thought. Systems theory is a profound perspective, one that has deeply marked my thinking, and it really deserves more than a footnote. For more on the subject, I recommend Joanna Macy's *Mutual Causality in Buddhism and General Systems Theory* (Albany, NY: SUNY, 1991).

Four Spiritualities

1. This essay is based on concepts developed in "Four Journeys to Divine Illumination," a sermon delivered in Kennebunk, ME, Feb. 25, 1990. I then chose to coordinate the Four Spiritualities with Jung's cognitive functions rather than with Keirsey's temperament theory, which is the more popular approach. Space prohibits detailing the dynamics of typology, particularly what Jung called the dominant, auxiliary and inferior functions, as well as their roles in consciousness and the unconscious. Still, I hope this essay will provide an adequate introduction to what I feel are critical issues for our emerging Unitarian Universalist spirituality.

2. Rolph Gerhardt, "Unitarian Universalists and other Personality Types," in *UUMA Selected Essays 1987* (Boston, MA: UUMA, 1987), pp. 113-127.

   In addition to this fine essay there are numerous introductory works available in any paperback store, such as

Notes

Kroeger and Thuesen, *Type Talk*, 1988; Hirsh and Kummerow, *Life Types*, 1989; and Keirsey and Bates *Please Understand Me*, 1978.

3. Theodore Parker, *Experience as a Minister*, (Boston, MA: Rufus Leighton, 1859), p. 117.
4. *Ibid.*, p. 159.
5. Martin Marty, *A Cry of Absence* (San Francisco, CA: Harper San Francisco, 1983).
6. *Singing the Living Tradition* (Boston, MA: Beacon Press), #274.
7. *The Koran*, Arberry, Dawood, and Pickthall translations compared. Arthur Arberry, trans., *Koran Interpreted*, (New York, NY: MacMillan, 1964). N.J. Dawood, trans., *The Koran: With Parallel Arabic Text* (New York, NY: Viking, 1991). Mohammed Pickthall, trans., *Meaning of the Glorious Koran* (New York, NY: Dutton, 1953).
8. Quoted in Silliman, ed., *A Selection of Services for Special Occasions* (Boston, MA: UUMA), p. 51.
9. If we are to concur with Roy Oswald in *Personality Type and Religious Leadership* (Washington DC: Alban Institute), 1988.
10. Ralph Waldo Emerson, "Circles," in *Essays: First Series* (New York, NY: Harper Collins, 1993).
11. Gia-Fu Feng and Jane English, trans., *Tao Te Ching* (New York, NY: Random House, 1989), pp.13, 31.
12. For a discussion of how Men Ko's concept, Mandate of Heaven, influenced the Enlightenment in the West and therefore us, see Herrlee Creel, *Confucius and the Chinese Way* (1949), particularly Chapter 15, "Confucianism and Western Democracy."
13. Channing, an introverted intuitive, was a mystery to his extroverted, sensing parishoners. Whether his auxiliary function involved a preference for feeling values or thinking principles warrants continued study.

Rethinking Children's Religous Education

1. Maya Angelou, from an interview quoted in *Facing Evil: Light at the Core of Darkness*, edited by Paul Woodruff and Harry A.

Wilmer (LaSalle, IL: Open Court Publishing Company, 1988), p. 22.

2. Earl K. Holt III, newsletter column in *The Unitarian*, First Unitarian Church of St. Louis, September 13, 1992.

3. Alice Blair Wesley, "Creative Worship: A Workshop," for meeting of Ohio-Meadville District, Unitarian Universalist Association, in Youngstown, Ohio, October 7, 1978, p. 5.

4. Gertrud Mueller Nelson, *To Dance With God: Family Ritual and Community Celebration* (New York, NY: Paulist Press, 1986), pp. 25-26.

Racial and Economic Justice: Hand in Hand *En La Lucha*

1. Robert Reich, *The Work of Nations* (New York, NY: Knopf, 1991).

2. Cornell West, *Race Matters* (Boston, MA: Beacon Press, 1993).

3. Frederic John Muir, *A Reason for Hope, Liberation Theology Confronts a Liberal Faith* (Carmel, CA: Sunflower Ink, 1994).

4. *Ibid.*

Can a Prophet Chair the Board?

1. Amos 6:1. See also James Luther Adams, "The Stabilizer and the Shatterer," *The Unitarian Universalist Christian* 1977, Spring/Summer, p. 52.

2. US Census Report, October 1994.

3. Quoted in D.B. Robertson, ed., *Voluntary Associations: A Study of Groups in Free Societies* (Richmond, VA: John Knox Press, 1966), p. 159.

4. H. Richard Niebuhr, *The Social Sources of Denominationalism* (Cleveland, OH: The World Publishing Company, 1929), p. 21.

5. David Reich, "Who Reads the *World?*", *World* 1993, January/February, p. 60.

6. Saul Alinsky, *The Professional Radical* (Evanston, IL: Harper and Row, 1970), pp. 29-30.

7. See Richard S. Gilbert's Collegium paper, "Terribly at Ease in Zion," Fall 1977. (Available from Richard Gilbert).

8. Quoted in Homer A. Jack, *Denominational Social Action* (B.D. Dissertation), Meadville Theological School, 1944, p. 73.

9. Harold Taylor, *A Plan of Education for the Unitarian Universalist Ministry* (Boston, MA: UUA, 1962), p. 41.

10. Angus H. MacLean, *The Wind in Both Ears* (Boston, MA: Beacon Press, 1965), p. 6.

11. Quoted in Max Lerner, *America As a Civilization* (New York, NY: Simon and Schuster, 1957), p. 273.

12. US Census Report, October 1994.

13. *Rochester Times-Union*, February 28, 1991, p. 6D.

14. See Isaac Shapiro, *No Escape: The Minimum Wage and Poverty* (Center for Budget and Policy Priorities, June 1987), pp. 1, 20.

15. See Juliet B. Schor, *The Overworked American: The Unexpected Decline of Leisure* (New York, NY: Basic Books, 1991).

16. See Barbara Ehrenreich, *Fear of Falling: The Inner Life of the Middle Class* (New York, NY: Harper Perennial, 1990).

17. *Rochester Democrat and Chronicle*, September 4, 1992, p. 6A.

18. World Bank, *Los Angeles Times*, October 21, 1984.

19. Paul Samuelson, *Economics* (New York, NY: McGraw Hill, 1980), pp. 79-80.

20. See Richard S. Gilbert's *How Much Do We Deserve: An Inquiry in Distributive Justice* (Lanham, MD: University Press of America, 1991).

21. William Ryan, *Equality* (New York, NY: Vintage Books), p. 73.

22. *The Changing Distribution of Federal Taxes: 1975-1990* (Washington, DC: Congressional Budget Office, October 1987), p. xiii.

23. Quoted in *Christianity and Crisis*, date unknown.

24. Lester C. Thurow, *Generating Inequality* (New York, NY: Basic Books, 1975), pp. 10-11.

25. Lee Iaccoca, quoted in *The Other Side*, via *Context*, November 1, 1987, p. 5.

26. See Sam Pizzigati, *The Maximum Wage* (New York, NY: The Apex Press, 1992), pp. 49-50 and Milton Friedman, *Capital-*

ism and Freedom (Chicago, IL: The University of Chicago Press, 1962).

27. Michael Wolff, *Where We Stand. Can America Make It in the Global Race for Wealth, Health and Happiness?* (New York, NY: Bantam Books, 1992), pp. 20-21.

28. See Fredric John Muir, *A Reason for Hope: Liberation Theology Confronts a Liberal Faith* (Carmel, CA: Sunflower Ink, 1994).

29. Pete Peterson, "Facing Up," *Harpers Magazine*, October 1993.

30. Walt Kelly, "Pogo Looks at the Abominable Snowman," quoted in Robert Cope, *Indictments and Invitations* (Boston: Council of Liberal Churches, 1959), p. 76.

The New Three R's

1. M.A. Stoddard, *Quarterly Review*, 1848, 84: 173-174.
2. Roger Fisher and William Ury, *Getting to Yes* (New York, NY: Viking, 1983).
3. Dorothy Soelle, *Political Theology* (Philadelphia, PA: Fortress Press, 1974), p. 76.

Liberating Religious Individualism

1. Theodore Parker, "The Transient and Permanent in Christianity," in *The Three Prophets of Religious Liberalism*, ed. Conrad Wright (Boston, MA: Skinner House Books, 1994), p. 139.
2. Robert N. Bellah *et al.*, *Habits of the Heart: Individualism and Commitment in American Life* (Berkeley, CA: University of California Press, 1985), p. 142.
3. *Ibid.*, p. 143.
4. *Ibid.*, p. 142.
5. *Ibid.*, p.14.
6. *Ibid.*, p. 144.
7. *Ibid.*, p.142.
8. Paul King *et al.*, *Risking Liberation: Middle Class Powerlessness and Social Heroism* (Atlanta, GA: John Knox, 1988), p. 6.
9. *Ibid.*, p. 61.
10. *Ibid.*, p. 39.
11. *Ibid.*, p. 40.

Notes

12. Unitarian Universalist Association, *Principles and Purposes* (Boston, MA: UUA, 1984).

13. Peter Berger and Thomas Luckman, *The Social Construction of Reality: A Treatise in the Sociology of Knowledge* (Garden City, NJ: Doubleday Anchor, 1966), p. 16.

14. *Ibid.*, p. 60.

15. King *et al.*, *Risking Liberation*, p. 101.

16. Richard Shaull, *Heralds of a New Reformation* (Maryknoll, NY: Orbis, 1984), p. 36.

17. The concept and power of objectivation is still a difficult one to discuss. When I delivered a part of this paper at a study group of colleagues, heads were nodding in understanding and agreement until this sentence. What happened, I believe, is this: The idea of objective reality is critical to a God concept. Colleagues were ready to agree with the objectivation process as applied to everything *but* God. In other words, they believe God is the only objective reality. The way I understand this is, too much is at stake in terms of a person's world order to objectivate God. I am not suggesting that God cannot be objective reality, merely that God is *personal*, objective reality.

18. Alice Blair Wesley, *Myths of Time and History: A Unitarian Universalist Theology* (Alice Blair Wesley, 1987), p. 20.

19. Sam Keen, "The Stories We Live By," in *Psychology Today* (December, 1988), p. 44.

20. *Ibid.*

21. Unitarian Universalist Association, *Principles and Purposes.*

22. Andrew Hacker, "Transnational America," *New York Review of Books*, November 22, 1990, pp. 19-24.

23. Conrad Wright, *Walking Together: Polity and Participation in Unitarian Universalist Churches* (Boston, MA: Skinner House Books, 1989), p. 164.

24. Fredric John Muir, *A Reason for Hope: Liberation Theology Confronts a Liberal Faith* (Carmel, CA: Sunflower Ink, 1994), pp. 39-58.

25. Charles Bayer, *A Guide to Liberation Theology for Middle Class*

Congregations (St. Louis, MO: CBP Press, 1986), p. 60.
26. *Ibid.*
27. David Rankin, "Thoughts Following a Suicide," *Portraits From the Cross* (Boston, MA: UUA, 1978), p. 29.
28. King *et al.*, *Risking Liberation*, p. 145.
29. Wright, *Walking Together*, p. 166.
30. Parker, *Three Prophets*, pp. 145-146.

The Church Green: Ecology and the Future

1. Richard Ostling, "Revelations," *Time*, Special Issue, Fall, 1992.
2. All quotes from James Luther Adams appear in his book (edited by Max Stackhouse) *On Being Human Religiously*, (Boston: Beacon Press, 1976).

A Theology for Phenomenal Women

1. Emanuel Kant, *Religion within the Limits of Reason Alone* (New York: Harper Collins, 1960).
2. Maya Angelou, "Phenomenal Woman," *And Still I Rise* (New York, NY: Random House, 1978).
3. David Hume, *Dialogues Concerning Natural Religion* (New York, NY: Free Press, 1972).
4. Ibid, p. 44.
5. Freiderich Schleiermacher, *On Religion: Speeches to Its Cultured Despisers* (New York, NY: Cambridge University Press, 1988), pp. 7-9.
6. Stephen Toulmin, *Cosmopolis: The Hidden Agenda of Modernity* (New York, NY: Free Press, 1990), p. 11.
7. Toni Morrison, *Beloved* (New York, NY: Knopf, 1987), p. 95.
8. Anne Carr, *Transforming Grace* (San Francisco, CA: Harper San Francisco, 1990), p. 102.
9. Mud Flower Collective, *God's Fierce Whimsey* (Cleveland, OH: Pilgrim Press, 1985), pp. 14-15.
10. Riane Eisler, *The Chalice and the Blade* (San Francisco, CA: Harper San Francisco, 1988), p. 164.
11. Phyllis Trible, *Texts of Terror* (Minneapolis, MN: Augsburg Fortress, 1984), p. 3.

Notes

In Generations to Come
1. W. Strauss and N. Howe, *Generations: The History of America's Future 1584-2069* (New York, NY: Morrow, 1991), p. 74.
2. *Ibid.*, p. 76.

From the Earth to the Moon
1. "The Flight of Apollo 13," PBS broadcast, 1985. (Rebroadcast 1994)
2. Mitchell Kapor, "Where Is the Digital Highway Really Heading?", *Wired Magazine*, July/August, 1993.

Recreating Religious History
1. Garry Wills, *Lincoln at Gettysburg: The Words that Remade America* (New York, NY: Simon & Schuster, 1992).
2. *Ibid.*, p. 38.
3. *Ibid.*

Into the Woods: In Search of Our Stories
1. *Into the Woods* opened on Broadway in 1987. For libretto see, Stephen Sondheim and James Lapine, *Into the Woods* (New York, NY: Theatre Communications Group, Inc., 1989).
2. One should also add post-structural, post-industrial, post-Christian, and possibly post-feminist culture.
3. These thoughts are generalizations that are easily prone to oversimplification. The lived realities behind such generalities are both concrete (e.g., the demise of public education in urban settings or our culture's lack of caring for children) and abstract (e.g., the chaotic tensions in intellectual disciplines such as philosophy and theology).
4. William Dean, *The Religious Critic in American Culture* (Albany, NY: State University of New York Press, 1994).
5. In earlier times, as we perceived common foes to be resisted, (e.g., religious orthodoxy), unity could be found in the solidarity of rejection.
6. One example is the American Roman Catholic experience.
7. My use of the singular presumes a plurality of stories; it is

used here for the sake of efficiency.

8. For instance, feminist Unitarian Universalist scholars are about the work of recovery in recollecting for public purposes the particular histories of women in Unitarianism and Universalism. As in the culture at large, the histories and contributions of women have, until the last generations, been more subtext than text in the official histories.

9. We are inclined to believe that if all reasonable people can sit down together a consensus can be reached, that there is a common truth to be had.

10. This phrase is taken from Rebecca Chopp, *The Power to Speak: Feminism, Language, God* (New York, NY: Crossroad, 1992).

11. Specifically, I have in mind the works of empirical theologians and philosophers, such as William Dean. For an overview of empirical theology see, *Empirical Theology: A Handbook*, ed. Randolph Crump Miller (Birmingham, AL: Religious Education Press, 1992).

Born of Woman, Born of Earth

1. Raphael Patai, *The Hebrew Goddess* (New York, NY: Avon Books, 1978).

2. Rachel Levy, *The Gate of Horn: Religious Conceptions of the Stone Age and Their Influence on European Thought* (London, England: Faber and Faber, Ltd., 1968).

3. Marija Gimbutas, *Gods and Goddesses of Old Europe, 7000-3500 B.C.: Myths and Legends and Cult Images* (Berkeley, CA: University of California Press, 1974).

4. Joseph Campbell, *The Masks of God: Occidental Mythology* (New York, NY: Viking Penguin, Inc., 1964).

5. Joseph Campbell, *The Masks of God: Primitive Mythology* (New York, NY: Viking Penguin, Inc., 1967), p.315.

6. Patai, *The Hebrew Goddess.*

7. "Breaths," poem by Birago Diop, music by Ysaye M. Barnwell, Barnwells Notes Co., 1980.

8. Sophia Lyon Fahs, *Today's Children, Yesterdays Heritage* (Boston, MA: Beacon Press, 1952), p. 113.

Notes

9. *Ibid.*, p. 115.
10. *Ibid.*, p. 117.
11. Quoted in Irene Diamond and Gloria Feman Orenstein, eds., *Reweaving the World* (San Francisco, CA: Sierra Club Books, 1990), p. 74.
12. *Ibid.*, p. 18.
13. *Ibid.*
14. *Ibid.*, p. 251.
15. *Ibid.*, p. 261.

Unitarian Universalism and Religious Purpose

1. Joyce Appleby, Lynn Hunt, and Margaret Jacob, *Telling the Truth About History* (New York, NY: Norton, 1992), p. 192.
2. Karl Marx, Fredrich Engels, *The German Ideology,* (New York, NY: International Publishers Company, 1970).
3. Rem B. Edwards, *Reason and Religion* (New York, NY: Harcourt Brace Javonovich, 1972), p. 14.
4. Michael Werner, "Humanism and Postmodernism," *Journal of the North American Committee for Humanism,* 1994, p. 19.
5. Khoren Arisian, sermon delivered April 1994 at the First Unitarian Society of Minneapolis.
6. Daniel Walker Howe, *The Unitarian Conscience* (Middletown, CT: Wesleyan University Press, 1970), p. 7.
7. Committee on Appraisal, *Our Professional Ministry: Structure, Support, Renewal* (Boston: UUA, 1993).
8. Barry A. Kosman and Seymour P. Lachman, *One Nation Under God* (New York, NY: Harmony Books, 1993).
9. Wilfred Cantwell Smith, *The Meaning and End of Religion* (Minneapolis, MN: Fortress Press, 1991).

Afterword

1. Conrad Wright, ed., *Three Prophets of Religious Liberalism* (Boston, MA: Skinner House Books, 1994), p. 136.
2. *Ibid.*, p. 122.